PEACOCK BOOKS

Editor: Kaye Webb

HELP!

Stuck for somewhere to live? Bored with your job? Know what to do when you're ill? Can you mend a fuse, iron a shirt, build a bookcase, boil an egg – or do you fancy working abroad?

Problems have a habit of disappearing when you know how to cope with them, and it was with this in mind that HELP! was written. It is designed as a lifesaver in moments of crisis, or to have around as a handy practical reference book for anyone starting out to live on their own away from home.

It tells you clearly and simply how to go about getting yourself a doctor or dentist, what your legal rights are, how to manage your money and even how you can go about meeting other people.

The thirteen different chapters incorporate the maximum of information as clearly and simply as possible, on everything from basic cooking to finding out about birth control, drugs and drink, and from buying a car to travelling abroad with your bike.

HELP! won't make you a fantastic cook, a famous interior designer or even the life and soul of the party, but it could set you off in the right direction.

Help!

Starting Out on Your Own

Barbara Paterson

Illustrated by Graham Round

Peacock Books

To ACDE with love from B
and thanks especially to D,
without whose support
HELP ! *would never*
have been finished

Penguin Books Ltd,
Harmondsworth, Middlesex, England
Penguin Books,
625 Madison Avenue, New York, New York 10022, U.S.A.
Penguin Books Australia Ltd,
Ringwood, Victoria, Australia
Penguin Books Canada Ltd,
41 Steelcase Road West, Markham, Ontario, Canada
Penguin Books (N.Z.) Ltd,
182–190 Wairau Road, Auckland 10, New Zealand

First published in Peacock Books 1977

Copyright © Barbara Paterson, 1977
Illustrations copyright © Graham Round, 1977

Made and printed in Great Britain by
Richard Clay (The Chaucer Press), Ltd,
Bungay, Suffolk

Designed by Treld Bicknell

Set in Monotype Times and Univers

CONTENTS

ACKNOWLEDGEMENTS

It will become obvious that a lot of this book has been lived through, and that for a lot of information and advice I'm indebted to very many individuals met at different times and in different places. To all of them I'm grateful.

Many specialists have also generously helped by giving freely of their time and experience. For professional reasons they don't wish to be named, but I'd like to thank them all – doctors, dentists, accountants, lawyers.

Representatives of groups and organizations also contributed. Many thanks again to:

> After Six
> Electrical Association for Women
> Release
> Paddington Law Centre
> Drive
> British Nutrition Foundation
> Careers Advisory Service
> Members of the Metropolitan Police at Shepherd's Bush and Hammersmith

And a big thank you to Liz St. Clair, who helped ferret out some figures, to Elaine Jacobs, Ingrid Holldorff and Aileen Price, who nobly helped with the final typing, to Jackie Andrews and Charlotte Paterson, who read it in typescript, and to Sally Tarrant-Willis, who compiled the index.

B.P.

NEW READERS START HERE

HELP! *is based on the belief that practically everything is obvious once you know it, but that very little is until you do.* This is a truth which becomes painfully clear the moment you're out on your own and find life exposing all the gaps in your knowledge. Here's where HELP! comes in.

It's not a book to read right through (though of course it would be nice to feel some of you might). It's to keep around until you're stuck: then you open it up and – let's hope – find what you need to know inside.

How you use HELP! depends on what you're looking for. If it's one specific piece of information – you want to know how to mend a fuse or whether you've got appendicitis – then turn to the index on p. 361 and look up the key word: fuses; appendicitis.

If you're bothered about something much broader – how to stop money slipping through your fingers, how to meet and make friends – then look at the full list of contents to see where and how your particular worry is covered.

To make it easy for you to pick out what you need, HELP! *is split into thirteen separate parts.*

Every part is self-contained, and tries, by including relevant topics, to foresee the kind of questions you may find yourself asking. (For example, Section VI also includes such items as contraception, long-term relationships, abortion, and caring for babies.) Turn to p. 5 for full details of what to find where.

Each part starts from scratch. Skip over what you already know, and stop at what's new to you. Where necessary, you'll find references to other bits in other sections which you might find useful. (You don't *have* to look them up, they're just there in case you do.)

HELP! has been metricated throughout. If you're still more at home with imperial measures, please refer to the complete conversion table on p. 357.

When HELP! *is not enough.* Sooner or later even HELP! may fail you When it does, don't despair: you can be sure that someone somewhere will be able to come to your aid.

If it's a practical problem, and you don't know where to start, a good place is your local library. The people there may well be able to suggest the right firm, government department, or organization. If it's some.

thing more abstract or complex, any of the groups mentioned in a relevant section of HELP! may be what you're looking for. (Check with the complete list on p. 353.)

Often your local Citizens' Advice Bureau (CAB) will be able either to help you directly or to put you in touch with those who can. Most CABs keep complete lists of local groups and organizations, especially those dealing with young adults. Many are open in the evenings. Don't be put off by the rather pompous name: most of those who work there are experienced, helpful, and non-stuffy.

Most of us manage in the end. I hope HELP! *helps to clear the ground a little at the start.*

Although the information, addresses and phone numbers are as up-to-date as possible, in a few cases they will have already changed by the date of publication. New laws get passed, people move, agencies go broke. Phone numbers in particular keep changing, but in many cases dialling the previous one produces an operator to tell you the new one: otherwise ring directory inquiries. Prices too are obviously not going to stay the same. Where they're included, it's to give you some *comparative* idea of what to expect, so you know whether you'll have to lay out pennies or pounds.

Because HELP! tries to be comprehensive, it touches on a number of highly specialized areas. Sometimes experts disagree. Where this happens, I have tried, after sifting through the relevant information and discussing controversial topics with specialist advisers, to give what seems to be the information currently adopted as most up-to-date and accurate.

There remains the awful thought that in the pages which follow I am likely to have let at least one error slip through. I pray fervently that it's not as drastic as the one published in a government-sponsored booklet which urged people to stew rhubarb leaves (*don't* do it – they're poisonous): but whatever it is they are, I apologize in advance.

A roof over your head

Your own door, your own key, your own way of life with your own kind of friends around, and no one to grumble at you or pester you with questions. It sounds tempting, it is tempting, and for many lucky people it does work out that way. But not for everyone. The problem is highlighted in London because of the sheer numbers of people it affects, but the situation is much the same everywhere. Every month there are fewer bedsitters than the month before and fewer flats for short-term lets, while prices rise and keep rising.

In the hope that forewarned is forearmed, here are some things to do, or avoid doing, which might help you avoid some of the nastier pitfalls.

1 BEFORE YOU LEAVE

Don't leave home without sufficient cash in hand to keep you going. You need enough for *at least* two weeks' rent in advance (plus, very often, a further two weeks' as a deposit against breakages and non-payment); money for accommodation while you're looking, for living expenses until your first pay packet arrives, and for essential phone calls, transport, newspapers etc. How much this adds up to depends on your chances of finding a job, whether you'll get paid weekly or monthly, what type of place you're looking for, how used you are to handling money and economizing. So work out for yourself the minimum you think you'll need – and then add as much extra as you can. Money melts in circumstances like these, and the more desperate you get the faster it goes. Obviously, the closer you are to just scraping through the bigger the gamble you're taking. The more surplus you have, the better your chances of survival.

2 STARTING-POINT

Most colleges arrange at least first-year accommodation for their students; many large organiz-

Leaving Home

Legally. Once you're eighteen you may leave home and live where and as you please, subject to the normal restrictions of finance, the law, the tiresome behaviour of others etc.

At fifteen you may not legally leave your home and the protection of your parents/guardians.

Between the ages of sixteen and eighteen your rights are not entirely clear, and what may happen depends on your character, sex, circumstances, parents, and — if involved — local police and welfare officers.

If you leave home during this period with the consent of your parents, and don't do anything to bring you up against the law, then you'll probably be left alone. But if you leave home against your parents' wishes, they may apply to the police to have you traced as a missing person. (If you leave a letter declaring your deliberate intention of leaving home, the police may refuse to consider you a missing person.)

If you're traced, or if it comes to the attention of the police that you're away from home and under eighteen, what takes place then depends on local practice and how you're living. If you're male, nothing is likely to happen, as long as you can produce proof that you can earn and keep yourself. If you're a girl, and especially if you appear to be 'in moral danger' — sharing a flat with a boy, keeping unconventional company — then you may well find yourself either on a train heading for home, or under a court supervision order, or under a care order.

If you're taken to court, you can apply through Legal Aid (see p. 341) for a solicitor to represent you. If possible consult your Citizens' Advice Bureau.

Emotionally. Some parents are awful (so are some children). But in the average family situation a teenager stalking out without consultation or agreement causes deep upset all round.

Everyone feels like making a break sometimes. Obeying sudden impulses is rarely the best course to follow; think very long and hard if you're tempted. Unless your life has been made miserable through violence or other abuse, please don't vanish without warning. You risk causing great and unmendable heartache, to yourself as well as to others.

(If you do walk out, you can save those you leave behind a lot of anguish by letting them know that you're OK, through the Alive and Well service. Ring 01–567 5339. You're connected with a tape-recorder, not a person: your call can't be traced. Give your message and the name and address to send it to. Your relatives or friends will then be contacted by letter and, if they wish, the message will be forwarded to them.)

ations run hostels for young people, some have lists of recommended rooms for apprentices and trainees. The YMCA and YWCA run hostels in most large centres: unfortunately, those in London are often booked up a year in advance. There are also many smaller hostels, some run by religious organizations, some (especially in London) to provide temporary homes for young people of specific nationalities. For details and addresses of hostels, ask either at the local Town Hall or central library; if you're from abroad, try your embassy. For London, the YWCA has compiled a list of over 100 hostels, both YWCA and others, mainly for girls and women; send a 40p postal order for their handbook *Staying in London* to the YWCA Accommodation and Advisory Service, 16 Great Russell Street, London WC1. The YMCA has a list of YMCA hostels only; send a sae to 83 Endell Street, London WC2. For females, Girls Alone in London Service has a small hostel at 69 Roseman Street, London EC1.

If you're offered or discover anything along these lines, don't automatically turn your nose up at it just because it's not the way you'd pictured yourself living. At worst, it will give you breathing space while you look around and see what alternatives you can find. At best, you might enjoy it, and since accommodation like this is often subsidized you could actually get the chance to put money away – which you'll certainly need when you do spread your wings.

3 NEXT MOVE

If you don't have or can't face any of these possibilities, then you're on your own in the open market.

Check these points *before* you start.

How much can you afford? Have you worked out the maximum rent you can pay? Be brutally realistic about this. If you haven't lived on your own before, and your ideas are hazy, try to get someone who has to help you work out an elementary budget (see also p. 323).

Don't forget that rent is only the beginning. Heating, light, baths are usually extras. If you've never paid for gas or electricity before, you may have little idea how expensive it is.

Check the rates of your local Gas and Electricity Boards, and remember these will be the minimum you'll pay. (The landlord/lady owns the meters and can set them at a higher rate.) Obviously, too, you'll have to spend more in the winter than the summer; the more space you have the more it will cost to heat; and the more time you spend inside the more you'll have to pay out.

Make sure your meter works. When you move into a flat/room with a meter, check that it's working. If it isn't, let your landlord/lady know *immediately*, or you could find yourself let in for large bills.

Do you want to share or not? Sharing with tried and tested friends can be the happiest way of starting on your own. The chance to share talk, company, friends, usually more than compensates for the occasional friction over cost-sharing, noise, washing-up. Problems seem far less daunting when you've someone to talk them over with. Without others around you could find you miss your family much more than you ever thought possible.

If you've no friend prepared to move at the same time as you, then try answering the ads for fourth girl or third male to share flat. Sharing with unknowns is obviously a risk, but it can work well; can give you company, facilities you wouldn't have in a bedsitter – separate kitchen, own bathroom – or simply the best chance of finding anywhere at all. However, you can't know in advance: you may find personalities incompatible or habits intolerable. Avoid any long-term commitments.

Mixed male/female flats are growing in popularity, but – especially if the other flat-sharers are strangers to you – can be even more hazardous and offer extra complications. Successful mixed-flat sharing demands a fair degree of common sense, experience, and

Be an early bird

If you have any choice at all, think ahead. This is essential if you intend to move any time around September. Schools and colleges re-open, people return from summer holidays, students arrive from abroad. Competition's fierce. There are many vacancies in July which vanish before autumn. It's worth taking a room earlier, and then paying a retaining fee, rather than swelling the September inrush.

self-assurance. Don't try unless you're sure you can cope. Even then, have second and third thoughts before deciding.

In spite of the benefits of sharing with others, for some people privacy and the desire for independence make living on their own essential. There can also be practical benefits – you have more control over your costs and the way you choose to live.

You know yourself better than anyone else does. What you'd prefer depends on your possibilities and temperament.

What are your basic priorities? Try to decide on your priorities – what you must have and what you can do without. *Remember that you're highly unlikely to find the kind of set-up pictured in films and magazines at the kind of price you can at present afford.* You increase your chance of finding somewhere bearable if you know what's important for you.

For example:

Do you need good cooking facilities?
Are you relying on public transport?
Must you have a telephone?
Do you want a central position?
Or peace and quiet?

Whatever your priorities, these will determine where you start looking, what you start looking for, and what you end up with.

After all, you're not settling somewhere for life. You can always move later to somewhere more along the lines you'd planned.

4 WHERE TO START LOOKING

Noticeboards. If you've chosen your area, start by looking at local newsagents' noticeboards.

Polytechnics and colleges also often have boards in their main buildings, and there's generally nothing to stop non-students walking in and taking a look.

Accommodation-available advertisements. Local papers vary. Where there are several, often only one carries the bulk of classifieds. Buy them all and see. The same applies to *evening papers.* In London, for example, the *Evening Standard* carries far more accommodation ads than the *Evening News.* The accommodation advertised in *dailies* is almost always at the top end of the price range, so bear this in mind if there's no money mentioned. Some *magazines* also carry accommodation ads. *Time Out,* the *New Statesman, The Lady* are all possible sources. Religious papers (e.g. *Universe,* the *Jewish Chronicle*), certain trade papers, minority magazines like *Gay News,* also have accommodation columns. but advertisers will naturally expect prospective tenants to fit into specific categories.

Accommodation agencies. Agencies vary. By law, they are not allowed to charge tenants fees for giving details of accommodation, but they can for providing services (e.g. ringing up landlords). A recent case indicates that an agency may also charge a reasonable fee for finding a tenant accommodation which he accepts.

It's not easy to find out in advance what each agency's behaviour will be, so unless you know (e.g. from a friend's recommendation) that a particular agency is both efficient and honest, it's probably simplest not to deal with them at all. At least steer clear of any agency which demands your cash before even handing you a list. (Sometimes this blackmail is disguised by being called a 'subscription'.)

If you want to avoid them, don't be trapped into contacting them by mistake. Where an advertisement lists several rooms-to-let with the same phone number it's clearly an agency's. Ads which give more than one phone number (unless there's one for day and

How the 1974 Rent Act can affect you

The 1974 Rent Act is a confused and complicated act which appears to have provided security of tenure at the cost of cutting down on the availability of rentable flats and rooms. It is possible that it may be reviewed or amended. At the time of writing, these are the provisions most likely to affect you.

The Rent Act divides tenants into *protected* and *unprotected* tenants. You're *probably* a protected tenant *unless* your landlord/lady lives on the premises, or you're a student in college property, or where board (e.g. breakfast) is provided, or you're in a 'holiday letting', or where accommodation goes with your job.

Whether you're a protected or unprotected tenant, the only way at present a landlord/lady can evict you is by giving you a *written* Notice to Quit, with twenty-eight days' clear notice, followed if necessary by then applying for a County Court Possession Order. (If you find yourself up against attempted illegal eviction or harassment, seek advice as below.) If you're a protected tenant, you can be evicted only if you have e.g. fallen in arrears with your rent or damaged property or caused annoyance to other occupants. Even an unprotected tenant may have a Notice to Quit suspended for up to six months by the Rent Tribunal.

Because it has become a long drawn-out and difficult process to get rid of even an undesirable tenant, landlords/ladies are becoming increasingly reluctant to take risks. The more glowing your references, the more settled your job, the better your chances. Ideally, you need to be able to persuade your potential landlord/lady that you're sufficiently stable to pay regularly and not cause havoc, but not so settled that you'll stay put for ever.

The complexities of the act need skilled legal interpretation. If you have any queries over security, Notices to Quit, what constitutes 'board', don't rely on amateur opinions. Go to any Neighbourhood Law Centre or Housing Advice Centre; or your Town Hall (ask for the *Harassment Officer* or *Legal Officer*) or your CAB.

one for evening) are usually agency ads too. If you do ring up and you're suspicious, ask for the address. A private advertiser will obviously be perfectly happy to give you this, but an agency won't.

5 LESS USUAL AVENUES

If none of the conventional ways turns up anything, try looking for

something less obvious. Many people have an odd room which they haven't considered renting. You might be able to tempt them by advertising yourself. First try the local newsagents' boards. Think of some reason why someone should want you as a lodger – perhaps you can give evidence that you're a particularly responsible and desirable tenant, or because you can offer services they might be glad of in exchange, or part-exchange, for rent. Babysitting. Housework. Gardening. Typing. Book-keeping. Music lessons. Don't just try one card, write out several and put them in as many newsagents' as possible – in different areas if you're not tied down to one.

If this doesn't work, try *putting an ad in the 'accommodation wanted'* column in local or evening papers. It can be worth the expense; prospective landlords/ladies often start by looking there. Make your ad as explicit as possible. Points you might mention are sex, job, reliability, area wanted, type of accommodation, maximum cost. A little extra money spent at this point can make the ad worthwhile instead of useless.

In London you could also try an agency called '*Beds-in-Homes*' which tries to put prospective tenants and houseowners in contact with each other. They inspect rooms, interview both parties, and do their best to match them successfully. They charge would-be tenants a fee (payable only if successful) from £3 to £5. Their address is 44 Langham Street, London W1, 01–637 3251.

Another possibility is joining in a *commune*, a group of people sharing a large house or flat. Arrangements are usually much more fluid than in the average shared flat, and the set-up varies from the simply squalid to the highly sophisticated. However, apart from personal invitations and the occasional ad in *Time Out*, you're unlikely to find the opportunity of joining one on your first time out. (In London, try the Communes Information Centre, 01–229 0730.) If you do, it clearly depends on the kind of commune and your own personality whether you find this a tempting idea or not. One word of warning – don't, unless you're very sure, part with a large sum of money as a joining deposit. If you find that after all commune life doesn't suit you, you may never set eyes on it again.

With the increasing difficulty of finding accommodation, *squatting* can seem ever more tempting; *but* it is often illegal; it can delay the provision of housing for families who are even more desperate; the stress and insecurity involved can push people, often unwillingly, into actual crime.

Living-in can be a launching pad. If you're still completely stuck, and despair of ever building up sufficient funds to get started, you might try a *living-in job* in or near the area where you hope to live. There are usually plenty of vacancies in both hotels and private homes, though most temporary or short-time jobs are in holiday periods. All your essential expenses are met. You can really save. And you have a base from which you can start to look around. Try domestic and catering agencies, ads. in local and evening papers, and (especially good for out-of-London jobs) *The Lady.*

First Steps

Buy a local street-map (and a bus-map, if one's available). Have plenty of change ready for phone calls. (If you're not used to telephones, see p. 257.)

Buy papers and magazines as early as you can after they appear. Check through the ads. Don't waste time on ones which are impossible because of cost or position, concentrate on and mark just those which might do. (If you're in London, and you can't tell from the all-number exchange where the accommodation is, you'll find a list of exchanges and districts served towards the beginning of each telephone directory.)

Start making your phone calls as early as seems reasonable. Think out beforehand what you're going to ask. Be polite, be precise. Make sure you know where the flat or room is. Write down the address. Make as early an appointment as possible to see it. If you're visiting several places, make sure you allow enough time for getting from place to place and for actually viewing them.

Second Steps

Have on you (somewhere safe) one week's rent (though sometimes a £5 deposit may be enough). If you have any references, take them with you (probably the best kind is one from a former landlord/lady: otherwise, bring one from your tutor, or employer, or anyone who's known you a respectable length of time). A banker's reference (to show you're credit-worthy) plus cheque and cheque card can also come in useful if you have them. Don't forget that you'll need plenty of money too for getting around — and there may be times when it makes more sense to take a taxi than wait for a bus.

Turn up when you say you will. Be civil, be cheerful, be clean. These may be bourgeois qualities, but no landlord/lady is out to import avoidable problems.

Don't be distracted by conversation from actually *looking* at the room or flat. Check the items which matter to you — whether the landlord/lady lives on the premises, how many electric points there are, how big the wardrobe is, or whatever. You'll never find everything you want. This is where clearing up your mind about priorities beforehand pays off.

Ask what, if anything, is included in the rent; whether there are restrictions on baths, visitors, record-players. If you're thinking of sharing, ask your prospective flatmates how they work out who buys what and who puts money in the meters, how they share out the housework, the cooking, the clearing up. Ask anything else which seems important. Don't leave it till later.

If you're interested *make up your mind*. Don't go away to think it over, it'll be too late. If your landlord/lady wants to clinch it then and there, and you hand over your first week's rent, get a receipt. If he/she or your prospective flatmates want time to make up *their* minds, leave a phone number where you can be reached.

The legal position of squatting and squatters is extremely complicated, since a great many laws and by-laws are involved. The opportunities, the realities, and the attitudes of different local authorities vary from borough to borough and from one part of the country to another. For some aspects of the situation in London see *Alternative London*, published by Wildwood House, 24 Floral Street, London W C 2, or contact Self-Help, 17 Prince of Wales Crescent, London N W 1, or the Advisory Service for Squatters, 2 St Paul's Road, London N 1.

6 FINAL REMINDERS

Don't sign any kind of agreement unless you fully understand what it involves. If there are ANY *words you don't understand, in whatever size print, take it to a solicitor first* (see also p. 340).

Beware particularly of signing an agreement in which you take sole responsibility for tenancy of a shared flat. Although it's possible to have a joint tenancy agreement, landlords understandably prefer to have only one person responsible. This can be a real headache, so watch out. You could find yourself accepting sole legal responsibility for payment of rent and for any damage caused.

If the landlord/lady asks for a *deposit in advance* as security against non-payment of rent or damage, ask for a receipt, plus a written statement of the circumstances of non-repayment. (If this is a non-refundable deposit, this is illegal and you should not pay it.)

If you have a weekly tenancy you should have a *rent book*. Make sure you do, and that every payment is entered into it.

If your rent seems unreasonably high, you can apply for a *reduction* to the Rent Tribunal (if you've a resident landlord/lady) or the Rent Officer (if you haven't) –

look in the phone book or ask at the Town Hall where to go. (If your room/flat is particularly inadequately furnished, it may be possible to have it reclassified as 'unfurnished', thus producing a different set of conditions with a different rent structure. Consult your Rent Officer or Citizens' Advice Bureau.) If the rent is not unreasonably high, but you still can't afford to pay it, it could be worth while asking your housing department if you're entitled to any kind of rent rebate: this depends on your income, health, job.

P.S. When you're really stuck.

What help you find varies from place to place. If you're desperate, start by asking at the Housing Department of your local Town Hall, or talk to the Youth Officer. Sometimes the department of Health and Social

Insurance

One of the hazards of bedsitter life is the depressing possibility of being burgled. Doors get left open, someone forgets to shut windows, locks are often child's play. Take the trouble to get some insurance. What it costs depends on where you live and what you have, but it won't be much. Don't think you have nothing worth taking. Just work out how much replacements would cost. Ask your bank for advice, if you have one, or call in or write to any insurance office.

Early Days

Moving in is often an anti-climax. Apart from minor annoyances, you're likely to find yourself faced with one of two basic difficulties, depending on whether you're on your own or sharing.

1. *Knowing no one at all.* Don't allow yourself to sit round brooding. Get out and about, no matter how exposed you may feel. Take a look at p.172. Relax, stop worrying. Give yourself time, and you'll find you do meet people and make friends.

2. *Putting up with people.* Maybe you never stopped to think that life away from home wouldn't be all harmony. It's not only your family that's hard to get on with. So are other people. So, horrid thought, are you. There's no point in getting het up over every minor provocation, or in letting yourself indulge in anti-social behaviour, such as keeping your record-player running at top volume after midnight. Don't expect everyone else to adapt to you: they won't. Make a start yourself, and you'll find most people only too willing to meet you half-way.

Security can refer you to a reception centre.

In London, if you need only short-term accommodation, the Budget Accommodation Service run by the London Tourist Board (4 Grosvenor Gardens, London SW1, 01–730 0791) will find you a student hostel or hotel on a day-to-day basis: the earlier you call the better your chance. For girls, GALS have an advice centre outside Euston Station at West Lodge, 190 Euston Road, London NW1 (01–387 3010).

The *Centrepoint Hostel* (St Anne's House, 57 Dean Street, London W1) opens at 11 pm and provides beds plus soup, coffee and advice for young people who have just arrived in London and have nowhere to go. They provide encouragement plus short-term accommodation – normally for not longer than three nights.

Outside London, there are some reception centres, and some advisory agencies, but too few. Ask at your CAB for possible addresses.

Home Sweet Home

No matter where you eventually hole up, the chances are that there'll be no one around to keep life running smoothly.

If you're plunged into darkness, *you'll* have to fix the fuse. If you drop your clothes all over the floor, there they'll stay till *you* pick them up. If you leave dishes unwashed, they'll grow dirtier and smellier and eventually mouldy until *you* do something about it.

Which can come as a nasty shock.

However, help is here, plus the assurance that it really takes only a very little time each week to keep your environment under control. And it's worth it – whether it's to keep you from getting too depressed, the landlady from giving you notice, or your girl/boyfriend in a responsive mind. Dirty tables, dirty dishes and dirty sheets are *not* conducive to romance.

So here are a few notions to help you keep afloat in your new go-it-alone establishment.

1 SHIPSHAPE AND BRISTOL FASHION

When a room looks tidy, it automatically tends to look clean – even if you haven't dusted it for a fortnight. When it looks messy, it automatically looks dirty – even if you swept it from top to bottom only yesterday.

So the simplest starting-point is to concentrate on finding, as no doubt someone has told you at least once, a place for everything and then putting everything in its place. It doesn't mean being obsessively concerned with tidiness but simply deciding where best to keep things, and automatically returning them there. Clothes belong in cupboards. Books on bookshelves. Tools in a tool-box. And so on.

Living in a small cramped space makes it both more important to be tidy and more impossible. If you're in rented premises, you probably don't have nearly enough room to put things. So take a hint from ship's cabins and caravans, and plan what space you have as well as possible.

What you need is

Places to put things

Somewhere to put small things. You can buy from Woolworth's sets of plastic and metal drawers in various sizes in which to put small tools, lipsticks, pens, stamps, bills, razors, rings – all the clutter which otherwise disappears under sweaters or newspapers. Or, very

economically, you can build up your own system by glueing together large match-boxes and putting round gold paper-pins in the drawer-bit for handles, exactly as you may have done at primary school.

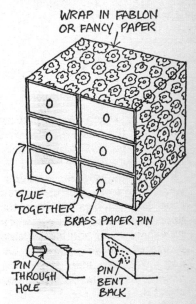

WRAP IN FABLON OR FANCY PAPER

GLUE TOGETHER

BRASS PAPER PIN

PIN THROUGH HOLE

PIN BENT BACK

WHOLE THING A SET OF PLASTIC BOXES: DRAWERS WITHIN A CABINET

Somewhere to put larger things. In most markets you can find a useful plastic article sold as a shoe-tidy. This is a set of several plastic compartments suspended from a coat-hanger, costing only a few pence. You can hang them anywhere, and can use them for shoes, scarves, pants, socks, screwdrivers . . .

In office-supply-shops, kitchen shops and stationers, you can

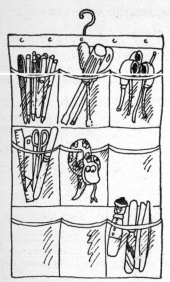

find a selection of trays and mini-shelves of various descriptions, which you can either use separately or stack together to house any number of flat things. Prices seem to vary considerably, so shop around.

Somewhere to put huge things. This isn't so easy. Anything which is large enough to provide resting room for large things tends to be large, and therefore expensive, itself. A pity the orange-box is practically extinct.

However, if you're near a street market you could try going down at the end of the day, especially Saturdays. Much produce still arrives in boxes and baskets (some of these are super) which only get thrown out.

Kitchen departments provide plastic laundry baskets: also square buckets and covered dustbins: which, while not beautiful, are cheap and provide plenty of space. They're also light and easy to carry around.

Or you could get whitewood chests (not usually very strong) or metal trunks which not only store quantities of stuff but can be sat on as well.

Shelves

If you want to make more of what shelves you've got, there are various drawer systems and space-saving mini-shelves you can attach to them which you can buy, quite reasonably, either by mail-order or in large department stores.

If you decide you need a completely new storage system, it'll probably have to remain an idle dream. Almost all need fixing in some way to the walls, which your landlord/lady is likely either to object to or subsequently claim as a fixture. But if you think it's worth investigating, your local do-it-yourself shop will advise you (see also note on p. 38).

You may already know the simplest, cheapest, quickest way to create an instant shelf system. All you need is planks of wood or chipboard plus ordinary bricks. Use the bricks at the side to build up supports to the required

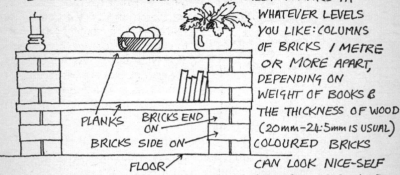

PLACE BRICKS AT RIGHT ANGLES, ROW BY ROW FOR
STABILITY: DON'T USE MORTAR: GRAVITY & WEIGHT OF
BOOKS WILL HOLD THEM: SIMPLY REST PLANKS AT
WHATEVER LEVELS
YOU LIKE: COLUMNS
OF BRICKS 1 METRE
OR MORE APART,
DEPENDING ON
WEIGHT OF BOOKS &
THE THICKNESS OF WOOD
(20mm-24.5mm IS USUAL)
COLOURED BRICKS
CAN LOOK NICE-SELF
COLOURED OR PAINTED

PLANKS
BRICKS END ON
BRICKS SIDE ON
FLOOR

level (use the fewest bricks necessary), place the plank on top, and continue building sandwich-wise. It's a perfectly sound method *but* it can be very heavy. Use your commonsense, and if you want to build higher than one or two shelves you'll need either to stick to the groundfloor or to take positive steps beforehand to find out if the floor and joists are strong enough to take the extra weight.

If you've any room for actual genuine extra furniture, you can still find excellent bargains from junk shops, *Exchange and Mart*, local papers and noticeboards.

Actually, the biggest single help to tidiness in a small space is the most enormous waste-paper basket you can buy. You need one large enough to swallow up newspapers and wine bottles, not just pieces of fluff and the odd envelope. Don't throw *perishables* in here though. Turf out your apple cores and dead flowers right away, or you'll have *smells*. (But see 'Waste Not Want Not' on p. 52.)

2 KEEPING DIRT AT BAY

However tidy you manage to coax yourself to be, you're still going to have to spend a few minutes once in a while keeping down the actual dirt. How often this seems essential depends on how many there are of you, how fussed you get, and how dirty the outside world is: once a week is probably pretty average.

Your actual den

1 Check round, and make sure you've thrown away everything you don't intend to keep.

Second~hand doesn't have to be second~best

With wood the price it is, you're unlikely to lose out if you buy any piece of well-made furniture in fair condition. If you use your eyes and take the trouble to find out a bit about what you're buying, you could find yourself with pieces which you like, are useful, and actually gain in value as time goes on. Look to see how pieces are made; at the joints; at the wood. Take out drawers to see the backs and underneath. Be careful to check e.g. in corners, under chair seats, to make sure there are no tiny holes which means woodworm; if you find any – unless you've somewhere to leave pieces while you treat them – play safe and don't buy. Restoring old furniture is possible, interesting, and money-saving: some helpful books are *Restoring Old Junk* by Michele Brown (Lutterworth Press, 1973) and *The Pauper's Homemaking Book* (Penguin, 1976).

2 Find a clean duster and set out to dust all horizontal surfaces – picture frames, shelves, window-sills, tables. Start with higher-up ones and work down. Try to mop up and absorb the dust; don't dash away at it, or you'll simply whisk it into the air. Don't try dusting round things. Pick up the flowerpot, carving, pine-cone: dust them, dust under them, and replace.

Once in a much longer while, dust vertical surfaces too.

3 If you have a hard (vinyl, linoleum or wood) floor or surround which has been accumulating *bits* you'll need to sweep it. (If you have to buy a broom, pick one with bristles which are neither too hard nor too soft. There is a cheap standard broom, painted red, black and yellow, which you can buy from Woolworth's and most ironmongers'.)

Sweep *away* from you or you'll

have to keep skipping round to avoid the mess. When you've got the bits nicely cornered, sweep them into a dustpan and empty them in the rubbish bin.

4 If you have a carpet you'll probably also have the use of a vacuum-cleaner. Vacuum-cleaners *won't* happily digest paper clips, pins and so on, so make sure you've picked all these up first or you risk damaging the motor.

If you haven't a vacuum-cleaner, a carpet-sweeper is a good substitute: cheap to buy if you have to pay for it yourself, light to use and nothing to go wrong, but keep it emptied and the brushes clean.

5 Polish any mirrors. A shiny mirror makes the whole room look clean. So though it may seem airs-and-gracey, it isn't. There are several mirror cleaners in bottles or sprays which make life easier. (Don't use furniture polishes by mistake.)

6 That, basically, is that. If you feel a rush of enthusiasm before a special occasion, you can go round with (a) a cloth and liquid detergent, wiping odd finger marks off paint etc. and (b) a tin of polish and rubbing up your best furniture. (But a lot of modern furniture is melamine-coated and doesn't need polish anyway: it's the older stuff that benefits.)

Your kitchen (or kitchen corner)

1 Throw away any worn-out scraps which may have escaped your eagle eye during the week.

2 Wash down all washable surfaces with a little liquid detergent in water. (Actually, if you've been clearing up as you go along – see p. 104 – there'll be practically nothing extra to do.) Don't use abrasives (Ajax, Vim etc.) on Formica, or you'll scratch the surface right off.

3 Wipe down the cooker, cleaning off all burnt bits. Abrasives are quite safe for most cookers, or there are various cooker-cleaner-pastes in tins.

4 If you use your oven a lot you should be prepared to clean it every month or so. This is not entirely for your landlady/lord's benefit: a really dirty cooker gets grease congealed on its roof which then melts and drips on to what you're cooking. Cleaning it isn't too much of a chore if you don't leave it too long and if you use one of the special sprays or cleaners. *Read the instructions carefully* before you start.

5 If you have a fridge you should defrost it every month: more often if it's small, and in hot weather. Leaving it until you get ice caked all over means it has to work harder, is less efficient and costs more to run.

Aim to do it when it's practically empty. Turn the fridge off, remove any ice-cubes and take everything out (you can leave this until the ice really starts dripping if it's hot or you're short of space). Leave the door open and hurry the melting process, if you want, by putting bowls of boiling water in the icebox. (Put newspaper on the floor round the fridge to soak up the inevitable mess.) You can shift a lot of the ice fairly wholesale, while it's melting, but *be very careful not to go prising away overenthusiastically with a knife* or you may cut an essential wire. When there's no

ice left, rinse the fridge out either with plain hot water or water with a little washing soda. (Avoid detergents. Most of them are scented and can leave smells behind, especially in older fridges.)

Put everything back.

Put the fridge on.

(See also p. 104 for 'Clearing up a Kitchen Chaos'.)

Your bathroom – if you have one

Leave no tide-marks in bath or basin when you use them. A wipe-around with a cloth plus a little cleaner if necessary should be enough. (In hard-water areas, putting a water-softener in the bath-water makes life easier.)

Once a week they'll need a thorough clean if they're to remain hygienic/respectable/free of stains. You can get a special bath-cleaning sponge which has a gentle scouring-pad on one side. This plus a bath-cleaning liquid or paste will do the trick – ordinary liquid detergent may be quite strong enough. *Don't put bleach in the bath. Don't use abrasives.* Do the taps too, and go round the fiddly bits with an old toothbrush if you're feeling fussy. Rinse everything well. Dry the taps with a soft cloth if you're keen on seeing them twinkle.

Your WC

The easiest way of keeping a lavatory clean is sprinkling a cleanser round it last thing at night several times a week. Use a lavatory brush first when necessary. Wash the seat, lid and thereabouts frequently with hot water and detergent. Add disinfectant if you like, and make sure to do this if anyone in the household has any kind of gastric infection. Put bleach in the pan if you want: see the bottle for amounts: *but don't use it with anything else.*

3 BRIGHTENING UP THE HOME

Alas, all the lovely articles in all the magazines throughout the year are unlikely to persuade the average landlord/lady/owner to let you lay one finger on their cherished property: so this will be a very short note indeed.

1 If you're one of the lucky few who get a chance to put your decorative ideas into action, don't forget that it costs no more to paint a strongly coloured or unconventional scheme (don't panic, you can always repaint it afterwards if it doesn't work out). Wear your oldest clothes. Put plenty of newspaper around to catch splashes. If you do flick paint around, wipe it off *then and there*, don't wait until it dries. Emulsion paint and some of the new gloss paints are water soluble until dry, which means you can clean brushes easily in water and

Beware!

Several ordinary household products can be dangerous if misused.

Bleach is among the most dangerous, and there are rarely adequate warnings about this on bottles. *Bleach will burn your skin* if you splash yourself accidentally (rinse quickly in cold water) or if you put your hands into water with too much bleach in it; it can also cause allergies. Use bleach only in the correct diluted quantities: and it's safest of all to use rubber gloves.

Detergents can cause unpleasant skin allergies, particularly the new biological detergents. If you or anyone else in your family has ever suffered from eczema or other allergies, regularly wearing rubber gloves could save you from distress.

Disinfectants and antiseptics are quite safe when used as they're meant to be. Drinking them is lethal. So make sure bottles are never put where they could be confused with something else.

Soda. Washing soda * is relatively harmless (though it can roughen your hands). *Caustic soda* is quite different and is what it says. Caustic. Which means it *destroys living tissue*, causing deep burns. Never confuse the two.

Aerosol sprays. All aerosol sprays work by using a propellant containing chemicals which can harm the lungs. So keep all sprays at a distance and avoid breathing in fumes.

In addition, some sprays are dangerous in themselves. Oven sprays can affect your skin. Fly sprays are poisonous and should never be used near food. Some scientists are dubious about their effects on people in an enclosed space: especially on children; and when used over a period of time.

Aerosols are under pressure (and therefore explodable) even when they're empty. Never leave them in the sun or near any source of heat: and don't puncture or attempt to crush them.

Never put any potentially dangerous substance (e.g.

methylated spirit) in a bottle or container designed for something else. This has been stressed over and over again, and yet every week people die because somebody somewhere thought this time it wouldn't matter.

washing soda + hot water is a cheap, effective cleaner for floors, cookers, sinks etc.

wash paint splashes off clothes (as long as you do it immediately).

2 If you're one of the majority, you'll have to rely on less far-reaching methods. What you choose depends on your personality and your cash supply; but it makes sense to concentrate on things you like, can take with you when you leave, and possibly – to start with – *large* things. A rug. A bedspread. A wall-hanging. All can help to change the feel of a room and make it yours.

3 You can make a considerable change in your room by simply putting away all loose bric-à-brac already there. (If your landlady/lord complains, say it's because you don't want anything broken.)

4 If you have even one separate 2-amp socket you can change the look of your room astonishingly simply by buying and using one new side-lamp. British Home Stores is a particularly good source of cheap well-designed lights.

5 If you have any space at all, you might consider buying any pieces of furniture you find either useful or elegant or both, from whitewood bookshelves to Victorian armchairs, depending on your tastes (see p. 28).

6 Use your frustration by noting down and remembering what you dislike about the room(s) you're in – and resolve to use this experience positively in the future.

4 TV OR NOT TV

Watching what you want when you want to. A friendly face on the box when you feel under the weather. News and nonsense – and all for a few bob a week.

It's all too easy, one wet and lonely afternoon, to walk into one of the TV rental shops plastered with welcoming posters and sign a form without realizing what's involved. But before you do, stop and consider these points.

1 Many rental shops are unwilling to let to students or tenants of furnished rooms, so that if you fall into one of these categories, they may insist you commit your-

When linen's not provided

"Linen's off dear..."

Most rented accommodation provides blankets and pillows but not linen – which means sheets and pillowcases.

If you can't rely on family hand-downs and have to buy your own, here's some help.

1. *Make sure you buy sheets big enough*

Old single beds are 2′ 6″ or 3′ wide by 6′ 3″ long. The new metric size is 100 by 200 cm. Even if your bed is the narrower 76 cm. (2′ 6″) width it's sensible to buy sheets with a 100 cm. (3′) bed in mind. Your next bed may be bigger, and while you can put wider sheets on narrow beds, you'll be very uncomfortable the other way round. So buy sheets *200 cm. wide*.

Sheets also come in various lengths. To my mind, the 275 cm. length is essential unless you're a very tiny person. Polyester-cotton sheets are often made in 260 cm. length: this is OK because these sheets shouldn't shrink. But keep away from shrinkable sheets. The few pence saved is poor compensation for having your toes stick out at the end.

2. *Sheets come in various materials and at various prices*

(a) *Cotton* sheets. Most people find cotton sheets very comfortable to sleep in. Good ones last for years, but they're getting more expensive all the time.

They're bulky and heavy when wet. So you'll need to allow for laundering expenses, either at your launderette or laundry.

Beware of 'special bargains' – they're often made of very thin cotton plus filler (a wash-out starch) to make them look better. (Rub the material between your fingers to test.)

(b) *Polyester-cotton* (various trade names). Comfortable to sleep between, but some people don't like them as much as cotton. They last fairly well.

You could wash them easily in a bath, even in a largish basin. If you have a spin-dryer, or somewhere you can easily leave them to drip, they dry quickly.

Prices keep changing. They used to be dearer than pure cotton, but are now generally cheaper.

(c) *Nylon*. Some people dislike sleeping between nylon sheets, especially in summer. Others don't mind at all. There are various textured nylon sheets which are less slippery and sticky. They last for years.

They take up very little room when wet, and are easy to wash, even in a basin. You can hang them up over a bowl or newspaper to dry. They've become very cheap.

3. *Duvets*

If the blankets you're given are paper thin or too few, you may prefer, instead of buying more, to splash out on a *duvet*. There are many different kinds and prices : consult *Which* (see p. 326). Generally, those filled with manmade materials are cheaper, washable, non-allergenic but less warm. Cleaning feather-filled duvets is expensive, but you rarely need to do this provided you treat yours sensibly and change the covers regularly. Nylon covers are cheap and washable but very slippery : ones in cotton or polyester-cotton could be a better bet.

self to a minimum of one year's rental – possibly more.

2 Increasingly, TV rental shops prefer to deal in colour TV with its bigger profit margins. If you stick to the more reasonably priced black-and-white, they may insist that you buy and don't rent. Examine all such propositions very carefully. Ask whether maintenance is included. Work out – if, as is most likely, you're paying a set weekly amount – what the total cost will be over the suggested period. (This may astonish you. I have been quoted payments totalling £150 for a set worth, new, less than half that.)

3 Inquire about aerials. Whether you rent or buy, any aerial necessary for adequate reception is your concern. (The TV shop may not tell you this if you don't ask.) In some areas a small portable

aerial for £1–£3 is adequate. In others, you may need a much more expensive roof-mounted aerial.

4 As with any form, or agreement involving money (see pp. 334 and 340), don't agree to any proposal until you fully understand what's involved.

5 Don't forget that you might, in any case, be better off with a second-hand set. Some TV shops have reconditioned sets with three- or six-month guarantees; or you can take a chance with sets sold through newspaper ads or cards at your local tobacconists. An £11 set lasted us for ages longer than the same amount spent on the cheapest rental set.

6 *And* there's the licence. Don't try to get away without one. People *do* get caught, and it *does* cost money.

5 YOUR FIRST TOOL-BOX

If you've never so much as handled a spanner in your life, you soon realize that it's very difficult to live on your own without a few elementary tools.

What kind you need, and how many, depends on whether you just want to fix plugs and hang pictures on walls, or whether you see yourself as a budding joiner. This list starts with things which come in handiest in an everyday way, and then goes on to others you're likely to need only once in a while. Start with the bare minimum and then go on to buy others as and when you need them.

Buy good tools. They cost money, but cheap tools not only fall to bits but can be dangerous. If you're completely inexperienced, look around for an ironmonger's, DIY shop or specialist toolshop, and take their advice.

1 *Screwdrivers*. They come in various types and sizes. To start with, buy

(a) a general-purpose screwdriver. It's useful to have one with a reversible blade which deals at one end with ordinary screws (with one straight line across) and Phillips screws (with a cross on top).

(b) An electrician's screwdriver. These are cheap, so buy two or three as they always seem to vanish. You need these for fixing plugs.

Later you can buy other screwdrivers as you need them: or you can get a cheap collection of driver heads with a detachable handle.

2 *Hammers*. Again, various types and weights. You need

(a) A tack hammer. This is a small light hammer without a claw which you use for knocking in picture hooks and so on.

(b) A claw hammer. With this you drive in nails with the rounded

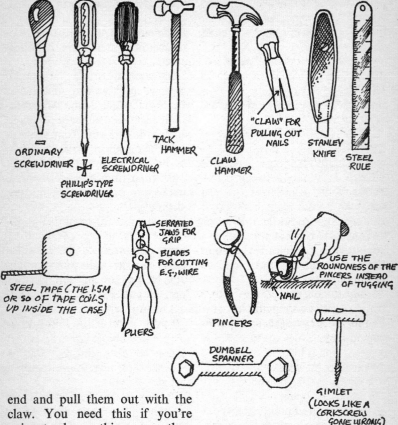

ORDINARY SCREWDRIVER

PHILLIP'S TYPE SCREWDRIVER

ELECTRICAL SCREWDRIVER

TACK HAMMER

CLAW HAMMER

"CLAW" FOR PULLING OUT NAILS

STANLEY KNIFE

STEEL RULE

STEEL TAPE (THE 1.5M OR SO OF TAPE COILS UP INSIDE THE CASE)

SERRATED JAWS FOR GRIP

BLADES FOR CUTTING E.G., WIRE

PLIERS

PINCERS

USE THE ROUNDNESS OF THE PINCERS INSTEAD OF TUGGING

NAIL

DUMBELL SPANNER

GIMLET (LOOKS LIKE A CORKSCREW GONE WRONG)

end and pull them out with the claw. You need this if you're going to do anything more than knock in light tacks. You can't use a tack hammer for heavier nails, it'll simply bounce off the head.

3 *Stanley knife* with changeable blades. You use this for cutting back wires, fitting plugs, trimming wallpaper, putty, paint off windows etc.

4 *A steel rule* and a *steel tape*.

You'll want the steel rule to use with the Stanley knife. An ordinary wooden ruler's no good, you'll only slice off bits. The tape measures up to 3 metres.

5 *Pliers*. Use these for gripping and holding. Can also be used instead of spanners for turning nuts as long as they're not too tight. Come in handy also for

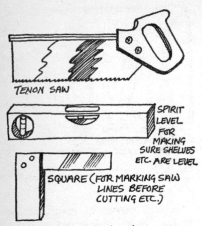

TENON SAW

SPIRIT LEVEL FOR MAKING SURE SHELVES ETC. ARE LEVEL

SQUARE (FOR MARKING SAW LINES BEFORE CUTTING ETC.)

opening stubborn bottle tops.

6 *Pincers*. Use these for pulling out nails which are either too deep or too stubborn for the claw of the hammer.

7 *Dumbell spanner*. Adaptable, cheap, and easy to handle.

8 *Gimlet*. The gimlet has a spiral end and starts holes for screws.

9 *Tenon saw*. This is a small saw which will cope with small sawing jobs, which is all you're likely to need in the ordinary way. If you want to go on and make things, of course, you'll need more than this. There are several other saws, all designed for specific tasks. At this point you'll need specialist advice.*

10 *Junior hacksaw*. For deepening slots in stubborn screws, and general metal-cutting purposes.

11 *Spirit level*. Optional extra,

but handy for putting up shelves etc.

12 *Square*. To use with the rule for accurate measuring of right angles.

Keep your tools together in one place where you can find them when you want them. All these will fit easily into a box or toolbag, which you can buy from around £1. (See your local shops, or small ads in e.g. *Exchange and Mart*.) Look after your tools. *Put* them safely away, don't hurl them from a distance.

Warning note. It's impossible to hang anything heavier than a picture on ordinary plaster walls. Drive in larger nails and you pull out chunks of plaster. If you want to put anything like shelves or a wall system you'll need (a) permission if the house isn't

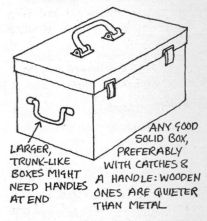

LARGER, TRUNK-LIKE BOXES MIGHT NEED HANDLES AT END

ANY GOOD SOLID BOX, PREFERABLY WITH CATCHES & A HANDLE: WOODEN ONES ARE QUIETER THAN METAL

If you're interested in carpentry and want to know more, you'll almost certainly find plenty of help in local evening classes.

yours, (b) Rawlplugs. These provide a means of plugging drilled holes with asbestos filler to take plugs which accept screws. Full details from your DIY shop. Reasonably easy when you know how, but there can be snags.

Helpful note. There's a whole range of modern adhesives which are extremely strong (they're used for sticking bits of aircraft together) and can be used by bungling amateurs like me to glue things together instead of relying on traditional craftsmanship. Make sure you use the right one: your shop should have the necessary information.

6 ELECTRICITY

Electricity can be a very complex subject. However, for most practical purposes what you want to find out is how to get and keep things working while avoiding accidents.

So, with these aspirations in mind, here are a few very basic facts you need to know.

Very basic facts

Basic fact no. 1

Most electricity in this country enters each household as AC (alternating current) at a rate of 240 volts (though there are still areas which have DC (direct current)), or where the voltage is not standard.

Basic fact no. 2

Electric power is measured in watts. Every piece of electric equipment you buy should have its power clearly marked on it. 1,000 watts are called one kilowatt (kW). The more watts, the more power, the higher the cost per hour. Roughly speaking, a piece of equipment which supplies heat costs more to run than one which doesn't. A light bulb, for example, can be as low as 20 watts – even the brightest in most homes is only 150, while even a small heater is 500 watts.

Basic fact no. 3

What kinds of electrical equipment you can use in your room(s) depends on what kind of sockets you find there; which in turn depends on when and how the building was wired.

If your sockets have *three square holes*, (a), then the wiring is recent and each socket is on a

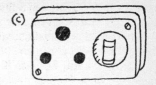

ring main. This means that you can plug into each one virtually anything you want from hair-dryers to 3 kW fires. (But you couldn't smuggle in a large electric cooker and install this. A cooker can use up to 15 kW and has to be connected to a special 30- or 45-amp socket.) There is one main 30-amp fuse; each plug also has its own fuse (which must be the correct one – see p. 42).

Perhaps the principal risk is to be tempted to plug into one socket (via an adaptor) pieces of equipment which together use more than 3 kW (e.g. a fast electric kettle plus a large heater). So bear this in mind, remembering that such overloading would danger-ously overheat and damage the socket.

If your sockets have *round holes*, (b) and (c), then the wiring is certain to be old. If your sockets have only *two holes each* (b), then they're either 2 or 5 amp. If the holes are small and close to each other, then they're only 2 amp,

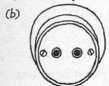

(b)

and will take only equipment like lights, tape-recorder, radio etc. If they're slightly larger (holes measuring 5 mm across and about 12 mm between the two), they're 5 amp, and you can use slightly more powerful equipment of up to 1,000 watts – like a hair-dryer or vacuum-cleaner. *However*, because these 2-amp and 5-amp sockets are related to all other 2-amp and 5-amp sockets on the same floor, what you can use in your sockets depends on what else is being plugged into the same circuit at the same time. Each circuit will not carry more than a certain maximum – of 500 watts for the 2 amp, 1,000–1,200 watts for the 5 amp. This means that if you (or you plus others) simultaneously plug in pieces of equipment which *together* exceed the limit, you over-load the circuit, the main fuse blows and chaos reigns. If your sockets have *three round holes* (c), these are earthed. The smaller sizes (2 amp and 5 amp) correspond in capacity to the sockets above *except that* you can use a 1 kW fire in a *3 pin* 5-amp socket. (*For why see p. 46.*)

If your three-holed sockets are larger, then these are proper power points which will take up to 3 kW each. You can use a fast electric kettle or a 3-kW fire or a small plug-in cooker. What counts is still the *total amount per socket*: if you use an adaptor because it's convenient, what you're using mustn't add up to more than 3 kW.

What this boils down to, obviously, is that a room with modern 3-pin square-holed sockets provides electricity in a more convenient, safe, more flexible way. One with older 3-pin round-holed sockets can be quite satisfactory, especially if there's more than one 3-point. A room with only 2-pin sockets restricts your use of equipment severely. (Which may not matter if, for example, there are gas fires and you don't want anything but lights anyway. See also p. 15 on flats.)

Why fuses matter

What fuses are

A fuse is a specifically provided weak point in a circuit. If anything goes wrong in either the wiring of the circuit or any individual appliance, the resultant surge of electricity overheats the fuse wire which melts away, breaks the circuit, and thus automatically cuts off the source of power. A fuse is a very important safety device which, *properly used*, immensely reduces your chances of

electrocuting yourself or setting the place on fire.

As you'll know if you've taken in *Basic fact no. 3*, fuses on older systems (with round-holed sockets) are part of the circuit and in a fuse-box: on new systems the plugs themselves are fused.

Why fuses blow

Whether in a fuse-box or a plug, a fuse blows for one of these reasons:
1 overloading of the circuit by having plugged into it either one appliance of too high a power or several appliances *together* using too much power.
2 a short-circuit in an appliance (caused by two wires touching which shouldn't).
3 a defective flex.
4 worn-out wiring.
5 corrosion and breakage of the fuse itself. The wire can weaken with age so that the fuse blows without anything else being wrong.

Coping with fuses

In plugs. When you buy square-pin plugs they're normally automatically sold with brown 13-amp fuses. These are the correct fuses if the appliance you want to put it on is over 750 watts. (You'll find the wattage marked on it.) But if the appliance is *under* 750 watts (hair-dryer, lights, radio, tape-recorder etc.)* then you need a red

* A fridge or vacuum-cleaner should have a 13-amp fuse although the loading is below 750 watts.

3-amp fuse. Ask for the fuse to be changed. If you're already using appliances without having checked the fuses in the plugs to make sure they're right for the wattage, do it now. *It's important that these fuses are correct.* If you're using a 13-amp fuse where there should be a 3-amp, your appliance (if faulty) can overheat without affecting the fuse at all, and so build up to a potentially dangerous situation.

Replacing fuses in square-pin plugs. Keep handy a supply of both 13-amp and 3-amp fuses.

When an appliance stops working (and there's money in the meter), first check to make sure there's nothing obviously wrong with it – no smell of burning or sign of overheating. If there is, then the fuse is just doing its job

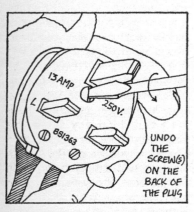

UNDO THE SCREW(S) ON THE BACK OF THE PLUG

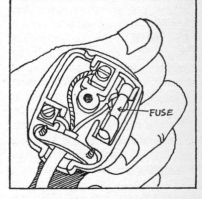

FUSE

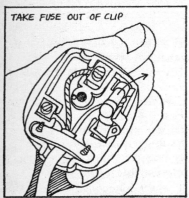

TAKE FUSE OUT OF CLIP

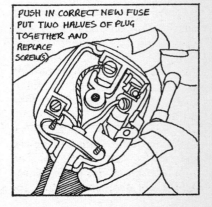

PUSH IN CORRECT NEW FUSE PUT TWO HALVES OF PLUG TOGETHER AND REPLACE SCREW(S)

and warning you that the appliance needs seeing to, and until you've fixed whatever's wrong there's no point in touching the fuse.

If you can't see anything wrong, then the fuse may have deteriorated with age. First, undo the big screw on the back of the plug, which will open into two parts. Pull out the old fuse. Push in the correct new one. Put the two halves of the plug together and replace the screw. Replug the appliance into the socket.

If it still fails to work, check that it's not the socket at fault by plugging it into another one. If it still won't go, then there's almost certainly something wrong with it even if you can't detect the fault. (If it's new, take it back to the shop where you bought it. If it's old, find an approved electrician specializing in small repairs; look for the letters NICEIC outside a shop. If you have any difficulty, go to your Electricity Board and ask there for the roll of approved electricians, or consult the list at your local library. Any NICEIC electricians must carry out work to approved standards, or make good any deficiencies at their own expense.)

In fuse-boxes. If you're living somewhere with older *round-pin* sockets (see also p. 40), none of your appliances has fused plugs. All sockets are connected to fuses in the main fuse-box.

Since this fuse-box may not be generally accessible, establish beforehand from your landlord/lady what the procedure is if a fuse blows. Some owners prefer to mend fuses themselves, which means getting hold of them. Others expect you to do it, which means being prepared and knowing how to.

Most important of all is doing your best to avoid blowing a fuse. If you plug faulty equipment into a socket you'll take everyone else's electricity away as well – tricky if the fuse-box is locked up and the landlord/lady ungettatable.

Once you're plunged into darkness, a sensible starting-point is to try to find out why. If there's a faulty appliance or socket-overloading anywhere on the circuit, the fuse will simply blow again the moment it's replaced. If no one comes up with a straightforward solution, then it may again be a case of a fuse's blowing with old age.

If all you need do is contact the owner, go ahead.

If you have to tackle it yourself, here's how.

Mending fuses in main fuse-boxes. Collect a torch, electrician's screwdriver, card of fuse-wire, pen-knife or scissors (and HELP! if you need it). Make sure you have the correct weight of wire: thinner wire for 2- and

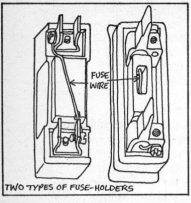

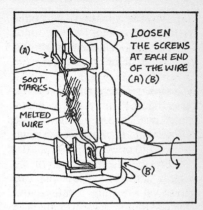

TWO TYPES OF FUSE-HOLDERS

FUSE WIRE

LOOSEN THE SCREWS AT EACH END OF THE WIRE (A) (B)

(A)

SOOT MARKS

MELTED WIRE

(B)

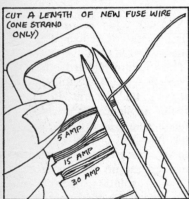

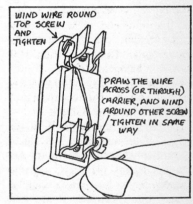

CUT A LENGTH OF NEW FUSE WIRE (ONE STRAND ONLY)

5 AMP

15 AMP

30 AMP

WIND WIRE ROUND TOP SCREW AND TIGHTEN

DRAW THE WIRE ACROSS (OR THROUGH) CARRIER, AND WIND AROUND OTHER SCREW TIGHTEN IN SAME WAY

5-amp fuses for the lighting circuit or 2-pin sockets, thicker 15-amp for fuses attached to 3-pin sockets. *Never mend a fuse with the wrong wire*: it defeats its whole purpose.

When you get to the fuse-box, the first thing is to *turn off the main switch*. You'll find a large switch or lever connected to the fuse-box. Push it in the opposite direction from the way in which you find it.

Open the fuse-box. You may have to undo a couple of screws to remove the lid. Inside you'll find plastic or china fuse-holders. If your house is efficient, you may find these labelled to correspond with the rooms they serve, which can help to speed matters. If not you'll have to take them out one by one to check which has the blown fuse. Usually you can spot this right away by soot-marks on the carrier left by the melting wire. If you don't find the fuse first time round, check again more carefully until you've got one with broken and/or melted wire.

Loosen the small screws at each end of the wire. Remove the old wire and clean up any mess. Cut a length of new fuse-wire (one strand only). Remove a neighbouring, unblown, fuse and keep it by you to make sure your repair duplicates the same pattern of wiring. Wind one end of the wire clockwise round the top screw and tighten the screw. Draw the wire across or through the carrier – according to type – to the other end, wind round the other screw, and tighten in the same way. The wire should fit without being stretched.

Replace your fuse (and the one you've taken for comparison). Turn on the main switch.

If the fuse immediately blows again there's no point in doing anything more to it until you find out what's making it go: but nine times out of ten all will be well.

Plugs and how to wire them

Appliances are sold without plugs. It's up to you to put them on.

You need the right kind of plug for your particular appliance and your kind of socket. If you haven't read *Basic fact no. 3*, do it now. It's important to understand *why* you can't just stick any old plug on any old flex and shove it into whatever socket you've got.

Basically, there are *four kinds*.

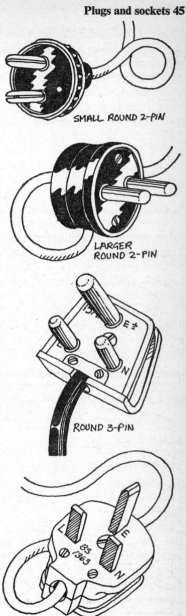

SMALL ROUND 2-PIN

LARGER ROUND 2-PIN

ROUND 3-PIN

SQUARE 3-PIN

Small round 2-pin, larger round 2-pin, round 3-pin, square 3-pin. What matters most is to remember that you can't plug into a small 2-pin socket any appliance rated higher than 500 watts, into a larger 2-pin one higher than 1 kW: you can only use anything with a higher wattage if you have either round or square 3-pin sockets.

Also, quite apart from the wattage, it's potentially *dangerous* to use any appliance with a casing made partly or wholly of metal *without using a 3-pin plug*. (Though some low-wattage but metal appliances – vacuum-cleaners, TVs – are double-insulated, and so can be safely used with 2-pin plugs.) This is because a 3-pin plug has an earth connection, so that if anything goes wrong with the appliance or its flex electricity rushes not through you but down to earth. This is why it's *never* safe to use, for example, an iron from a 2-pin socket. (Or through an adaptor from an overhead light-fitting – where, quite apart from the risk of electrocution, you can with the weight of the flex pull the whole fixture plus wiring from the ceiling.)

So get the right plugs for the right appliances for the right sockets. If you're in any doubt, call at your local Electricity Board and ask for their advice. *And then take it.*

Flexes and wiring codes

Flexes have a central core of either two or three wires, each covered with different-coloured plastic for inner insulation, and

Your local Electricity Board will wire a plug for you if you buy it there and ask nicely (which obviously means taking the appliance along). It will also wire plugs for appliances you buy there : so will some other shops : discount stores generally won't.

If you'd feel happier learning from practical experience under supervision, the Electrical Association for Women (25 Foubert's Place, London W1, 01–437 5212) gives short one-day courses for only £2 (including lunch). They have many other branches throughout the country, offering similar, often more flexible, sessions. (Not just for girls, males welcome too.)

then an outer insulating cover of either plastic or fabric. The different colours of the inner plastic insulating covers tell you what kind of wires run inside.

When you have *two wires*, one red and one black, the red is live and the black neutral. If one is brown and one blue, the brown is live, the blue neutral. If the wires are the same colour, the live wire should be marked either by a longitudinal ridge or a plastic sleeve.

When you have *three wires*, they may be coded according to the old British standards, in which case red = live, black = neutral, and green = earth; or according to the new British (European) standards, in which case brown = live, blue = neutral, striped green/ yellow = earth.

It's important that these wires go to the proper place inside the plug.

When you open the plug (see ahead p. 48) you'll find letters by the terminals (the little screws inside) or by the pins outside, which tell you where each wire goes. L = live. N = neutral. E or ⊥ = earth.

If you're wiring a *2-core flex to a 2-pin plug* the red (brown) live wire goes to the L (live) terminal. The black (blue) neutral wire goes to the N (neutral) terminal.

If you're wiring a *2-core flex to a 3-pin plug*, connect the red (brown) live wire to the L (live) terminal, the black (blue) neutral wire to the N (neutral) terminal, and leave the third terminal blank.

If you're wiring a *3-core flex to a 3-pin plug*, connect the red (brown) live wire to the L (live) terminal, the black (or blue) neutral wire to the N (neutral) terminal, the green (or green and yellow) wire to the E (earth) terminal.

Never wire a 3-core flex to a 2-pin plug.

Wiring your plug

Whatever kind of plug you're wiring the procedure's the same. You need an electrician's screwdriver, a Stanley knife (or something similar), and a certain amount of patience.

Take the plug and unscrew the small screw(s) that hold it together. Loosen the flex-holder screws. Put the screws somewhere safe so they won't roll away. Handle both parts of the plug carefully so bits don't fall off and get lost in the carpet. Put both bits down (1).

Take the flex. Bend it about 35 mm from the end and nick it with your knife. Cut round carefully *without* damaging the inner coloured insulation (2). If the flex has a fabric cover, wrap insulating tape around the cut end.

Splay out the separate two or three covered wires inside. Lay the flex across the plug (3) with the covered end of the flex just across the flex-grip (a). Push each

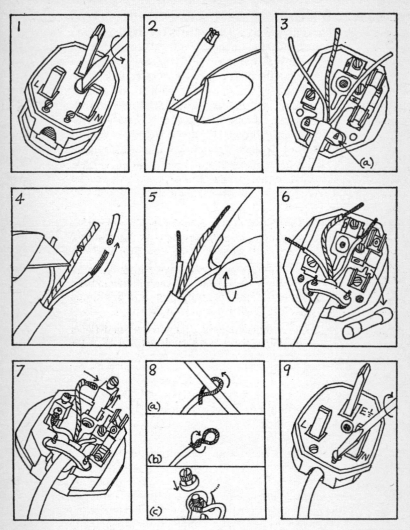

individual wire into shape by each terminal it's going to connect with. Cut each wire off 12 mm beyond each terminal. The wires will be different lengths.

Pick up the flex and cut round the inner insulating cover on each wire about 12 mm from each end, going slowly and being careful not to damage any of the inner wires. If you do cut any of these you'll have to start again, as relying on too few strands could overheat them. Strip off the inner covering, leaving the wires bare (4). (You can get wire-strippers to do this, but a knife is quite adequate as long as you don't rush things.)

On each wire, twist all the separate strands together neatly (5).

Push the flex under the flex-grip, making sure you get the end of the outer covering inside the case, and spread each wire out by its terminal. (If the fuse is in the way of the live terminal, take it out.) Check to make sure you've got the right wire in the right place (6).

Connect each wire to its terminal, starting with the earth.

If your terminals have a hole in the pillar beneath the screw, fold over the exposed end of the wires, twist together, poke through the hole, and screw down firmly (7).

If your terminals have nuts and washers, remove each nut and washer in turn. Twist each wire in a loop and lay this clockwise over the correct terminal. Replace the washer and nut (8c). Screw down firmly clockwise. Make sure none of the insulation is trapped under the washer.

Screw down the flex-grip (9).

Your plug should now be ready. Check to see that the insulation on each wire goes right up to the terminal, and that there aren't any loose bits of wire anywhere inside the plug. See that the wires lie in the grooves provided for them without being twisted. If you've removed the fuse, put it back.

Replace the cover on the plug and screw it up.

Congratulations!

Electricity is safe when used as it's meant to be – but not otherwise. Check now *through the safety-first items below.*

Electricity costs money – note the comments on p. 14.

7 SAFETY FIRST

Young people on their own probably spend less time under their (rented) roof than practically any other age group, and you're probably alert and agile enough to avoid many potential accidents. Still, since none of us is sensible, sharp-eyed or possibly even sober 100 per cent of the time, it's a sound idea to take at least the most obvious precautions.

Gas hazards

All gas is explosive.
Older (town) gas is poisonous.
Gas fires. Check tubes and connections, particularly if they're old.
Gas cooker. Don't turn on rings without lighting them.
Be extra careful *never* to turn on

the oven without lighting it. (This could cause an almighty explosion once the door's opened.)

Don't leave gas ring(s) on at a low light all night to keep the chill off: they could blow out.

Gas leak. Never look for a gas leak with a naked flame. (Very obvious: it happens.) Call the Gas Board *immediately*.

Gas water-heater. See you, or your landlord/lady gets it serviced regularly. If it's in the bathroom, it's safest, though shivery, to leave the window slightly open.

Gas slot-meters. Never put money in a slot-meter before making sure all appliances are turned off.

If several of you share the same meter, work out a system. The simplest way is to make whoever puts the money in responsible for a quick check. Remember accidents caused this way happen pretty frequently, particularly in cold weather when people go to bed leaving fires on.

Electric hazards

Always use the correct plugs and fuses (see p. 41).

Don't use worn cables or wires.

Don't run flexes under carpets or mats.

Don't overload by plugging too many appliances into one adaptor (see p. 41).

Don't pull out a lead from a kettle without first switching off at the plug.

Don't pull a plug from its socket by tugging it out by its flex.

Electric fires. Don't move a fire close enough to anything burnable to set it alight.

Don't leave it where anything (coat, towel) can fall on it.

Don't push it, still plugged in, under furniture or out of sight. (Someone could switch it on by mistake.)

Never take an electric fire in the bathroom.

Electric cooker. Remember surfaces stay hot, though black, long after being turned off. Don't touch them or leave anything on them.

Electrical equipment. Don't buy cheap electrical equipment of unknown origin. Make sure that whatever you buy has on it the seal from the British Electrical Approvals Board. (Some very expensive equipment, especially foreign equipment, may not have this seal and be perfectly safe, but this isn't the case with cheaper goods.)

TV. Switch off and unplug at night (especially if it's colour).

Paraffin hazards

If you have an old paraffin heater, it may be unsafe to use it at all. Check with your ironmonger.

Don't buy a second-hand heater. (New heaters have safety devices old ones lack.)

Fill it outside if at all possible.
Store paraffin somewhere it won't
get knocked over.

Open-fire hazards

Leave a fire-guard – preferably a
fine-mesh guard – in front of an
open fire when you're out of the
room.
Don't leave wood in front of it to
dry out overnight. It can burst
spontaneously into flame.

Drying hazards

Don't dry anything (clothes, tea-
towels, sleeping-bags) close to
fires or naked flames.
Don't hang anything on strings
over cookers, or leave on fire-
guards, or over fan-heaters.

Mixed hazards

Don't let pans or kettles burn dry:
particularly electric kettles.
Put hot kettles, teapots, coffee
pots, where they won't get upset.
Don't leave pan handles sticking
out.
Don't leave pans of oil or fat
heating on the cooker (see p. 94).
Don't walk away from the ironing-
board leaving the iron on. If you
have to answer the phone or the
door-bell, switch off first.
Don't leave cigarettes in ash-
trays to overbalance and tip out.
Don't smoke in bed. (This causes
1,000 fires a year.)
Don't drop matches into waste-
paper baskets.

Don't have a boiling hot bath,
especially if you've eaten or drunk
too well. (If you do feel yourself
coming over all faint, pull out the
plug.)

8 FIRE!

All fires feed on oxygen.
Without oxygen, a fire dies.
So, no matter what kind of fire's
involved, the aim in dealing with
it is to cut off its source of air.

Small, non-oil, non-electrical fire

Throw on water and/or smother
with heavy rug, coat, to keep out
air.

Electrical fire

If the fire's caused by a single
appliance, *switch it off and unplug
it*. Then throw water on it. If more
extensive – fire in a socket – *turn
off the electricity at the mains* and
then use water. If you can't
switch off the electricity, *don't use
water*: throw on a heavy rug,
blanket etc.

Oil-fire (on cooker)

Don't use water, as it will simply
spread the flames. Cover with a
lid, if possible, or a heavy damp
cloth if not.

Paraffin heater fire

Throw on buckets of water from
as far away as possible – at least
six feet.

For anything but a small fire which has only just started to catch –

CLEAR EVERYONE
OUT OF THE HOUSE
RING 999 FOR THE
FIRE BRIGADE
SHUT ALL DOORS AND
WINDOWS IF YOU'VE TIME

If anyone's clothes catch on fire, trip them up, *throw on any rug, coat or blanket you have handy, roll them in it, and beat out the flames.*

For what to do next, and for all other cases of accidents involving personal injury, see pp. 124–9.

9 WASTE NOT WANT NOT

When you start on your own you're bound to buy some mistakes. Food goes bad before you eat it because you bought too much at once. Blankets shrink. You don't like the shirt you chose. You never really use the mixer you coveted.

Don't get too upset about this. It's inevitable, part of the price of gaining experience. Find out what's gone wrong and why; and then see you don't do it again.

Sometimes we have to live with our mistakes – but not always.

There's nothing grasping about trying to recoup some of your money by selling second-hand something in good condition which you simply don't like or have found out is impractical. The blanket you shrank may be too small for you but fine for a child. The cheapest way of advertising is with a card in a local shop. If this doesn't work, try *Exchange and Mart* or your local paper.

Never just throw away anything which has life left in it. Old clothes, cutlery, crockery, books – local organizations, churches, scouts, guides, children's charities all want these for jumble sales. So do charity shops like Oxfam, War on Want, Help the Aged.

Some councils, scout troups, churches, collect old newspapers. Some are starting to collect glass. Several charities collect milk-bottle tops and all kinds of foil. Don't think it's worth so little it doesn't matter. It adds up. I know of one local branch of a charity which raised over £500 from foil collecting.

So if you can help, please do. You're performing a socially valuable action in recycling materials; helping the organizations concerned; and the individuals who buy for pennies what you find useless.

Nourishing Nosh

When you first start living on your own often your diet is the first thing to suffer. Local canteen food is dull. Restaurant food's too dear. You may not know one end of an egg from another. Or you feel as long as you eat something it doesn't much matter what.

Fortunately, most young adults are extremely resilient. Missing the odd meal from time to time, or eating other even odder ones consisting of chips and chocolate, does little harm provided that your standard eating pattern is sound. But days or weeks of snacks, or months switching from feast to famine, do no one any good.

It's not hard to eat well, eat sensibly, and enjoy it. As a bonus you're more likely to have:

a good figure
clear skin
energy
peaceful nights
an amiable temper
good health
Among the other gains of good food are a positive attitude to life and being able to keep going – whether at parties or work.

It's all too easy to eat badly and suffer for it. Among other disagreeable consequences, you may find yourself with:

a poor figure
spotty skin
that dead-beat feeling
insomnia
a nasty temper
shocking colds
Among the other lesser penalties of a poor diet are a bad digestion, rumbling stomach, bad breath. Among the more serious, anaemia and depression.

It takes a bit of know-how and practice, but it is possible to eat well and relish it even if you haven't got cash to throw around. And the biggest money-saver, and the best guarantee of food the way you like it, is to know how to make your own meals.

1 FINE FOODS

A little of what you fancy may do you good, but too much of it will make you sick, fat or spotty. All food is fuel – only your body is far more complex than a car.

Everything you eat provides calories which your body converts into heat and energy to keep you going. Different kinds of foods also affect your body in different ways.

Your body needs a balance of foods to develop properly. A good body and good looks depend more than anything else on good food. Good – not expensive.

Here's what you need	*Why you need it*	*What happens if you run short*
Protein. You get this from *meat, fish, eggs, cheese; split peas, haricot, butter and kidney beans, lentils, nuts;* some also in *cereals, bread, and potatoes.*	Proteins build and maintain actual body tissue. Adequate protein means you have firm, not flabby, flesh, good muscles, energy, resistance to disease.	Your skin, body, muscles suffer. You tire easily, fall ill more quickly.
Fats and oils. Butter, margarine, lard, oils.	Essential to body tissue, especially nervous tissue, and for a healthy skin.	Your skin, hair and body are affected (but most British diets contain plenty of fats).
Vegetables and fruit.	Provide a large share of essential vitamins, especially vitamin C from citrus fruits, fresh green vegetables and potatoes. The roughage – fibres, skins etc. – particularly from uncooked fruit and veg. helps to make sure your insides work properly.	You catch colds easily, feel lethargic, may suffer from constipation. (The average British diet has too little fruit and veg.)

Carbohydrates. Cereals, bread, rice, potatoes, pasta.	Fill in the gaps – provide the bulk needed to prevent you feeling hungry; also provide roughage (especially brans, wholemeal bread and muesli).	You'd feel hungry and get thin. (This rarely happens. You're far more likely to eat too much and get fat.)
Milk.	Provides protein (see above) vitamins A and D (see below) and calcium.	

Other elements you need include:

Minerals. Apart from calcium (see milk) your body also needs minute proportions of other minerals to function properly. As long as you eat a properly balanced diet you get these automatically. There's only one mineral deficiency – of *iron* – which crops up with any regularity, causing anaemia (see p. 130). If you have ever been, or still are, anaemic, include regular helpings of iron-rich foods such as liver, kidney, and green vegetables.

Vitamins. There are a number of elements in foods, which have been identified and given letters from A–K, which are essential to good health. Again, however, as long as you eat sensibly you'll get plenty.

Things you don't actually *need*:

Tea and coffee. These are stimulants, without calories except when you add milk or sugar.

Alcoholic drinks. Most provide plenty of calories but not much else. But wine, especially red wine, is a source of iron and other trace elements.

Sugar. There is no requirement whatever for sugar: it provides no useful food element. Sugar, sweets and heavily sweetened cakes, biscuits, fruit syrups etc. can be positively damaging. Eating sweets and sweet stuffs in quantities ruins your appetite for proper food, makes you fat, gives you spots, rots your teeth. The British eat more sweets than anyone else in the world. They have some of the worst teeth too.

Your eating plan

There is no one perfect balanced diet absolutely right for everyone. On the whole, a tall well-built person needs more than someone who's small and slight. Someone heaving bricks around needs more than someone else immured behind a desk. But doctors don't yet know much about metabolism, the ins and outs which explain the rate at which food gets burnt up and used as fuel. Unfairly, some small skinny people can eat more than big hefty individuals.

This eating plan's only approximate. What matters is that proportionately it's OK. If you find that following it means you eat too much (or too little) you'll need to cut down (or increase) right along the line – not simply cut out all the vegetables and add boxes of chocolate biscuits.

How much each day?

Proteins. 2–3 helpings a day of any of the foods mentioned on p. 54. For each helping approximately:
100 gm raw meat (excluding bone) *or*
50 gm cooked meat (ham, etc.) *or*
125–150 gm fish *or*
50–75 gm cheese *or*
100 gm + of dried peas, beans or lentils *or* 100 gm nuts *or*
1–2 eggs. (An egg a day is a good idea, but eggs for every meal will upset your stomach.)

or any combination of these, e.g. lentils and cheese, bacon and beans etc.

Fats and oils. 25 gm a day (which should include butter or margarine for their vitamins A and D).

Vegetables and fruit. At least one vegetable and one piece of fruit. Two vegetables and two pieces of fruit are better. (One vegetable should be green, one fruit have plenty of vitamin C – orange, lemon, grapefruit.

Milk. 6 dl. (1 pint).

Carbohydrates. As much as you need to fill in the gaps after you've eaten other, more vital, foods. *And no more.* Carbohydrates which provide other elements (e.g. potatoes, bread – especially wholemeal – rice) are *much better* than jam puffs or brandy snaps; they also provide bulk and roughage.

Tea and coffee. What you like, within reason, but remember that too much may make you irritable, take away your appetite, and – if you take sugar – overload your sugar intake. (2 average tsp. sugar weigh 14 gm.)

Alcohol. A moderate amount only, if at all. Beware if you find yourself using alcohol as a substitute for food (see pp. 278–288).

Sugar. The least possible in any form. If you've a sweet tooth, or catch yourself eating doughnuts instead of dinners, watch out. Remember, when sugar destroys the balance of your diet, your health, figure, teeth and skin all suffer.

When to eat what

How you distribute these goodies between different meals is up to you entirely. It depends partly on how you live, how well you cook, whether you're forced to eat out or not and how hard-up you are. But four points:

1 *Breakfast*. The main thing is *do have it*. I know experts keep advising this in a monotonous way, and I know people keep right on not having it. But recent tests show that lorry-drivers who skip breakfast have considerably more accidents than ones who don't. Which means that if *you* skip breakfast you are e.g. more likely to quarrel with the boss, jam your machine, end up doing work twice.

Your blood sugar drops right down during the night. Even a cup of tea or coffee (preferably with milk) is better than nothing. A proper breakfast is better still. And after all, to cook and eat a fried egg plus a slice of toast or bread and butter takes no more than 10–15 minutes at most.

2 *Your main meal*. Make one meal a day your main meal, and try to eat it in reasonable calm. Whether you eat it at midday or in the evening depends mainly on your living-pattern; what matters is avoiding a whole succession of snacks bolted down at speed – a

sure recipe for indigestion and bad temper. It should have protein, vegetable(s), fruit, and as much carbohydrate (potatoes, rice, bread) as you think enough.

3 *Your third meal*. See that your third meal of the day, whenever you eat it, is as well balanced, even if less substantial, than your main meal. Not coffee plus cream cake, but a roll and butter with cheese, apple, milk.

4 *Down with in-betweens!* People often nibble away out of habit, not hunger. If you really do get peckish, pieces of cheese, carrot, apple, are better than biscuits. Or, if you're doing heavy physical work, you might find a thermos of Bovril or Marmite – if you like them – more sustaining than coffee or tea.

Don't be a Mother Hubbard

Always have a few handy foods which keep well. Dried milk; eggs; tinned sardines, tuna, frankfurters; tinned and dried soups; spaghetti; meat sauce; crispbreads and crackers. What you choose depends on your cooking and storage facilities, but see that you always have something around to feed yourself and friends. Replace your store as you use it.

'But I can't afford to eat properly'

I'd be the first to agree wholeheartedly that it's much easier to eat well and sensibly if you've got

Problem Corner

So you feel you're too fat?

You've only got to use your eyes to see for yourself that many of us are overweight. Doctors keep telling us that we eat too much. Magazines and newspapers are full of diets and slimmers' hints, so it's not surprising that many of us are very figure conscious indeed.

But oddly enough, though many people who ought to slim don't, others who shouldn't try do. So before you become agitated and start cutting down, make quite sure that you need to.

There are several different figure types. Some people are born to be rounder, heavier-framed, more muscular, than others. People of the same height in perfect health can have quite different weights. You're not too fat just because you weigh more than the lightest person you know.

You probably *are* overweight if (a) your stomach bulges past your hip bones; (b) your bottom and thighs are flabby and soft even when you tighten your muscles; (c) you can pinch a good handful of flesh away from your rib-cage.

Why?

If you are overweight, the first thing to do is work out why.

Is it recent? If so, have you changed your way of eating? Dropped regular meals for chips, biscuits, cakey-snacks? If so, you need to change back – fast.

Or are you eating the same but cutting down on exercise? If so, you'll either have to eat less or walk more.

Have you been putting on weight gradually? Then your

pattern of eating is probably wrong. Check back to *your eating plan* (p. 56) and see where yours is different.

Do you succumb to temptation and fall for luscious pastries? Then change your travelling route, or leave extra money behind.

Are you a sweet nibbler? This alone could tip the balance. Don't have any sweets on you.

Have you given up smoking and taken to other titbits to reward yourself? Try eating raisins or cubes of cheese.

Do you eat because you are bored? Then find some outside occupation (see p. 204); or if you nibble because you're sitting still, keep your hands occupied – try knitting, or carving, or embroidery, or play with worry beads as the Greeks and Arabs do.

If you think you need to lose a great deal of weight, then you must consult a doctor first. You should never go on to crash diets of any kind for longer than a day without medical advice. Many of these are basically unsound and could be damaging.

Losing weight. If you only want to lose a few pounds, then you can do it on your own by adopting the eating plan on p. 56, taking to heart the warning against sugar, and cutting down on carbohydrates (especially cakes and biscuits).

The safest way is to lose a little at a time and keep on losing it steadily.

If you've been eating the right food but too much of it, then keep eating the same kind – but only half as much. And/or exercise. Walk instead of using the bus. Cycle instead of taking the car.

There are various clubs and organizations which can provide help and encouragement. One with branches in many different areas is the Weight Watchers' Club for both males and females. (For your local branch write to Weight Watchers Ltd, 1–2 Thames Street, Windsor, Berks.) If you're serious about slimming, and feel you may lapse, these can provide just the stimulus you need. They also publish a helpful book, *Weight Watchers – a way of life,* 75p + 15p post.

Problem Corner continued...

So you think you're too thin?

For those struggling desperately to lose weight it seems like a bad joke to realize that there are actually people who complain of being too thin. But if you've a salt cellar neck, skinny wrists and bony thighs, you can feel quite as conspicuous as if you were fat.

If you're not just thin, but desperately thin, and if you also have any other reason for feeling you're in less than perfect health (if you tire easily; get breathless; cough; vomit), then you *must see a doctor.* Describe your symptons, and let him/her decide whether or not there is any medical decision which needs taking.

But if you're skinny but full of pep and vigour, eating well, rarely tired, then you're probably just a live wire destined to stay that way. What about the rest of your family? Your parents, brothers, sisters? If they're thin too, it's probably a family trait. You may have to accept it.

If you're really set on thickening up, check these points.

Do you give yourself enough time to eat? Or are you always on the run? Do you enjoy eating? Or do you find your food unpalatable? (This can happen when people eat too much institution food.) Do you worry a lot? This can both prevent your eating properly and burn up energy in nervous tension.

Make deliberate efforts to sort out your problems (see also p. 129). Seek help where necessary. Try to calm down and relax.

Ironically, it's much harder to put weight on than lose it. Your doctor may be able to give you specific advice: otherwise, drink more milk, eat plenty of cream, butter and potatoes. Eat soup before your meals. Nibble nuts between meals. Have a sweetened milk drink at bedtime. Do, in fact, all the things that overweight people are warned against! (But don't eat sweets in quantities, or you'll eat even less for your main meals and may end up thinner still – but spottier as well.)

You may still not succeed in putting on more than the odd pound or two. Console yourself with the knowledge that you'll probably stay extremely fit and healthy to a fine old age. And *never* tell your plumper friends how impossible you find it to put on weight!

plenty of cash rolling in: but it's not true that a good diet *has* to be expensive. Sprats and coley are as nutritious as sole – and just as tasty. Kidneys and liver well cooked are luxury items in other countries. Fresh fruit costs less than cakes.

The less money you have, the more imaginatively you have to plan, buy and eat. It can be done. Remember that it really is false economy to cut down on essential foods. Over a period – weeks or months, depending on what kind of credit your diet has built up in the past – not only your health but your shape and looks certainly suffer.

Beating eating out

There's one main drain on most young adults' purses: the fact that they're forced to eat out at least once a day.

When you eat out, you pay not only for the food itself, but for wages, insurance, fuel, rent, rates, VAT and profits. Take-away food is cheaper, because overheads are less: but none the less, whenever you buy prepared food it's seldom you can avoid spending over the odds. The only exception is when you eat in subsidized canteens, as in schools, colleges and many larger welfare-conscious firms. Cooking standards of course vary, but if you have the chance of eating a meal which, in effect, is being partly paid for by someone else, it's common sense to make the most of it.

One other popular form of subsidy is luncheon vouchers. Because today they rarely begin to cover the cost of a meal, you may prefer to stack them together for a better lunch twice a week; especially if on the other days you take a packed lunch.

If there's nothing like this going

for you, think twice before you fall into the habit of *regularly* dropping in at your local café or fish and chip shop or take-away. Remember you'll be paying roughly two to three times what the food is worth. And with rare exceptions you pay high prices for pre-cut sandwiches too.

If you possibly can, why not take a packed lunch instead? You can pick things *you* enjoy and eat them when you feel like it. It's true it'll take a few minutes to put together – but then think of the time you'll save by not queueing midday.

What about the social aspect? This can present problems. If everyone else is trotting off every day it isn't easy to explain that you honestly can't afford it without starving in the evening or next day.

Compromise. Eat out once or twice a week, and be too busy the other times. Or say you're on a strict diet and limited to a half of bitter or one coffee or whatever. Or, if it's possible for anyone's flat/room to be a central meeting-place, suggest everyone brings along a modest contribution (ham, tomatoes, bread).

Packed Food

Packed food needn't be boring, time-consuming – or even cold.

You don't *have* to take sandwiches. Try rolls and butter in a plastic box.

For protein, take sliced cooked meats, cheeses (many varieties), pâtés, tinned fish.

With the help of thermos jars as well as flasks you can take hot stews, soups, drinks.

For vegetables you can choose any kind of raw salad thing (see salads, p. 97). Plus salad dressing (in a screw-top jar). Take fresh fruit too.

And there aren't many places you can't get milk around the corner.

(If you're putting on weight – or even if you aren't – you'll find a good selection of tasty packed lunches in *The Slimmer's Cookbook* by John Yudkin and G. M. Chappell (Penguin, 1963).

Coping with Fancy dinners out

When you're the guest

There's no reason why being taken out to eat in a fancy restaurant should be anything more than a pleasant – if expensive – way of passing the time.

But it can be an ordeal. And often is.

So the first thing to remember is *don't fuss*. If you're being taken out, it's up to your host/hostess to look after you, cope with where to sit, help you to choose, and so on.

If you want to get rid of your coat a waiter will take it – unless, in a large restaurant, you've already left it in the cloakroom. If you're a female, someone will pull out the seat for you ; and, as you sit down, will push it in towards the table. No need to yank at it in a frenzy.

Look at the menu. Most restaurants offer two different kinds. If you choose the *table d'hôte*, you have a limited selection of dishes, and you (or in this case your host/hostess) pay a fixed price for – generally – three courses. If you eat from the *à la carte* menu, you pick whatever you want and pay for each individual dish. A few restaurants only offer a *table d'hôte* : others only offer *à la carte*. Which offers the best value depends on how much you want to eat and how good the cooking is.

An *à la carte* menu is normally divided into sections. What these are depends on whether the restaurant is English, French, or something more exotic. A typical menu might include appetizers/fish/meat/cold dishes/vegetables/desserts/savouries/cheeses : but an Italian restaurant, for example, would have a section on pastas (spaghetti-type foods), a fish restaurant would be devoted – obviously – to fish, a Chinese restaurant often divides its menu into chicken dishes, pork dishes, rice dishes, etc.

Many menus are written in French, which can be a problem if you've forgotten most of what you learned at school. Here are a few common words. *Potages* – soups. *Poissons* – fish. *Entrées* – main meat dishes. *Agneau* – lamb. *Veau* – veal. *Légumes* – vegetables. *Petits pois* – peas. *Haricots verts* – beans. *Fromages* – cheese.

If most of the menu remains a total blank, pick a couple of items in each section to ask about. Don't feel awkward about it. Many terms used in menus are in any case incorrect, misunderstood, or dreamed up by the restaurant concerned.

A conventional meal today would be a starter (soup or melon or pâté etc.); a main course (meat or fish); afters (cheese or dessert). If this is too much for you (it is for me) you can either choose a main course alone; or starters plus a main course; or main course plus afters. (A more elaborate meal might have four or five courses; fish as well as meat; and so on.)

Decide on the main course first. This makes it simpler to decide what, if anything, you want besides. If you want to concentrate on fish, you probably won't want fish to start with: if you settle for steak and kidney pie, you won't feel like apple pie to follow.

If you do end up eating several courses, don't be baffled by the cutlery. The waiter will remove what you don't need. After that you work from the outside in.

If you're asked what you want to drink, please yourself. If you have no idea, ask for suggestions. If you're not used to drinking, the main thing is *not to drink too much* (see p. 281).

Whoever is taking you out presumably wants you to have a good time. So do. Don't shout, giggle, get drunk, fall into the soup, or off your chair, and you stand a better chance of being popular all round. Incidentally, don't forget your host/hostess's pocket. If you don't know how well off he/she is there's no need whatever to set out to beggar him/her. Use your common sense.

When you're host/hostess

This is hardly likely to happen to you out of the blue or without a little preliminary reconnaissance.

But if you have to/want to and you're new to it, the simplest thing is to ring the restaurant and reserve a table. Saves hanging around wondering whether you will/won't get in.

If this is a private and not a business occasion make sure you can afford it. *Time Out* (for London), local newspapers, friends, may all help to give you some idea of what kind of cash is involved. Never take anyone anywhere you feel you can just about manage. You'll be stuck if you can't. Pick somewhere more modest, and be prodigal.

You'll be shown to your table, helped to sit down. It's now up to you to ask your guest(s) what he/she/they would like. Offer suggestions if they seem uncertain. Don't force them to eat more than they want. Ask the waiter to explain items on their behalf.

If you want to order wine, conventionally red goes with meat, white with fish. If you know nothing about wine, most restaurants have a house (or carafe) wine which is modest in price and perfectly acceptable (while if you pick from a wine list at random you may pick one hideously sweet). The wine waiter takes your order.

The bill is an elaborate thing these days. On top of the separate items you often get:

(a) a cover charge ('couvert'). This is an arbitrary sum per eater which is supposed to include the table setting — i.e. anything from use of a paper napkin to damask all over, garlic bread, olives, and tit-bits. You have to pay it and like it.

(b) VAT.

(c) Service charge 10–15 per cent. The service charge should go directly to the staff. 10–15 per cent of the sizeable bill you'll get is a considerable amount. I don't myself see any reason why you should be blackmailed into paying still more on top. (Restaurant staff: if you're not getting this, what's your union doing about it?)

Note: It is almost impossible to eat out well and cheaply. Which is not, in many cases, the restaurant's fault. Be prepared to pay.

It's up to you, your personality, your financial situation, to decide how best to handle this side of it.

When you do eat out, use your skill to get the best food value for your money. Pick whichever meal seems to provide most protein and vegetable. Fill up the gaps with potatoes, bread or rolls, never with high-priced high-carbohydrate low-food-value cakes, biscuits or fancy gateaux. Water is free, so unless you're going to pine away without tea or coffee, give a cuppa a miss.

2 FUSS-FREE COOKING

First steps

You may have anything from bare ckg. fac. to a complete kitchen, and obviously the better your equipment and the more space you have the easier it is to be an all-round cook. But even if you've only one gas ring or a roaster–toaster, or even – at a pinch – just an electric kettle, it is possible to prepare yourself adequate and tasty meals.

But no matter how constricted you are, you need:
– some basic equipment
– some idea of what to buy and where
– some understanding of the main rules.

Glance at what follows; leave out what seems impractical for you and go ahead with the rest.

What you need before you start

1 small sharp knife (blade 9 cm. long).

1 larger heavier sharp knife (blade 16 cm. long).

Don't think you can do without these. It's impossible to prepare food easily and quickly with just any old table knife. You can buy knives like these in many ironmongers and sometimes Woolworth's. Wooden handles are less slippery. See that the cutting edge of the blades is paper thin, and that the point is a real *point*, not a blunted end.

If you can afford it buy too:

1 even larger heavier chopping knife (blade approx. 20 cm. long, broader, heavier).

1 knife sharpener. Either of these

kinds is cheap and easy to use.

1 chopping board. Plain wood is best.

1 potato peeler. I find the swivel type quickest. A potato peeler like this means you can peel potatoes, carrots, apples etc. very quickly and thinly.

1 wooden spoon. Better than a metal spoon for stirring foods as they cook, because it won't scrape pans or get too hot to hold.

1 sharp serrated bread knife.

1 fish slice. (Not just for fish, but turning eggs etc. too.)

1 measuring cone. Cheaper than scales, takes up less room.

2 saucepans. 1 small pan (1–1·5 litre), 1 larger pan (2–3 litre) – with lids.

Buy heavyweight pans only. (Plain aluminium is best.) With these you can fry as well as stew; food won't stick or catch nearly so easily.

1 frying pan (16 cm in diameter). Cheap thin frying pans are useless for practically everything except frying eggs. *Make sure your frying pan has a flat bottom*.

1 asbestos mat. To help stop food catching, especially if your gas or electric ring doesn't adjust down

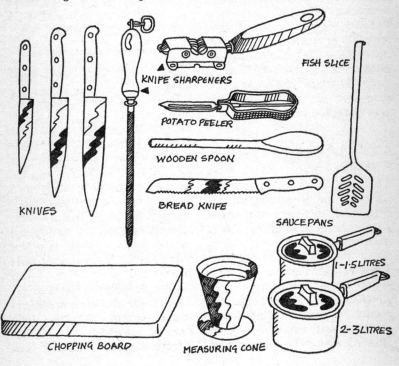

KNIFE SHARPENERS

FISH SLICE

POTATO PEELER

WOODEN SPOON

BREAD KNIFE

KNIVES

SAUCEPANS

1–1·5 LITRES

2–3 LITRES

CHOPPING BOARD

MEASURING CONE

as far as it should.

1 casserole with lid. 1 litre size convenient to start with. Stoneware is best. Earthenware's more fragile, glass needs more cleaning.

1 large basin.

1 colander.

1 tin opener.

1 grater. Metal. Plastic isn't sharp enough.

1 rotary beater. The cheapest kind will do, but won't last.

1 dish mop.

1 gentle scouring pad. (Nylon or similar.)

1 harsher scouring pad. (Metal – but use only in emergencies, e.g. badly burnt pans.)

1 or 2 mopping-up cloths.

...not utensils, but very important:

1 kitchen timer. Just about the only secret in good cooking is to have everything done just right – neither overcooked (and either pappy or burnt) or undercooked (and either impalatable or plain inedible). Experts may cook by the hairs of their wrists, but beginners certainly can't. Perhaps

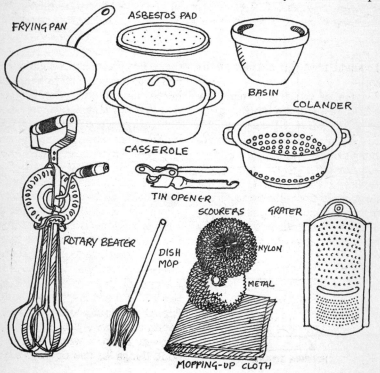

FRYING PAN

ASBESTOS PAD

BASIN

COLANDER

CASSEROLE

TIN OPENER

ROTARY BEATER

DISH MOP

SCOURERS   GRATER

NYLON

METAL

MOPPING-UP CLOTH

APRONS

I FEEL SO MANLY IN MY BUTCHER STRIPE APRON...

1 PAIR RUBBER GLOVES

FRIDGE

I should have put a timer at the top.

1 apron. If you're a he-man buy a he-man's apron – butcher stripe or plain white. Even if you're daintily female you need something practical and covering.

1 pair rubber gloves. Again, not romantic, but practical. You can do most kitchen chores in gloves if you try, and if you don't want dishpan hands there's positively no reason why you should have

KITCHEN TIMER

them. Buy cheap lightweight ones, and since one is bound to wear out faster than the other, don't forget that you can always turn an extra one inside-out (blow it) to use on the other hand.

A fridge. There now, I can hear you gasping. Well, it is a bit of a jump, I admit, from pennies spent on gloves. But on mature consideration I really believe that having a fridge is the one thing which makes eating in your own hovel a truly practical and economical proposition. If a room is warm enough for you to cook or work in it's not going to be cold enough to store perishable food.

With a fridge, you can buy only once or twice a week. You can cook things for two or three days at once and leave them without any worries. You can buy market bargains when you pass without feeling they're going to go bad before being eaten. And no bothers about mice or flies.

You can get a perfectly good second-hand fridge from £5–£10. Try your local paper, newsagents' cards, or *Exchange and Mart*. You can always sell it again later.

Stocking up

To start with, buy only what you want when you want it.

Then try looking ahead and buying for three or four days at a time. That way, you'll stock up on the kind of goods, particularly *dried goods* (flour, cereals, salt, tea etc.) that you want without having to think too hard.

When you're buying *packaged goods* choose a clean shop in preference to a dirty one, and check any date stamps visible.

Larger sizes generally work out proportionately cheaper than smaller, but don't buy in quantity unless you've got enough room for storage, are sure you'll finish whatever it is before it goes bad, and know having more won't mean you eat too much. Prices may vary from shop to shop, but unless you've a lot of time to spend in shopping around, it makes better sense to pick one shop and stick to it. Prices over a period generally average themselves out; and you'll get more individual service, especially from smaller shops, once you're known.

When you buy *frozen foods*, make sure they're always completely frozen, and never buy from an overloaded fridge. Food in these fridges may defrost and then refreeze, which could be dangerous.

Frozen fruit and vegetables are dearer than fresh ones in season at that moment (see p. 79). Fish may sometimes be cheaper (but see p. 76). Prepared uncooked meat (beefburgers etc.) is quick and tasty but usually compares in price to the dearest fresh meat (see p. 72). If you buy pre-cooked meat (in beef dinners etc.) you almost always pay heavily for the small (generally unweighted) portion of protein.

Tinned foods vary enormously in quality. Some meat, fish and vegetables are worthwhile, others overcooked, overpriced and tasteless. Test and see. Tinned fruit is expensive, usually in a heavy syrup, and fattening.

Fresh foods are both more interesting and more complicated. Remember, whatever you're buying, that (1) it almost always costs more if it's pre-packed in any way; (2) it'll often cost more if the shop is in an expensive area.

Choosing meat

There are three ways you can

buy meat.

1 *Pre-packaged* in separate poly-thene-wrapped portions from fridges in supermarkets or self-service stores.

Advantages

(a) You know exactly what you're paying.

(b) If the labelling's good, it tells you what you're getting and possibly even how to cook it.

(c) If you're buying from a well-kept shop with efficient stock-control, you can be sure that the meat is clean and uncontaminated.

Disadvantages

(a) You have to take what's there, which may mean getting two chops instead of one, paying good money for fat.

(b) The labelling may be un-informative or even wrong.

(c) If the shop is *not* well kept, the meat may be of doubtful freshness. Don't buy pre-packed meat which is damp, limp or sweating.

(d) You'll almost certainly be paying a higher price than for meat sold over the counter.

2 *Pre-cut meat sold from the window* (which may or may not be refrigerated) in a butcher's shop.

Advantages

(a) No embarrassment, because you can decide what you want before you go in the shop.

(b) You can both pick and choose and buy small quantities.

(c) It's usually a few pence cheaper than pre-packed meat. (But note what the relative prices are, and keep your eyes open.)

Disadvantages

(a) If the window isn't refrig-erated (most aren't) the food may not be as fresh as it should be. This is particularly important in summer. *Don't buy food on which flies and wasps are gorging themselves.*

3 *Meat not pre-cut* and perhaps not even in the window at all: the old-fashioned butcher's shop.

Advantages

(a) More hygienic. The meat is generally in cold store – especially in summer – until actually needed.

(b) If the butcher's friendly (most are) he'll cut for you exactly what you want when you want it, even if you only want a small quantity, and will mince and bone cheaper cuts.

(c) Usually no dearer than but-chers offering less service, and often cheaper than super-markets.

It's easiest to start in the super-markets, especially when you know nothing at all; but if you're often cooking for one, and count-ing the pennies, it makes sense to pluck up courage and head for a proper butcher.

What meat to buy

There are many different cuts of meat, which you'll find clearly described and identified in any good elementary cookery book (see p. 103). These are the points to remember.

The dearest carcass meat. Meat which has little tissue (gristle) running through it, a small proportion of fat (or none), a small proportion of bone (or none). This meat needs nothing to make it edible but the bare cooking process – frying, grilling, roasting. It's either quick or simple or both, but the cost per portion is high. Meat like this includes: *Beef –* sirloin, fillet, rump steak, topside, ribs etc. *Lamb –* chops (chump, loin, neck) leg, shoulder. *Pork –* chops (chump, loin), fillet, leg, hand.

The middle range of meat. This has a much higher proportion of connective tissue, a higher proportion of fat, and/or a higher proportion of bone. Generally, it needs cooking by a longer process (stewing, casseroling) and often other ingredients added for flavour. It's just as nutritious as more expensive cuts, at least as tasty (can be more interesting) and cheaper (but watch the cost of those extras). Meat like this includes: *Beef –* chuck steak, leg, shin, skirt. *Lamb –* middle neck. *Pork –* spare ribs, best end of neck. (You can also often fry or grill these.)

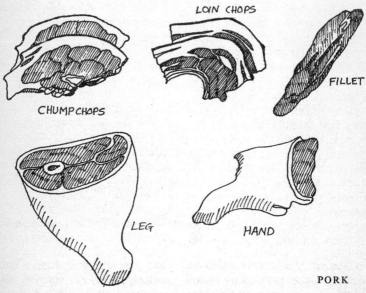

LOIN CHOPS

CHUMP CHOPS

FILLET

LEG

HAND

PORK

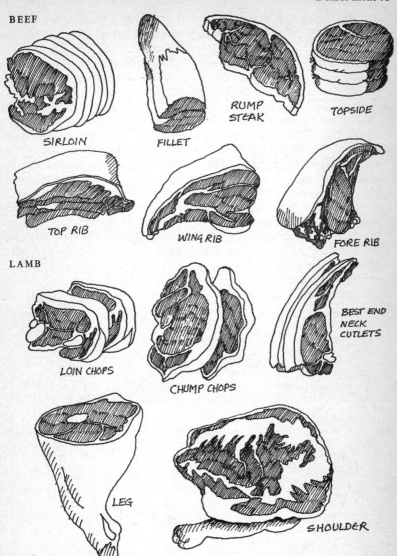

BEEF

SIRLOIN

FILLET

RUMP STEAK

TOPSIDE

TOP RIB

WING RIB

FORE RIB

LAMB

LOIN CHOPS

CHUMP CHOPS

BEST END NECK CUTLETS

LEG

SHOULDER

Cheapest of all. Meat which has a much higher proportion of connective tissue, bone or fat. Meat like this includes: *Beef* – anonymously labelled 'stewing steak' (chopped up fatty bits and pieces

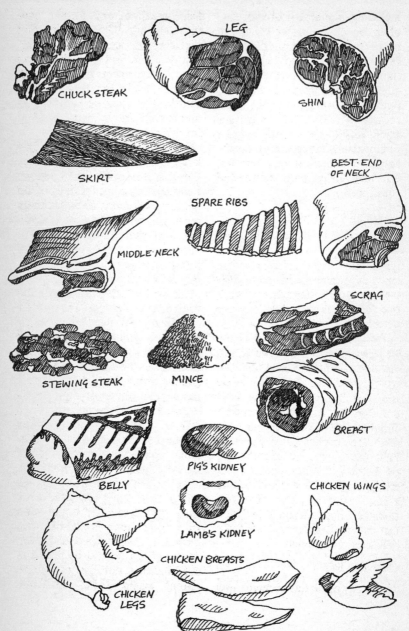

CHUCK STEAK

LEG

SHIN

SKIRT

SPARE RIBS

BEST·END OF NECK

MIDDLE·NECK

SCRAG

STEWING STEAK

MINCE

BREAST

BELLY

PIG'S KIDNEY

LAMB'S KIDNEY

CHICKEN WINGS

CHICKEN LEGS

CHICKEN BREASTS

including, e.g. scraps of shin etc., often by no means as cheap, in proportion to better middle-range cuts, as it ought to be), mince (minced up version of the above – quality varies from butcher to butcher). *Lamb* – scrag end, breasts ('TENDER SWEET BREASTS' as a local butcher optimistically labels them). *Pork* – belly. Some belly is very very fat, but lean belly both stews and roasts well.

Bargain basement

Kidneys (all kinds) and liver (all kinds except ox liver) are as quick and simple to cook as the most expensive meats, taste delicious (properly treated) and work out cheaper as you need little per person.

Chicken. Most butchers sell chicken pieces or half a chicken if you ask them. Small frozen chicken pieces seem to me absolutely tasteless, but maybe I've been unlucky. Marks and Spencer's cunningly sell chicken portions divided into packets of the same kind (all wings, or drum-sticks, or breasts). Wings come very cheap, and if you salt and pepper them, butter slightly, and grill them till crisp (see pp. 93, 95) you can eat them skins and all for a delicious cheap meal.

Choosing fish

You may never have bought 'wet fish', as they used to put over fishmongers', in your life, and perhaps you see no point when you've got a fish and chip shop handy. But, again, fish you cook yourself works out cheaper than fish cooked for you and it's so quick and simple that it's ideal for beginners.

If you're one of the surprisingly large number of people who say they just don't like fish, I confess I was the same until it dawned on me just how many varieties there were, and how easy it was to add this and that for very different flavours. And remember, fish is a first-rate source of protein, vitamin D (oily fish) and iodine.

It is best to try and find a good fishmonger. Standards vary tremendously. In the best, you get plenty of choice, fresh fish sold from a refrigerated window, the size of fish or portion you ask for. (In the worst, you may find no more than three or four kinds exposed all day on an open counter to dirt and flies.) Many of the best fishmongers tactfully label their fish 'skate', 'cod', 'squid', and so on to help you choose. Be adventurous. When you're buying a *whole fish*, make sure the eyes are bright and sticking-up, not dull and flat, skin gleaming, flesh plump and firm. *Pieces of fish* should be firm and solid looking, not limp or watery.

Some *supermarkets* sell fresh,

non-frozen, pre-cut fish, poly-thene-wrapped from the fridge. It may be fresher and safer in hot weather than from a fishmonger, but you have an even more limited choice than with meat. Since fish deteriorates quickly, it is particularly important to buy from a store with a sound repu-tation and high turnover.

One of the most popular ways of buying fish is *pre-packed and frozen*. This can work out as cheap or even cheaper when the fishing's bad; a lot dearer when it's not. There's little choice, and the cheapest fish is never avail-able.

What fish to buy

With fish, price is less closely connected with taste and easy cooking than is the case with meat.

Herrings and mackerel are con-structed much the same as trout, cook as simply, taste as good; but are cheaper. Various white fish fillets are not unlike in taste and texture, but vary in price de-pending what fish they've come from.

So: basically you can choose from three different cuts, so to speak, but you'll find different prices in each category.

1 You can buy *whole fish*, gener-ally from 15 cm–37 cm long. These can be either round fish (herrings, mackerel, trout) or flat fish (plaice,

soles, dabs). Round fish are oilier, have more flavour, and are richer in vitamins A and D. Flat ones are drier and blander. Whole fish need cleaning (gutting) – the fishmonger will do this if you ask.

2 You can buy *fillets* cut either from much larger fish (cod, coley, haddock etc.) or from the flat fish above (especially plaice). These are slabs of fish containing (theo-retically) no bones.

3 You can buy *steaks* – a chunk of fish plus a largish piece of bone – cut mostly across the body of large fish (cod, halibut etc.).

Fish costs fluctuate almost more than any other food, but provided it's fresh whatever fish is cheapest is the best bargain. *Coley* is generally one of the cheapest filleted (therefore non-bony) fish, which looks dark on the slab but goes white when it's cooked. Mackerel is often the cheapest round fish, and if fresh is delicious.

Shellfish can also be a good buy, particularly mussels in season. Mussels must be *shut* to be fresh. Simple to do. Consult a good cookery book.

Smoked fish (smoked haddock, finnan haddie – the bright yellow fish – kippers) can be surprisingly economical and delicious.

Bargain basement

Kipper fillets. They are absol-utely scrumptious, almost bone-

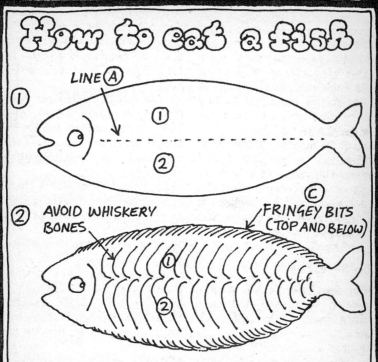

How to eat a fish

① LINE Ⓐ
① ②

② AVOID WHISKERY BONES
Ⓒ FRINGEY BITS (TOP AND BELOW)
① ②

Most fish actually come neatly marked out into sections. All that's missing is printed instructions.

If you look at the fish on your plate you'll see from the patterning on the skin a line running lengthwise along it (line A). Underneath this runs the backbone. Remove the skin if you want. Underneath you'll see the fish divides neatly into sections 1 and 2, with the grain running diagonally from the centre towards the tail. Slide a fork (or knife) down into the fish along the line A, and gently pull the flesh upwards and sideways, in the direction of the grain, away from the backbone. This comes away quite neatly and without any bones. (You may run into a little trouble at the head with long whiskery bones, but if you go carefully, continuing to use your fork to

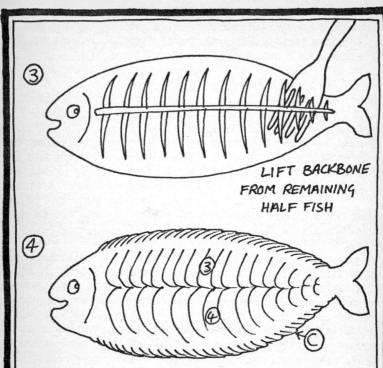

LIFT BACKBONE
FROM REMAINING
HALF FISH

pull the flesh away from the bones without breaking them, you'll do all right.)

Don't bother with the fringey bits around the edge (C). These are packed full of tiny little bones. Leave well alone.

When you've finished sections 1 and 2 the backbone will be exposed. Slide your knife (or fork) underneath, and lift away the whole backbone. (You'll probably get more whiskery bits at the top. Slide your knife underneath to remove them.)

Now you can see sections 3 and 4. Polish them off in the same way, still ignoring the fringey bits at C.

This is a pretty effortless method of eating a fish. The thing to do is to proceed fairly slowly, and to avoid snapping off bones which then smuggle their way into your mouth.

free, and relatively cheap. You can also eat them raw with potato salad or brown bread and butter. Best ones are oak-sawdust-smoked.

Sprats. They are also very cheap and tasty. You can eat them bones and all if they are small enough. Otherwise, split down the front, flatten out, pull the tail forwards and the backbone will come away. Dust with flour and fry (see p. 89).

Choosing vegetables and fruit

When you buy *frozen vegetables and fruit* you're paying for the convenience of having them prepared and cooked for you. Fresh vegetables in season are almost always considerably cheaper.

Pre-packed, generally pre-washed vegetables in supermarkets are also more expensive. Sometimes, too, they are far from being as fresh as they should be. Look carefully at the contents of any package misted on the inside with condensation.

The best source for fresh fruit and vegetables is a good *greengrocer* with a high turnover who buys and sorts stock daily. If you've a fruit and vegetable market within reach, you're in luck. You can see what you're buying, prices are more competitive, and the stock changes daily.

When you're choosing, see that
– all green stuff is green and not yellow, crisp and not drooping.
– cauliflowers are white. (A small patch or two of yellow or black doesn't matter too much, but ones which are black all over aren't worth buying.)
– root vegetables (carrots, swedes, potatoes etc.) are firm and not dry and wrinkled.
– fruit looks fresh, not bruised or over-handled. (Though it may be worth buying damaged pears, peaches etc. at a much reduced price for chopping into fruit salads.)

Bargain basement

Most tomatoes, oranges, grapefruit, bananas, melons are marketed in Britain well before they're ripe; with the consequence that when they reach the right point for eating they're often considered 'over-ripe' and sold off cheap. Look out, especially in markets, for e.g. tomatoes dark bright red (but still firm), grapefruit darker in colour than usual, bananas flecked with black. They'll be both cheaper and better than anything else (a rare combination).

Storing food

Packaged goods. These will keep well in the packets in which you buy them (that's what they're designed for) *provided* that, once opened, you intend to eat them

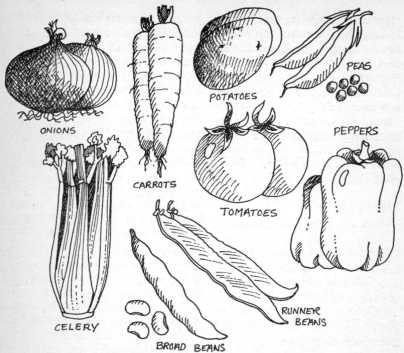

ONIONS

CARROTS

POTATOES

PEAS

PEPPERS

TOMATOES

CELERY

BROAD BEANS

RUNNER BEANS

reasonably quickly. But you will need to empty them into e.g. old screw-top coffee jars if (a) you've opened them so carelessly you have left a dirty great hole for flies to whizz in, (b) you propose keeping them some weeks, (c) you've limited storage space, so food may pick up unwanted smells or (d) *you think you have mice.*

Fresh foods. These are more of a problem. If you have a *fridge* (see p. 69) fresh meat and cleaned chickens keep 4–5 days: mince, kidneys, liver, 1–2 days. (Put meat on a plate covered loosely with paper. If it's closely confined it sweats. If totally uncovered it dries out.)

In the vegetable box, fresh fruit and vegetables will keep 4–7 days; root vegetables considerably longer. Even with a fridge, fresh fish and shellfish should be eaten the same day. Once cooked, fish (not shellfish) will keep 2–3 days.

If you've a cold north-facing *larder*, fresh foods will keep in the winter about as long as in a fridge, in spring/autumn half as long, in summer hardly at all.

If you've nowhere but your room to keep food, you can really only buy in advance packaged goods, eggs, root vegetables, and hard fruit. Meat, fish, green vegetables, you'll have to buy as and when you need them.

Bread. Proper baked bread keeps much better than packaged sliced. It may dry out (makes good toast) but won't get mouldy. You don't *have* to keep it in a bread bin. Mine lives in a massive stoneware casserole with a lid, which was dear to start with, but can also be used for cooking, fermenting wine, or serving up masses of hot soup or punch.

DOWN WITH NUDITY! NEVER LEAVE FOOD UNCOVERED AND EXPOSED

Pre-cooking

Wash your hands before you start

Most food needs preparing in some way. You have to peel, slice or chop. Here's how to go about it.

When you peel with the swivel peeler mentioned on p. 67, hold the handle *only* – don't try to put your finger on the blade as you would with a knife. Some people peel more easily towards them,

SLICING A LARGE POTATO

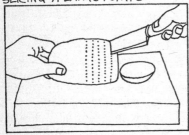

others peel away from the body.

When you slice. The larger the object you want to slice, the heavier the knife and the longer the blade you need for maximum efficiency. You need either to

CHOPPING ALMONDS ETC.

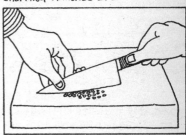

move the blade to and fro, or to apply pressure downwards to allow the weight of the blade to do the work. Which works best depends on the shape of the blade, its size and its weight. You'll have to experiment.

If you're slicing e.g. a large potato, cut a thin slice off the bottom to provide a flat non-slip surface.

If you're using a serrated knife (for e.g. tomatoes) the wiggly bits

CHOPPING AN ONION

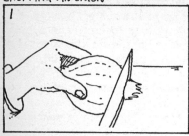

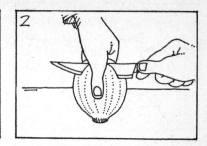

ONION FROM ABOVE: CUT BROKEN LINES, HALF-TURN, CUT SOLID LINES, ROOT UNDERNEATH ALL THE TIME

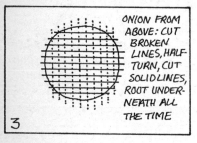

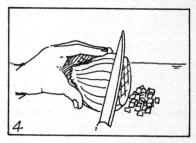

do the work. Saw the knife to and fro, take it slowly, and don't try to exert pressure downwards.

When you chop. You need your heaviest knife. Put the herbs or almonds or whatever on the board, hold the handle in one hand and the blunt edge of the point in the other, and chop to and fro in an arc.

Two special easy ways –
to chop an onion

1 Slice across the stalk end and remove the skin.

2 Place the onion on the board with the root end down. Hold firmly. Slice downwards towards the root.

3 Turn the onion in a half circle. Hold firmly. Slice down towards

the root at right angles.

4 Turn the onion on its side. Slice down across the onion. The onion will fall neatly chopped in bits.

5 Throw away the skin and root, and rinse knife and board quickly in cold water to stop yourself crying.

to cut chips

1 Peel the potatoes.

2 Take each potato. Cut a thin slice lengthwise off the bottom to make a base.

3 Place the potato on its base. Cut a thin slice off the side and discard.

4 Slice regularly downwards, holding the potato together with the other hand as you do so.

5 Carefully turn the potato over

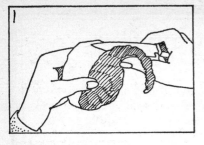

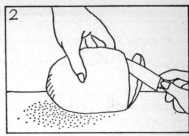

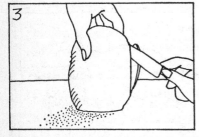

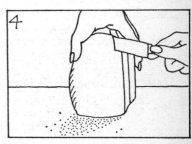

so the new straight-cut-edge is down. (The starch in the potato helps to keep it all stuck together.) Slice regularly downwards towards the new base.

You now have a chipped potato. This method takes no time at all. Obviously, the larger the potato, the more chips the quicker.

To prepare:

Vegetables. Root vegetables need peeling, after which you can either leave whole, slice across or slice lengthwise. Sprouts need the outer leaves removing and a cross cut in the base. Cabbages, greens etc. need the outer leaves removing, and the rest then sliced. (But the outer leaves are often usable, for e.g. cutting into soups.) All vegetables need thorough washing, if sluggy or insecty, in salted water. (But avoid leaving in water for longer than a few minutes. The vitamins drain out.)

Meat. It may need excess fat removing; and, for stewing steak, cutting into same-sized pieces leaving gristle and skin out.

Fish. It may need scaling (do it with a sharp knife against the way

Look sharp!

Kitchen knives, peelers, slicers, are all potentially dangerous tools and will cheerfully cut, peel and slice *you* if you mishandle them. I have three scars on my left hand to prove it.

So : when you use a knife remember

(a) Always use a sharp knife, a blunt one is far more dangerous. It skids.

(b) Always cut on a chopping board. Otherwise you're thinking more about the consequences of your cutting than about what you're actually doing.

(c) If you've washed the vegetables etc. before you attack them, dry them. It stops them sliding.

(d) Keep the two hands close together to give stability and control to the cutting hand : but don't let the holding hand stray into the way of the blade. Especially, make sure the index finger (pointing finger) doesn't stray forward into the path of the cutting edge. I've watched it happen.

the scales lie – but often the fishmonger does this for you) – or the skin removing. (This can be done, more easily, after cooking.) The fishmonger usually cleans/guts it for you (see 'Fish', p. 76).

The smaller the size you chop either vegetables or meat into, the quicker it cooks. All pieces should be roughly the same size, otherwise some bits get overcooked while others stay uncooked. If you cut vegetables too small you end up with soup, and, if you cut meat too small, you end up with something that looks like cat food.

N.B. After you've cut raw meat, wash both knife and board. Never put food you're going to eat uncooked (ham, tomatoes) on an unwashed board used for raw meat, or cut it with the same unwashed knife. (This can cause food poisoning.)

Cooking made clear

Note: There's more than one way of ending up with similar results, and most recipes have variants. If you've been taught other methods or recipes, then use them. But if you're a beginner, you can follow all these suggestions with reasonable confidence.

Basic Methods

No matter what your source of heat, *there are only a limited number of ways you can cook. What you end up with depends on what ingredients you use, how they're prepared, how you combine them, and how long you cook them. Here are the basic methods.*

On top of the cooker

Cooking in liquid

(usually in water, but you can use stock or milk).

Method. You put the ingredients in a pan, barely cover with liquid (use the least possible, but make sure everything's covered), add salt, pepper, any other flavourings necessary and bring to the boil. Once the liquid is bubbling, adjust the heat as low as possible while still keeping the water gently moving (this is called simmering), put on a lid (to prevent the kitchen steaming up and keep the flavour in the pan where it belongs) and leave until cooked. (If your pan is nearly full, with the

The time element

Obviously, stews and casseroles take a fair time to cook, and you won't want to come back, prepare your meal, and sit around waiting for two or three hours while it cooks. So what to do?

1 Consider buying a pressure cooker. (You can sometimes find bargains in kitchen sales.) With this you can cook vegetables and stews in about one third the normal time.

2 Prepare a casserole the night before and in the morning leave it cooking in the oven at a very low temperature. (See *Leave it to Cook* by Stella Atterbury, Penguin, 1968.)

3 If you have a fridge you could cook an enormous stew, say every four days: then each night cook up a portion with added bits and pieces to make it taste different. Tomatoes one night, olives the next, a little curry paste (Patek's is excellent) and so on. (But see note on page 89.)

Any of these suggestions make cooking cheap and tasty stews a practical possibility.

liquid near the top, then you'll need to leave the lid slightly crooked and only loosely fitting with room for the steam to escape. Otherwise the pan boils over.)

You can cook any of the cheaper cuts of meat, chicken pieces, bacon joints and almost all vegetables like this. (You could cook expensive cuts of meat like this too, but there wouldn't be much point to it: and you can cook fish but with care to avoid making it tasteless. See pp. 87–8.)

If you're cooking *meat, cut-up chicken, bacon,* you end up with a sort of stew. What kind of stew depends on what kind of meat and what other ingredients you add to it. How long it takes depends on how long it takes the longest-cooking item in the stew to become tender. (This is generally the meat: but it could be e.g. haricot or kidney beans.) Times for meat vary according to its quality and the size it is cut up into. Here are some very approximate times.

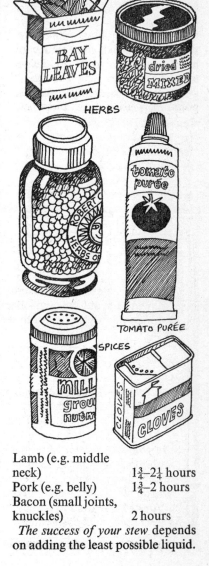

HERBS

TOMATO PURÉE

SPICES

Young roasting chicken joints	30–45 mins.
Old boiling fowl pieces	2–3 hours
Good quality, medium expensive steak suitable for stewing (e.g. chuck)	$1\frac{3}{4}$ hours
Cheaper stewing steak (e.g. leg)	$2\frac{1}{2}$–3 hours
Lamb (e.g. middle neck)	$1\frac{3}{4}$–$2\frac{1}{4}$ hours
Pork (e.g. belly)	$1\frac{3}{4}$–2 hours
Bacon (small joints, knuckles)	2 hours

The success of your stew depends on adding the least possible liquid.

(But it must *cover* what you're cooking. The bits that stick out can cook only in the steam.) Choose the best-sized saucepan for what you're cooking. What else you put in depends on what you're aiming at and what you have around.

You can add onions, carrots, potatoes, peas, celery, tomatoes, peppers, beans etc. You can use vegetable stock for the liquid: or add Marmite or stock cubes; or wine; or cider; or water plus flavouring plus 1 tbsp. vinegar; or even milk (good for chicken and pork).

(The various ingredients in your stew keep their flavour best if you fry them gently for a few minutes before you start: then add whatever liquid you are using.)

You can also try all kinds of *flavourings*: bay leaf, herbs (many varieties, not just the old parsley – experiment – but start with a little. They're strong. A pinch of the most flavoursome, e.g. thyme, to 1 tsp. of e.g. parsley is usually enough). Tomato purée. Spices (e.g. nutmeg). Stock cubes. Capers. Olives. Various kinds of salts (onion salt, garlic salt, celery salt).

Salt and pepper: you need approximately 1 flat tsp. salt, a good sprinkle of pepper, per $\frac{1}{2}$ kg of meat (none for bacon).

CAPERS   OLIVES

GARLIC SALT   ONION SALT

Obviously, if you add to your stew right at the beginning *all* the ingredients of various cooking times at once, some will be cooked long before the others. In a sense this doesn't matter – most of the flavour passes into the liquid part. But if you want the vegetables etc. to stay whole you'll need to add them at intervals.

You *can* boil *fish* but it's rarely a good idea, as most of the flavour vanishes into the liquid. (There's no point anyway, since almost all fish can be cooked better and quicker by other methods.)

You can, however, cook *finnan haddock in milk* (takes 3–5 mins.) and cook kippers by placing them in a jug and pouring boiling water on top (5–10 mins.). You can also make a delicious *fish soup* by putting bits and pieces from the fishmonger (make sure they're for human consumption) in a pan with onions or tomatoes, or whatever, simmering for 5–10 minutes and then removing the bones. Thicken if you like and/or add herbs (basil, dill, fennel, are good).

Start *timing* from the moment the water comes to the boil. (See 'Timing' on p. 91.) Boiled vegetables should be cooked in the shortest possible time in the least possible water. This gives the best flavour and the most vitamins. They should also be bitey, not limp or soggy. Once cooked, drain off the liquid (experienced cooks keep this stock for soup), put the vegetables back in the pan over a low heat until the surplus moisture dries out and they don't look wet. Most vegetables are improved by then adding a walnut-sized lump of butter and turning them in this until they're coated and gleaming.

If you're cooking *vegetables* like this you end up with plain boiled vegetables. Here's how long they take:

Beans (french/runner)	10–25 mins.	
Broad beans	5–20 mins.	
Cabbage	3–12 mins.	(It should be bitey – not squashy.)
Cauliflower (in sprigs)	5–15 mins.	
Celery	15 mins.– 1 hour	(or longer – depends on coarseness)
Courgettes	5–10 mins.	
Haricot beans (soaked)	2–3 hours	
Lentils	25–40 mins.	
Marrow (chunks)	5–10 mins.	How much salt to add? About
Parsnips	5–15 mins.	$\frac{1}{4}$ flat tsp. to 1 pint water;
Peas	10–25 mins.	but different vegetables take
Potatoes	17–25 mins.	different amounts. Always
Red cabbage	7–10 mins.	start with a little. You
Spinach	3–7 mins.	can add more right up to the
Sprouts	4–8 mins.	last moment, but you can't
Turnips	5–15 mins.	take it out.

MARMITE   STOCK CUBES

(*A better method* of cooking many vegetables, especially green ones and courgettes and marrow, is to fry them gently first in an oil/margarine mixture, then add about 1 cm of water, and cook them in this, stirring at intervals, until they're done and the water absorbed. But this does require attention. If you're not careful, you end up with the vegetable either half-raw or burnt to a cinder.)

If you want to add a sauce, see 'Thickening' on p. 94.

If you chop your vegetables up extra small you get vegetable soup. Mixed vegetable if you use mixed vegetables, potato if you use potato etc. You'll probably need to add a bit of Marmite, or a piece of a stock cube, for extra flavour. You can also add, e.g. chopped hard-boiled eggs, tiny pieces of fried bacon, cheese on top, for extra protein. *Soups are dead easy.* Also hot, tasty, comforting and *cheap*.

Shallow frying

You need a frying pan plus fat (a) to prevent the food sticking to

When heating up can let you down

It's safe to reheat casseroles etc. or fry up left-overs, *if* they have been covered and in the cool, away from the flies and infection, and *if* they are thoroughly reheated : either brought to the boil and kept at boiling point for several minutes, or fried so that the heat penetrates through.

But partly heating, or heating up food which has been left hanging around unchilled, is dangerous. So is using the oven to barely warm through cooked meats, pies or sausage rolls. Be particularly careful with pork and with anything which contains pork.

No food should be reheated more than once. See also *Left Over for Tomorrow*, Marika Hanbury-Tenison, Penguin, 1971.

Dried protein foods

Dried beans, peas, lentils etc. are all protein-rich foods. Peas and beans should theoretically be soaked overnight, but you can skip this if you pour *boiling* water over and leave for several hours. After this, you need to simmer them *slowly*, in water or stock, for 1–3 hours or even longer, depending on variety and age. Don't add salt until they're nearly tender. (Buy your dried foods from a shop with a rapid turnover. Two-year-old dried haricots won't cook in a month of Sundays.) Foods like red lentils or soya splits cook much faster, in half an hour or so, even without soaking.

All cooked peas, beans etc. are delicious with onion, tomato, parsley, butter and so on. Those that stay whole and firm are good drained and served cold with a vinaigrette (see p. 98).

You can find various soya-based meat substitutes. Perhaps the ground mince-type are the most successful. Do the initial soaking in a well-flavoured stock.

the pan and (b) to prevent dryness and add flavour to whatever you're cooking. You can use oil, lard, butter, margarine. For most purposes a mixture of half oil, half margarine is good. The more fat there already is in what you're cooking, the less you need in the pan to start with (e.g. for sausages you need no more than a few drops to grease the pan, for shallow-frying chips you may need it about 1 cm. deep depending on the size of your chips and how many).

You can fry any small cuts from the expensive grades of *meat* (chops, fillet steaks etc.); any *fish*; *sausages*; *bacon*; *onions*; *tomatoes*; *mushrooms* – and also, if you chop them up fine enough and stir–fry them Chinese style, many vegetables (*carrots*, *cabbage*, *cauliflower* etc.) which we would never normally think of frying.

Method. Heat the fat until it's very hot but before it starts to smoke. Then put in whatever you're frying, leave it for a few seconds until the heat has seared the outside (turned meat brown, dried the potato chips, or what-

Timing Problems

All the timings are approximate. It would be nice to be able to say 'Put the carrots on at 6.30 and take them off at 6.45 and you'll have perfect results.' But you can't be that precise.

How long exactly something takes depends on the heat of your oven, cooker, gas ring; how large your pan is; how much you're cooking; how small you've chopped everything; how fresh the food is; and so on.

But what the timings show is how long *comparatively* everything takes. You can see that cooking potatoes in the oven takes much longer than on top. That spinach cooks quicker than carrots. That chops are ready before stews.

And you can also work out how precise you must be.

You need to be extra particular over timing if you're (a) cooking quickly and with a high heat or (b) cooking something which needs only minutes to be ready. If you're grilling fish, you only have a few minutes leeway between well cooked and frizzled up. If you're cooking cabbage, even less between tenderness and slush.

On the other hand, if you're (a) cooking something slowly with a gentle heat or (b) cooking something which takes a long time to be done, an extra 15 or even 30 minutes more or less isn't going to bring disaster.

Once you've a little experience, you'll be able to adjust the timings to the way you yourself cook. Meanwhile, there's no substitute for using your timer, keeping an eye on what's going on, and *trying and testing* whenever necessary.

COORDINATION

If you want to be sure you get several dishes cooked and ready together at the same time, the simplest way is to make a list. Work out the time you want (or expect) to eat, and then work backwards.

Supposing you want to eat at *8.30 pm* – stew, boiled potatoes, sprouts. The stew you think will take 2 hours – the longest; so it will have to start *cooking* – all preparation done before – by *6.30 pm*. The potatoes take next longest (20 mins.) so they should go on at *8.05 pm.* (allowing for the time taken for the water to come to the boil). The sprouts take least time of all; say 7 minutes; so they should go on at about *8.18 pm.*

Once you get expert you won't need to write this down, but it's a help to start with.

ever) and then carefully turn over and sear the other side. Next adjust the heat down (probably to around half heat, but this is impossible to say, as cookers vary so much). You have to have the heat high enough to keep the oil/fat hot enough to continue the cooking process, but not so fierce that it burns the outside before the inside's cooked right through.

When you're frying foods which take a comparatively long time (e.g. chops) and you don't want a crisp outside, then you can cut down smells and splutters and increase the moisture content by placing a lid on the frying pan (so that the food cooks partly in its steam).

Successful frying takes both trial and error and your kitchen timer. Until you're really experienced, it's very difficult to know how well

whatever you're frying is doing merely by looking at it (especially with e.g. chops and sausages; much easier with chips). You need to *know* how long it has been sitting there to *know* that it's sufficiently done.

Here are approximate times. The simplest way is to divide the time in two, and turn the chop etc. over at half-time.

Lamb chops	15–20 mins.
Pork chops	20–25 mins.
Chipolatas	10–15 mins.
Big sausages	20–25 mins.
Fish steaks and fillets	5–10 mins.
Tomatoes (half)	5 mins.
Bacon rashers	2–5 mins.
Onions	5–10 mins.
Chips	10–15 mins.
Mushrooms	2–5 mins.

Again, the thinner the chops/

chips/fillets the quicker they cook.

You can fry most things without any kind of coating. If you want to add bulk or make a change you can add *batter* or *egg-and-bread-crumb* coating. (Consult one of the cookery books at the end.) The only time when you need to use a coating is when whatever you're cooking is so damp it may stick to the pan (e.g. fish). The simplest way is to dry it on kitchen paper as well as possible and then sprinkle very thinly with seasoned flour.

Don't forget that hot fat *burns*. Put the food in carefully with a pair of tongs, don't just fling it in. See that it's as dry as possible. (Shake chips first in a towel, for example. It's the reaction of water on oil that makes that nasty spluttering.)

When you've finished frying, if the food is particularly oily (chips usually are, mushrooms sometimes), put it on kitchen paper to absorb the excess fat.

Most people enjoy fried foods, but too much isn't good for your digestion. Don't grab the frying pan every day, or you may wish you hadn't.

Deep frying

Deep frying, involving a large quantity of oil or fat, is potentially a very dangerous method, unless you have a deep enough pan (most aren't) and nothing near to catch

fire. Hot oil can bubble up to well over twice its original depth when food is put in, and then overflow and catch fire. *Oil can also burst into flame spontaneously* when it reaches a high enough temperature. (There are over 11,000 oil fires – mostly from chip pans – each year.)

Practically anything you want to fry can be shallow fried, *including chips*. Don't try deep frying at all unless you've had plenty of experience and really know what you're doing.

Grilling

Grilling is very similar in effect and technique to shallow frying. Light the grill and allow it to become red hot. Place the food on the rack in the grill pan, and then – as with frying – adjust the heat to allow the food to continue grilling until cooked right through without burning.

Almost all foods which can be shallow fried can be grilled (but not potatoes or onions): that is, *sausages, chicken, bacon, most fish, expensive cuts of meat, kidney, mushrooms, tomatoes.*

For times, check the list for shallow frying as they're virtually the same.

If the food you're grilling is very dry (chicken joints, mushrooms) you need to put a little oil or melted butter on top before grilling.

How to thicken Sauces, Stews, Soups etc.

To *thicken*: means to make a liquid denser, creamier. This is the simplest of several methods. You can thicken stews and soups exactly the same way, and use the same method whether you're cooking on top of the cooker or in the oven.

Estimate the amount of liquid in the soup/stew you want to thicken. (If you can't estimate, drain it off and measure it.) Then, for each half pint of liquid, put 1 flat dessertspoonful of cornflour* in a basin, add 1–2 tbsp. cold water or milk, and mix to a cream (only takes a few seconds). Then, slowly, stir it into the soup/stew. Keep stirring until this is well blended in. (To start with, you may find it simpler to stir this into the liquid alone, and then add this mixture to the rest of what you're cooking. But once you've got confidence, you just pour the cornflour mixture slowly and directly into the pan or casserole.)

If you're cooking on top of the stove, keep stirring while you bring the whole lot gently up again to boiling point, then adjust the heat *right down*† and cook for 3–5 minutes.

If you're cooking inside the oven, just put the casserole back inside and leave it for a further 15–20 minutes.

*Beginners: *Make sure you use* cornflour, *not ordinary flour. (Flour thickens perfectly well, but it's trickier to handle and can go lumpy.)*

†Warning: *When you're cooking or reheating anything which contains starch, whether you've made it or it's tinned, whether it's soup or stew, it can catch and burn very easily. So if you want to heat it up on top of the cooker, keep the heat low. (You may need your asbestos mat.)*

If you have more liquid, you need more thickening (mixed in the same proportions). If you want it thicker still, add more cornflour pre-mixed in a paste in the same way, not just tipped in.

You can make most stews/soups more velvety by adding a small walnut of butter with the thickening.

If you want to make a sauce to go with *vegetables*, use cornflour in just the same way, but mix it to a cream with $\frac{1}{4}$ pint of milk and add to $\frac{1}{4}$ pint of liquid in which the vegetables have cooked. (Or adjust quantities to taste. It depends how strongly flavoured the stock is.) You can also add cream; parsley; cheese etc., etc.

Grilling is better for you and less fattening than frying.

In the oven

Note: Most ovens after lighting take 10 minutes *plus* to reach their correct cooking temperature. So remember to light yours at least ten minutes before you need it.

Baking and roasting

Strictly speaking, *baking* is cooking food in the oven by placing it without liquid or fat on an oven rack or a baking sheet. *Roasting* is cooking food with a little fat but without extra liquid. The two terms have become confused and one is often used to mean the other; however, when you're working from a recipe it will generally be perfectly obvious which one is meant.

Baking proper is for *cakes, bis-cuits, pastry, bread*, a few cuts of meat, some fish, a very few vegetables. You can only bake food which contains enough fat or moisture to prevent it from drying out when exposed to the direct heat of the oven.

You can bake *chops, sausages* and *chicken joints* by placing them on a grill in a baking pan containing a little oil, in the middle or top of the oven. Chops and sausages take from 30–45 minutes or longer in medium oven (no. 5, 360–75°F), chicken joints 20–35 minutes, depending on the size. (Though since the results are very similar to grilling, while it takes longer and uses more fuel, there's little advantage in using this method unless you have the oven on anyway.)

You can also bake *whole round fish*. 20–35 minutes in a medium oven (no. 5, 360–75°F).

Potatoes, onions, marrows all bake successfully. See the potatoes and marrows are well scrubbed, and leave the skin on the onions.

Times vary according to the heat of the oven and the size of the vegetable.

Approx. –

potatoes 1–1½ hours in a medium
oven (no. 5, 360–75°F)

onions 45 mins.–1¼ hours in a
medium oven
(no. 5, 360–75°F)

marrows 1½–2¼ hours in a medium
oven (no. 5, 360–75°F)

You can do them at either lower or higher temperatures, and adjust the time accordingly. Potatoes and onions are cooked when they are soft when squeezed, marrows when you push a skewer in at the fat end without resistance.

Roasting (sometimes called baking)

You roast by placing the food in an open dish or pan in a little fat (oil, lard, butter or dripping) and leaving it in the oven until cooked. Even with basting (spooning the fat now and again over the top of the food) this method is again only suitable for food which won't dry out in the oven heat. The hotter the temperature, the quicker it cooks – and the more it evaporates.

You can roast larger joints of meat, chickens etc., large whole fish.

It's an easy method. You don't have to watch anything while it's cooking, but you have to be reasonably accurate over timing. (Consult a cookery book.)

Roast-stewing

(My name) – often called baking, sometimes pot-roasting, sometimes braising.

You place the food in a little fat (oil, lard, butter, dripping) in a casserole or baking dish, sometimes after frying it on top of the oven for a few minutes first. You season it, cover it with a lid (sometimes adding 1–2 tbsp. water or other liquid first) and place it in the oven where it partly roasts and partly cooks in its steam. A medium heat is usually used.

You can use this for small joints of meat (under 1 kg.) which would otherwise dry out when simply roasted, for all kinds of fish, and for most vegetables except green ones.

Approximate times in a medium oven (no. 4–5, 360–75°F)

Fish fillets, steaks, and small whole fish	20–30 mins.
Tomatoes	20–30 mins.
Carrots (sliced or cut in segments)	1 hour plus
Parsnips, pumpkin	1 hour plus
Courgettes	30–45 mins.
Celery	1½–2 hours

Leeks	30–45 mins.
Apples	45 mins.– 1 hour
Pears	much longer, sometimes hours

Casseroling (or cooking in liquid)

The food-to-be-cooked is put in a casserole (covered baking dish), sometimes pre-fried to seal and add flavour, and then barely covered with liquid. (Water, stock etc. – see p. 87 for appropriate suggestions.) Once the contents of the casserole are at simmering temperature (which may be reached either in the oven or by pre-cooking on top of the stove) you can set the oven at a low or very low temperature – just enough to keep the heat from dropping below simmering.

You can cook any of the cheaper cuts of meat (plus vegetables) like this; also fish plus vegetables.

Times vary: from 2–3 hours in a slow (no. 2–3, 325–50°F) oven to 6 hours or more in a very slow oven for meat; from 30–45 minutes (no. 3, 350°F) for fish. (You need to time it from the moment when the casserole reaches simmering point and really starts to cook.)

As with stews on top of the stove, the secret is to pack the meat and vegetables as neatly as possible into the casserole and to use the least possible liquid. All kinds of vegetables and flavourings can be used (see also p. 87). If you want to thicken your casserole when you put it in the oven (see p. 94) you can: it's much less likely to stick than on top of the stove. Famous specialities like *coq au vin* and *bœuf en daube* use variants of this method.

If you want to cook a one dish meal you can prepare a meat and veg. casserole, as above, and top it with a roof of sliced potatoes instead of a lid.

Salads and such-like

If your idea of salads is a plate with four lettuce leaves, one tomato, one sliced beetroot, then you might be agreeably surprised to know how good salads can be and how many kinds there are.

Many vegetables can be eaten raw, as long as they're cut or grated finely enough. Many cooked vegetables can be enjoyed cold, especially with a flavoursome dressing.

For added protein you can choose between cold meat or chicken, cooked meats, hard-boiled eggs, cooked fish, tinned fish (tuna, mackerel, sardines), and many kinds of cheese. Or you can have a hot course (soup, or fish and chips, or sausages and potatoes) followed by some kind of salad to provide the vegetable bit.

Almost all salads are *much much nicer* with a French dressing (often called vinaigrette). If you haven't tried salads like this please have a go. (Don't be put off if you've had French dressing on salads in restaurants and not liked it: it's often mixed carelessly with too much vinegar and salt.) If you've felt in the past that salads were boring, this may help to change your mind.

The easiest way *to mix a French dressing* is to do a lot at once and keep it handy in a covered jar or bottle. However much you mix, the proportions are the same: 1 part vinegar (preferably wine) to 3 parts oil, plus salt and pepper to taste. Fill the jar or bottle rather less than a quarter full with vinegar. Pour in oil (groundnut is cheapest, olive the strongest flavoured) until 12 mm. or so away from the top. Add 1–1½ flat teaspoons of salt and a sprinkle of pepper per pint. Put on the lid. Shake to mix.

You'll have to shake it every time you use it as the contents separate out. You'll need 1–4 tbsp. per salad, depending on its size – enough to leave each leaf or vegetable glistening without a pool of surplus underneath.

This is basic French dressing. You can vary it by adding, to every 3–4 tbsp. you use, e.g. ¼–½ tsp. French mustard, a crushed garlic clove, garlic or onion salt, chopped chives, chopped herbs.

You can add these dressings to all kinds and combinations of vegetables. Here are some suggestions.

Raw vegetables

Plain *lettuce*. (Several varieties. The outer leaves, especially of Webb's and cos, can be used by cutting in thin strips diagonally across the leaf. Tear the other leaves in largish pieces.)
Tomatoes. (Sliced – nice with basil sprinkled on top.)
Any kind of *cabbage*, white, green or red (cut into four, cut out the core, and with a heavy sharp knife cut into thin strips across the point of the wedges. Red must be cut particularly fine or it can be indigestible. White cabbage gives coleslaw. Add thinly sliced onion, and/or chopped apple, and/or sultanas pre-soaked in a little water to make them swell.
Watercress. Good and decorative with peeled thinly sliced oranges.
Grated *carrot*.
Chopped *celery hearts*.
Thinly sliced *chicory* with *beetroot*. If you've never liked pickled vinegary-beetroot, try freshly cooked from the greengrocers.
Cauliflower. Good either raw or cooked, but slice thinly if raw.
Brussels sprouts. Take off outer leaves and slice.
Peppers, green and red.

Cooked vegetables

French beans. Good with tomato.

Potatoes. Must be firm and waxy, not floury. You can add chopped apples, onions, chives.

Cauliflower.

White haricot beans
Butter beans } all useful
Kidney beans } in winter.

Lettuce salads should be dressed just before eating, or they go dead and slimy. Most others (including cabbage) are improved by being dressed an hour or so before eating so the flavours have time to combine.

Wash all raw vegetables well before using. The easiest way with green stuff is to leave it soaking in salted water for a few minutes (not too long or you lose vitamins). If your lettuce is limp, you can revive it by making the water tepid, not cold. Be particularly careful with watercress – you sometimes get small snails clinging to the leaves. Rinse well in a colander under the cold tap, if necessary leaf by leaf or sprig by sprig.

Salads look best in wooden bowls (lettuce) or on undecorated plain strong-coloured plates or dishes.

What to eat with what

Some combinations of food taste better than others. Here are a few ideas.

Fix on your main dish first. This is the most important and probably the most expensive.

If it's a runnier kind of food (stew, for example) then serve firm non-runny vegetables with it. Peas, carrots, cabbage, not leeks in a white sauce. If it's a dry kind of food, serve juicier vegetables (e.g., with chops, tomatoes, cauliflower cheese etc.) or make a sauce or gravy.

If it's crispy, serve nothing liquidy with it. (Fish in batter and chips – *not* damp spinach.)

Don't forget that instead of serving vegetables *with*, you can serve salads *after*.

Avoid serving a plateful of foods of similar colours. White fish plus white potatoes plus white onions look dreary – even drearier on a white plate.

If you're serving more than one course, the other course or courses should complement and not repeat. Not fish soup followed by grilled plaice. Not steak and kidney pudding followed by plum duff. Not tomato salad followed by ham and coleslaw.

If you're at all interested in food you'll soon find all this out for yourself. Experience soon shows you that you enjoy best the kind of meal that provides contrasts of taste, colour and texture; not one which is a kind of muddle.

Try to put hot food on hot plates. Pre-warm them in the oven at the lowest heat or on a rack over the cooker.

Handy extras

Things to do with eggs

Boiled eggs. Bring water to boil in a small pan. When it is boiling, lower the egg(s) into the pan with a spoon. (Don't put in eggs straight from the fridge – they'll crack.) Bring back to the boil, then turn heat down. Time accurately. For medium-boiled eggs: $4\frac{1}{2}$–5 minutes (large), 4–$4\frac{1}{2}$ minutes (standard). Remove from water immediately. If the eggs do crack, add a little vinegar to the water.

Hard-boiled eggs. Boil the eggs as above, but leave for 10–12 minutes according to size. Pour off the water, run cold water into the pan and leave.

Fried eggs. Put butter, oil, or bacon fat into frying pan. Break egg into cup and slide egg into pan over low – medium heat. (Too hot fat will toughen it.) If you like the white to get creamy on top, put on a lid. Take it off the heat before it's quite cooked, as it'll go on cooking in the hot fat.

Baked eggs. Break the egg(s) into a greased shallow baking dish and place in a medium oven for 10–15 minutes. (You can also add, e.g. tomatoes, fried onions, asparagus or whatever for a complete meal.)

Scrambled eggs. Put 2 eggs in a basin, add 4–6 tbsp. milk plus pinch of salt and pepper. Beat with a fork. Melt a knob of butter in a small saucepan or frying pan over medium heat. Put in the eggs. As they start to cook, stir very gently with a wooden spoon, lifting the eggs from underneath away from the bottom of the pan. (You may need to take it off the heat to do this.) Eggs need only a low heat to set. If you let the heat rise too high, the eggs will either burn, separate, or turn into a gritty-looking heap. Remove from the heat before they're quite set. (You can also add chives, cheese, $\frac{1}{2}$ tsp. Marmite, chopped tomato etc.)

Omelette. Omelettes are a cinch. Since you can add all sorts of things to make a change (fried mushrooms, onions, tomatoes, chopped ham, herbs, fish etc.) it's worth knowing how to make a perfect one. Recipes vary. This is mine.

To each egg, add 1 dessertspoon water plus 1 dessertspoon milk, pinch salt and pepper. Beat well. (A two-egg omelette will fit a 16 cm frying pan neatly and serve one person.) Have a long broad-bladed knife handy.

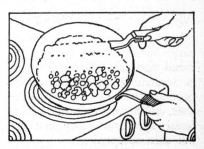

Let the pan dry out over gentle heat. Put in a good knob of butter. When it's melted and finishes bubbling, but *before* it turns brown, take the handle in one hand; pour the mixture into the centre of the pan with the other, tipping and turning the pan as you do so to allow the egg mixture to run evenly over the surface.

As you continue to tip and turn the pan, pull the mixture away from the edge with your knife, so the raw mixture runs in to take its place. In 1–2 minutes the mixture will be virtually set, but still with a slightly liquid top. Put the filling on to one half of the omelette. Slide the knife under the other half, and flip it over on top of the filling. Your omelette is ready. (Some people say the outside shouldn't be browned at all, but I prefer it ever so nicely golden.)

Take a plate (pre-warmed). Hold it over the omelette. Turn the omelette pan upside down and the plate right side up simultaneously. The omelette will drop on the plate. Success!

Breakaway from bread and jam

Bread and something is always easy: but it doesn't have to be bread and jam. Better for you is something which has more positive food value. Cheese. Marmite. Bovril. Sardines. Tomatoes. Smoked salmon! (You can get bits quite cheaply.)

And, if you've got a grill, toast-and-something hot is comforting and nutritious. Cook something (perhaps with a sauce) separately and then put it on the toast. Chopped kidney. Sliced mushrooms. Scrambled eggs.

Or toast one side only, turn over, and top with e.g. cheese or sardines to grill in position. A good variant is *pizza bread*. Toast one side. Turn over. Spread wall-to-wall with margarine. Put sliced tomato on top. Put under grill until tomato is soft. Take out. Sprinkle thickly with grated cheese and oregano. Add anchovies and olives if you're feeling authentic and extravagant. Put back under the grill to melt the cheese.

Or you can make pancakes

They're quick, simple, can be stuffed with any oddments, sweet or savoury, and need only flour, egg, milk, salt. For the recipe see any basic cookery book (p. 103). The batter can be made in a few minutes: there's no need to leave it to stand.

Cooking ahead

I hope you feel you know enough to start cooking with optimism and enthusiasm. When you want – as you soon will – recipes and ideas to expand your repertoire, you'll find in any reasonable bookshop an enormous number of cookery books to choose from.

Nice rice

With many dishes you can serve rice instead of potatoes. Chopped up meats, fish, vegetables in any kind of sauce, all combine well.

The best rice is long-grain patna. It's becoming so hard to find good-quality rice today that my favourite recipe (add twice the volume of water to gently pre-fried rice, bring to the boil, then cook *very slowly* under a lid for 15–20 minutes, turn off, leave for another ten) doesn't always work. You'll need to experiment. The following method is fairly reliable, but even so unless the rice is reasonably good you may end up with squashy outsides and hard middles.

Cooking rice

Rinse the rice well in a sieve under cold water. Bring a large panful of water to the boil. Add salt ($\frac{3}{4}$–1 dessertspoon to 4 pints). Tip the rice in the boiling water. Bring it back to the boil. Simmer gently for 7–15 minutes. Test by pinching a grain of rice in your fingers. It's done when it's slightly resistant but you can't feel any hard centre.

Drain in a colander. Pour boiling water through it. Make holes at intervals with a wooden spoon handle. Leave for a few minutes to dry out.

Super Spaghetti

— and macaroni, tagliatelle, vermicelli. You'll find any number of different kinds of pasta in most delicatessens : also excellent sauces (Buitoni's meat sauce is first-class) to serve with them or make your own.

Bring a large pan of water to the boil. Add salt – about 1 dessertspoon to 4 pints. Pour in the pasta. You need about $\frac{1}{4}$ lb. per person for a main meal. Wind the spaghetti gradually round the pan as it softens. Turn down the heat. Cook uncovered for 17–23 minutes. It's done when you can pinch it apart but it still resists slightly. Drain. Melt butter or heat oil in the pan. Return the pasta and stir round until it's coated.

When you've finished cooking, wrap all rubbish in newspaper and throw it away. (Don't leave perishable bits sitting for days in your bin.) Replace lids, make sure no food is left uncovered. Fill used pans with cold water. Put all cutlery, handles up, in a jug of soapy water.

And if it now all looks too much, see below 'Clearing up a Kitchen Chaos'.

Here are some which, as recent beginners, you might find particularly helpful.

Cooking in a Bedsitter, Katharine Whitehorn (Penguin, 1963). A really clear no-nonsense book which understands your limitations, and explains how to cook both simple meals for one and fancy meals for several.

The Penguin Cookery Book, Bee Nilson (Penguin, 1952). An excellent first cookery book. It's sensibly cross-referenced, and has in it comprehensive recipes for practically everything you might want to cook in the ordinary way.

The Pauper's Cookbook, Jocasta Innes (Penguin, 1971). Assumes you've grasped the basics of cookery, and gives a good selection of interesting recipes for using e.g. cheaper cuts of meat (if such things exist).

Good Food on a Budget, Georgina Horley (Penguin, 1969). This is a fatter book with selections of recipes arranged month by month for what is in season, and so is practical to help you plan.

The Vegetarian Epicure, Anna Thomas (Penguin, 1974). Some interesting and unusual recipes for non-meat cooking.

After these you might like to try one or some of the specialist cookery books which explain Polish, French, Chinese, Indian, Italian cookery. Remember, once you understand the basics of cookery, there's no reason why you shouldn't confidently experiment, and, because other nation's cuisines reflect the kind of food available, you'll find in certain areas much more scope and variety than you would if you stuck only to conventional recipes.

However, avoid getting too many cookery books too soon. You won't bother with them, and they'll sit in the kitchen unopened getting covered with coffee rings. Buy one at a time, and absorb what seems useful to you out of it. Only then go on to another.

3 CLEARING UP A KITCHEN CHAOS

Put back into cupboards or on shelves everything which has a home. The mess will start to look less menacing.

Put away (into a fridge if you have one) any left-overs which might come in handy. (Gravy, 2 potatoes, 3 tablespoons of grated cheese etc.).

Get rid of any others that won't. If your neighbours aren't on an anti-bird kick, you can dispose of a lot of cooked-food scraps – rice, peas, bacon rind etc. – by putting them on your window-sill or flinging them on the lawn. You will thus simultaneously keep your local sparrows happy and your dustbin clear.

You are now ready for washing-up

Pour water out of soaking pans. (If you've forgotten to soak them, pour water *in* and leave them till next time round. You're likely to ruin both your temper and the pans if you simply go at them with a scourer.)

Empty away any tea leaves, coffee dregs etc.

If you have running hot water and a sink, put first in second. If you have to heat the water on the stove, use a bowl and put the kettle on again. It's easier to wash dishes in four bowlsful of hot water than one sinkful of tepid.

Add a dash of washing-up liquid. You may need two or three splashes, depending on how much water/many dishes you have and how concentrated your particular poison is. *You will not gain anything by putting in more than you need.* All you'll get is slippery dishes which will slither from your fingers to the floor.

Wash glasses. You'll probably need a dish-mop or a cloth to remove grease-smears, lipstick etc. If you're a perfectionist, rinse them under the hot tap.

Tip all the cutlery into the bowl (unless you've anything bone-handled or precious) and leave it to soak off the gunge while you get on with the rest.

Cups and bowls next. Wash them and stand them upside down to drain.

Now the plates. If they're particularly gooey, you might leave them to soak for a couple of minutes while you feed the cat or whatever. Wash them, rinse if necessary, and balance them up-side-down against the cups to drain. (If you've got a plate-rack you're in clover. Just arrange accordingly.)

Take out the cutlery, which by now should be virtually self-washed. If not, give a passing rub. If your water has got unpleasantly greasy, rinse under the tap or with hot water from the kettle. Stand all the pieces fork–spoon–blade

How to rescue a really burnt pan

Fill with water past burn level, add 1 tsp. – 1 tbsp. detergent or washing soda, bring to the boil and leave to simmer away gently for 2–3 hours if necessary. Then tip out the water and rinse well. Most good thick pans come clean in the end. If your pan is thin, by the time it's burnt it's probably buckled as well and not worth saving.

down in a large jug.

Mixing-bowls, if any.

Now for the pans. Wash out non-stick pans with *only* a mop or a sponge, or pretty rapidly the non-stickness vanishes. A gentle scourer* is best for most things. If you've got nasty burnt-on bits fighting back, don't waste time and energy scrubbing away. Leave the pan to soak a little longer.

That, by and large, is that.

While you're around, wipe down anything which is wipeable down. Cooker, table, bread board. It won't take more than a few minutes, and it'll look more approachable next time you face it.

Throw away the water. If it's particularly squalid, catch the worst bits in a strainer or sieve and transfer to a rubbish bin. *A blocked drain can cost anything from £5–£25 to clear.*

Rinse out the sink.

Put the dish-mop, cloth, scourer etc. where they can dry exposed to the air, or they will *pong*.

Drying-up

With any luck you'll hardly need to do any.

If you've washed in hot water, and rinsed if necessary, you can leave everything draining away on its own. And you can tell any critics (how dare they!) that that's the most hygienic way.

* *Beware of coarse harsh metal scourers. They can leave the insides of pans so badly scratched that food becomes progressively harder to dislodge. They're particularly lethal to frying pans. Take care, or you'll find your fried eggs clinging to the bottom like limpets.*

Medical Matters

You've got to be well to work. You want to be fit to get the most out of living. And since this is one of the healthiest times of your life, with any luck you'll have no problems.

But sometimes things go wrong. When you leave home, and your pattern of life changes, your body's rhythm gets thrown out. You may suffer from minor but tiresome things like constipation or fatigue. Or you worry about what will happen if you *do* get ill. Who'll look after you? What about money? How do you know when to go to a doctor? How do you know what doctor to go to? Stress and strain cause tension or even lead to acute depression.

If you know what to do if you fall ill, you're more likely to keep well, less likely to worry and better able to cope if things do go wrong.

1 POSITIVE PLANNING

No one is 100 per cent healthy from January to December. But by taking preventive action you can cut down on the number of times you succumb to minor illnesses, you're less likely to have them turn into major ones, and you'll even help yourself guard against accidents.

Good food first

Your body's best defence against infection is the right amount of the right food (see p. 56). Both physical and mental troubles can often be traced at least partly to an inadequate diet. Accidents, too, happen more easily when you're below par. Eating sensibly won't automatically guarantee either health or happiness, but it's certainly a sound start, so check back.

Sweet sleep

Your body needs sleep. You've probably got enough vitality to work hard, play hard, have several late nights, even miss the occasional night's sleep altogether, without suffering any drastic effects, but if you lose out on too much sleep too often, your body will begin to protest. You'll feel lethargic, catch colds easily, maybe show signs of mental stress, get weepy, quarrelsome or depressed, depending on your temperament. Whatever the pressures on you, try to make sure that as a general rule you get a good night's sleep – then you'll miss it less when you don't.

How much? There's no hard and fast rule. If you do tough physical work you need more sleep than if you sat at a desk all day: but even so, people's requirements vary. Some manage on less than six hours' sleep. Others need eight. Most young adults seem satisfied with about seven. If you need a gong to wake you and go round yawning till midday, then you probably need more than you're getting. If you wake easily and feel unbearably bright and bouncy then you're doing all right.
Note. If you're sleeping eight hours a night and still feel exhausted, then see your doctor. It could be anaemia, or a sign of some other illness. Or it *could* be acute boredom. Possible? Then you might consider changing some of the circumstances of your life. See pp. 316 and 204 on work and liking your leisure.

Keep fit

Yes, well. I know lots of people leave school determined never to climb another rope or kick another football in their lives, but all the same, it's a mistake to abandon exercise altogether. This is especially important if you're going to spend most of your time studying in libraries or at a sit-down job. A reasonable amount of exercise helps to keep your body functioning properly. Girls in particular suffer if they suddenly cut down on games and sports: there's evidence this helps to cause bad stomach cramps during menstruation.

Include some exercise in your

everyday life. Walk instead of catching the bus. Use the stairs and not the lift. Cycle instead of driving. Once or twice a week do something more demanding. Go dancing, or swimming, or skating, or canoeing. Many otherwise expensive pastimes – squash, fencing, badminton – can be enjoyed relatively cheaply through classes attached to Adult Education Institutes or Polytechnics. (Ring your local college, or the Local Education Officer: telephone number under your Council or Town Hall.) In some areas you may be lucky enough to have a gymnasium attached to your swimming pool. If you've always enjoyed team games, look for a local amateur side you might join.

If you suspect – and your figure already shows – that you're not getting the exercise you need, make a positive effort to get out and find something you enjoy.

2 PLAY SAFE

As a child, you're likely to have been immunized against:

diphtheria	measles
tetanus	polio
whooping-cough	German measles
smallpox	(girls only)
TB	

So the chances are that you've received the various injections etc., and are partially protected against these diseases.

If you haven't, it might be worth asking your doctor about getting immunized now.

For most young adults probably the most immediately important out of the list above is a smallpox vaccination, especially if you want to travel. Many countries will not accept you without the relevant certificate, and sometimes these regulations are enforced at a moment's notice. Don't forget either that you'll be sorry if you wait until just before you want to leave – you may not be able to swim for at least a fortnight. (If a woman in the first three months of pregnancy is vaccinated against smallpox, the embryo may be deformed. So if you're in the first stages of pregnancy, or think you may be pregnant, *you should not be vaccinated.* You won't necessarily be asked if you're pregnant, so bear this important fact in mind.)

Trouble Areas

(a) *Sexual organs.* Quite apart from worries about shape, size etc. (see p. 138), many young people worry about the possibility of contracting some sexual disease, and, less seriously, about the chances that their sex organs may in some way be offensive. (i) You're extremely unlikely spontaneously and without infection to contract any kind of sexual disease. (For further information on VD see p. 118.) (ii) Provided you wash or bath regularly, you're not in the least likely to smell. Note for females: *be very wary indeed of using vaginal deodorants.* Doctors are highly sceptical about these. At best they're unnecessary. At worst they're downright dangerous. They can destroy some of the body's natural defences and dry up essential lubricants: some contain chemical elements of very doubtful safety (see p. 140).

(b) *Feet.* No one feels romantic with ropey feet. Corns, bunions, calloused heels, are all avoidable. Try to get shoes that fit (see p. 149). Wash your feet daily. Cut your toenails straight across, and keep them short. This prevents (a) ingrowing toenails and (b) holes in socks/tights.

(c) *Teeth.* In some odd way we're all inclined to think that teeth are dentists' business and nothing to do with our general health. We are, of course, quite wrong. Our teeth are very much part of us, as we realize the moment we get toothache. Badly decayed teeth can be killers. So if your teeth aren't all they might be at the moment, get them put right. (Not nearly as threatening as it sounds – see p. 133.) And if they are healthy, keep them that way, with the right food, lots of chewy fresh fruit and veg, and thorough cleaning.

Other could-be important vaccinations are against measles (if you haven't had it in childhood, the adult version can be nasty), polio and TB, and – if you're female – against German measles if you've so far escaped it; as you probably know, catching German measles during the first three months of pregnancy could mean serious risk to the embryo. When holidaying abroad, vaccinations against cholera are often advisable (start them three weeks before you go): if you're visiting certain parts of the world (e.g. India, South America) injections of gamma globulin beforehand reduces the real and unpleasant risk of infective hepatitis. (No one may suggest this, so find out.)

Only your doctor can say whether or not you could or should be vaccinated. Ask for advice.

There may be a modest charge which varies according to what it's for, why it's given, and the individual practice, but rarely exceeds £1. (See also p. 235.)

3 BE PREPARED!

Even the fittest person catches the

Brush your teeth at least every morning and evening. Brush up and down, behind and in front. Rinse very well – toothpaste contains sweeteners which can actually damage teeth if not washed away. Buy a new toothbrush regularly. A soft, balding one is useless.

odd cold, even the best organized has the occasional accident. Here's what to do when things go wrong.

How ill is ill?

What bothers many young people is wondering whether they'll be able to look after themselves if they *are* ill; how to know when they're ill enough to go and see a doctor; how to know when they're ill enough to want a doctor to come and see *them*. For every one who rushes off unnecessarily to the surgery there's probably another one who ought to go and doesn't. Doctors aren't always much help either. Some say that ill people should never try self-cures, others, that too much of their time is wasted on minor illnesses.

It's not easy to avoid treading on medical toes, and certainly no book can replace individual medical advice. But what I've tried to do is suggest – first for illnesses and then for accidents – when you might reasonably be expected to look after yourself; when you might seek medical help; and when you certainly must.

Category 1

When you're mildly ill, but feel reasonably confident that you know what's the matter with you, that you've had it before and know what to do.

The body is, in fact, well equipped to take care of itself, and – especially if fortified by previous good health – rapidly defends itself. In most minor illnesses the most sensible action you can take is to go to bed for twenty-four hours with a large jug of fruit squash and some aspirins and leave your body to get on with it. In addition there are some other simple steps you can take.

Cold. Go to bed. Keep warm. Drink plenty of fruit squash. Two soluble aspirins in water every four hours may help relieve headache or sore throat, though they don't actually cure. (There's some evidence that a large dose of vitamin C taken at the first sign of a cold stops it developing. If you want to try, ask at any large chemists for 1 gm. Vit. C tablets and take one when a cold first threatens.)

Cough. Ordinary cough following cold. Traditional remedy of hot lemon juice (real lemon) with large teaspoon of honey works well. Various cough sweets and cough medicines can prove soothing. *Don't smoke.*

Flu. As for colds – go to bed, keep warm, drink fruit squash. Two soluble aspirins taken every four hours will probably make you feel better, though again they're not curative.

Sore throat. Take aspirin every four hours. Have plenty of hot drinks, especially hot lemon and

Read this before you take to your bed

One difficulty in being ill when living on your own is that people aren't necessarily going to be running around looking after you — especially if they don't know. So, when you do feel ill, be sure to tell someone *before* you take to your bed. If you're sharing a flat or living in communal surroundings, ask someone reliable to pop their head round the door in a couple of hours to see how things are going — after all, you'd do the same for them, wouldn't you? If you're on your own, but you've got a telephone, ring up and let someone know: arrange for them either to ring back or call on you later. If you're absolutely alone, have no phone, know no one, pluck up courage to ask the most friendly-looking person you see around — there *must* be *someone* — and explain the situation: or if you positively can't find the nerve, ring your local branch of the Samaritans (number in your directory), tell them what's up, and arrange a set time for you to ring them back.

The reason for all this is so that if your illness does unexpectedly take a turn for the worse, someone will rapidly find out and be able to do something about it: and which is far more likely, to prevent you from lying there worrying that your illness *might* suddenly deteriorate with no one knowing a thing about it. This is particularly important if you have no phone handy: you may have to rely on someone contacting the doctor for you.

honey. Various throat tablets from the chemist may prove helpful. Wait and see. If after twenty-four or forty-eight hours your sore throat is much worse, you could be in for one of a number of illnesses. Consider yourself to have reached Categories 2 or 3.

Mild stomach pains. If you've reason to think the cause is indigestion (i.e. if you've gobbled down food in a hurry, or too much of it) lie down with a hot water bottle. An indigestion tablet may be soothing. *Never take a laxative for any kind of stomach pain.*

Vomiting. Lie flat and keep warm. If you're reasonably sure you've been sick because you've eaten or drunk unwisely or too much, you'll recover rapidly once your stomach's got rid of what's bothering it. Wait a couple of hours and try a little plain water. If even this makes you throw up, try instead a little salt water (1 teaspoon salt to 3 dl – $\frac{1}{2}$ pint – of water).

Diarrhoea. If you suspect you know what's caused it (e.g. too much fruit, food you're not used to, possibly a virus attack because several others have it) then you'll probably be on your way back to normal within twenty-four hours. A kaolin morphine mixture can help; 1 tbsp in a little water. *In cases of either acute diarrhoea or severe vomiting, eat nothing for 24 hours.*

You can take plenty of water-with-flavouring fluid (i.e. fruit squashes, or tea with lemon) but *no milk.* Warm drinks are easier to take than either hot or cold. *If you don't know what's caused the sickness or diarrhoea, or if it continues, see Category 2.*

Constipation. You won't get constipated as long as you eat a proper diet and don't rush off to catch the bus just as nature calls. Eat plenty of fruit, and foods with roughage – wholemeal bread and raw vegetables – and drink plenty of fluid: maybe get up earlier to give yourself more time: but don't brood about yourself and don't worry. And don't try laxatives until you've given your healthy, relaxed way of life time to work – at least a fortnight. Laxatives can actually create a fresh cycle of constipation.

Headache. Peace and quiet and an aspirin. But a bad and persistent headache may be a sign that you're catching one of a number of illnesses, so see Categories 2 and 3. (*Note:* oddly enough, hunger can cause a bad headache. If you haven't eaten for hours, have a light meal before you settle for the peace and quiet. You may find it does the trick.)

Rash. If you have no temperature and feel quite well, your rash is probably nothing significant – due to heat or some odd allergy. Dust it with talc if you like. If you have a temperature and/or it persists, you're into Category 2.

Fever (higher than normal temperature with sweating, shivering etc.) shows only that your body is fighting back some infection. Remember that what your temperature is *in itself* means very little. It's only part of a whole picture. Normal temperature anyway varies. Your own particular normal temperature (taken by mouth) could be from 97·2°F (36·2°C) to 99·5°F (37·5°C). Your temperature is at its lowest in the morning and highest in the evening.

If you have a slightly raised temperature (up 1 or 2 degrees, and feel slightly ill), take it easy, go to bed if you feel like it, and see what, if anything, happens over the next twelve to twenty-four hours. If your temperature continues to rise, you start to feel iller, or other symptoms show up, you've moved to Category 2 or 3.

Meanwhile, be prepared to throw blankets on or off as you feel cold or hot, and have plenty of fruit squash handy. A handkerchief soaked in cologne on your forehead is surprisingly soothing.

Menstrual pain: cramps, sickness etc. If you're in real pain, take two aspirins and lie down with a hot water bottle: if you're only mildly upset, often exercise is better. If you only start having trouble after changing a job, moving house, leaving your family etc., it may be something in your new way of life which doesn't agree with you. Are you eating very differently? Exercising less? Try readjusting and see if this does the trick. *If you suffer from real pain every time your period comes up, don't just endure it, you're in Category 3 and should visit your doctor.*

Warts. This may seem an odd thing to finish up with, but people who suffer from these often worry about them quite unnecessarily. These small hard spots *have nothing to do with cancer*, and often go as suddenly as they come. If you want to hurry their departure, and have no friendly neighbourhood witch, your chemist will sell you a wart-removing liquid. Use it regularly, carefully and persistently (you may need to keep it up for several weeks) and your warts will go.

Category 2

There are times when you're not quite happy with the way you feel, but you're not certain whether it's sensible to take up the doctor's time.

When whatever you thought you had – your cold, headache etc. – seems to be getting worse, not better

When your temperature keeps going up (over a period of days)

How to take your temperature

Look at your thermometer. Twist it until you see the thread of mercury. If it's at or above the normal temperature mark (98·4 ° F–37° C) you need to shake the thermometer until the mercury sinks right down to say 97° F. Hold the non-bulb end between your thumb and fingertips, hold it at arm's length, and give a sharp flip with your wrist – two or three times if necessary. If you're not used to doing this, try it over a bed or at least over a carpeted floor. (The thermometer could fly out of your fingers and smash.) Once you've shaken the mercury down, put the thermometer in your mouth under your tongue (obviously without biting down), and leave it there for two minutes. Take it out, twist it so you're sure you see the mercury clearly and read the temperature. (Your thermometer is probably marked at 1° intervals; with each degree split into tenths. You needn't bother too much about the small intervals. It's knowing *about* what your temperature is that can be of help – whether it's 99° F or 103° F.) After using a thermometer, rinse it in dilute antiseptic before putting it away. *Don't* rinse in boiling water.

When, without feeling dramatically ill, you have symptoms which are new to you

This is when it makes sense to ring up your GP and ask. He/she may be able to set your mind at rest quite easily. Or you may be advised to call. Or your doctor may prefer you to wait a little longer to see if there are any further developments. Either way, you'll know that you're sharing your worry with someone with experience – someone you can call on again as soon as you think it's necessary.

Many practices today, particularly group practices, have a fully qualified SRN working for them full time, or a district nurse who visits the surgery for part of the day. If this is the case at your surgery, you may prefer to speak to her to start with. Simply ask to be put through to her when the receptionist takes your call. She is fully qualified to give advice in many circumstances; if she can't, she will say so, and will arrange for you to see the doctor if she thinks it necessary.

If you're answered by an answering service, the person on the other end of the line may again be a qualified SRN; this happens in some practices. It's worth asking. If not, leave a message explaining what's wrong and asking the doctor either to ring you back (if you're on the phone) or to call if he thinks it necessary.

Warning note from a doctor. Advice from a fully qualified SRN backed by training is thoroughly reliable, but advice from a nurse in training or a medical student may be no more accurate (though probably no less) than from your next-door neighbour. Don't take it as gospel, particularly if what you want to know is or could be important.

Category 3

There are other times when you *must* see a doctor.

When you feel really ill

When you've been feeling mildly ill for a long time and don't seem to be improving

When any of the illnesses in Category 1 seem to be developing complications (when what seemed to be a cold combines with back pains: when influenza turns to bronchitis and so on)

When you find yourself with any of these symptoms:
Continued loss of appetite
Continued loss of weight
Generalized fatigue (not because you've had several late nights in a row, but when you feel tired all the time even when you get plenty of sleep)
Persistent headache
Wanting to pee more often, or finding it hurts when you do
Unusual cough or shortness of breath

Unusual vaginal discharge. (This means *unusual*. A slight clear regular discharge is completely normal: one which is heavy, or oddly coloured or strong-smelling isn't.)

Penile discharge

Unexplained rash lasting longer than a day

Unexplained bleeding from any part of your body

Continued, or recurrent, pain anywhere

Sores that don't heal (particularly sores around sexual organs)

Unexplained growth or change in birth-marks or moles (very unusual)

Boils around your nose or on your upper lip (also unusual)

When you see a doctor because you have one of these symptoms, it doesn't mean that there is necessarily anything wrong at all. What it does mean is that *you* can't decide – it takes skilled medical help. So don't ignore these signs. They just could be important.

Surgery or home visit?

You should call at the doctor's surgery whenever you reasonably can. If you want to see the doctor for most of the causes above, for example, there's no reason why you shouldn't be able to do the visiting yourself. But, clearly, ask the doctor to call if you're too ill to make the journey. If you suspect you're suffering from an infectious illness – mumps, chicken-pox etc. – ring and discuss with the nurse what would be the most sensible course to take.

Never call a doctor out at night unless it's a *real emergency* that can't wait until morning. (For what to say to the doctor – see p. 246).

Two fears – appendicitis and VD

Most stomach pains are *not* appendicitis,* but when you're living on your own there's always the nagging dread that this time it might be. Appendicitis takes different forms in different people: though sometimes it's accompanied by a high temperature and sickness, it isn't always, and a high temperature, sickness and stomach pains doesn't necessarily mean you've got it. A doctor's advice is that you should visit your GP *at any time you have a stomach pain which lasts longer than six or eight hours*, or if you have a stomach pain (especially with vomiting) which *keeps getting worse* even though you're lying down quietly. It probably still isn't appendicitis, but you need an expert opinion. Don't try to diagnose yourself.

* *If it's on the left-hand side it almost certainly isn't.*

Some Symptoms of VD

	Gonorrhoea	Syphilis
1st stage :	2–10 days after infection : a burning sensation on passing water ; a discharge of pus from the penis ; a vaginal discharge ; *but over half the girls in the first stage of gonorrhoea show no signs whatever.*	9–90 days after infection (average 25 days) : a small sore oozing a colourless serum on or near the sexual organs, sometimes elsewhere ; generally painless and so often (especially in a girl, where it may be internal) unnoticed. Often heals without treatment within a few weeks.
2nd stage :	from weeks to months later : flu-like symptoms ; or stomach pains ; or inflammation of the Fallopian tubes (girls). These symptoms may be painful and conspicuous or (especially in girls) virtually undetectable.	1–2 months later : mild illness with sore throat ; sometimes *non-itchy pinkish rash;* slight temperature ; loss of appetite. These secondary signs look like many other illnesses : only specific tests can show whether or not syphilis is present.
3rd stage :	May lead to sterility, arthritis, eye infection ; may affect the eyes of a new-born baby : in later years will cause pain in intercourse.	May take up to ten years to develop : affects the nervous system, brain, arteries.

There are also a number of other illnesses which affect the sexual organs which may be transmitted by sexual intercourse but can also arise for at present unknown causes. Among the more important are non-specific urethritis (with symptoms in men which closely resemble the early stages of gonorrhoea) and trichomoniasis (which can cause an unpleasant inflammation of the vagina, but is often symptomless in men).

The only safe response, as with any infection whatever of the sexual organs, is to seek medical advice. Girls in particular are too ready to endure irritation and even pain sooner than ask for help. Don't put up with anything like this hoping it will go away. Treatment will make sure it does.

For further information: write for a booklet to Health Education Council, Middlesex House, Ealing Road, Wembley, Middlesex; or to the Family Planning Association, 27 Mortimer Street, London W1A 4QW; or to *Family Doctor*, 47–51, Chalton Street, London NW1 1HT.

VD is not one disease but several, the most common in Britain being syphilis and gonorrhoea. Gonorrhoea is the second most frequent notifiable disease in the country. Both are spread only by intercourse, or near-intercourse, involving close contact of the sexual organs – whether heterosexually or homosexually. Further on you'll find listed some of the symptoms: but the most important thing to remember is that *anyone can catch VD: and that there won't necessarily be any signs to prove it.*

The commonest age in girls for catching gonorrhoea is fifteen to nineteen years, and in men, twenty to twenty-four years. So bear in mind these facts:

1 If you come into sexual contact with someone who has VD you are highly likely to catch it.

2 Catching VD has nothing to do with clean habits, class, race, education, job or anything else – any more than catching measles has.

3 Love offers no kind of guarantee against VD. If your sexual partner has it, you'll get it, no matter what the relationship between you.

4 Since the initial signs of both syphilis and gonorrhoea can be

both overlooked or non-existent (see panel) it's quite possible for your sexual partner to assure you honestly *but mistakenly* that he/she isn't infected. You can only be certain your partner (and you yourself) are not infected if neither of you has had any previous sexual relationships.

5 The greater the number of sexual contacts the more the risk.

6 You can catch VD without being repeatedly open to risk. One brief contact is enough to pass it on.

7 A sheath (French letter – see p. 194) gives some – but not complete – protection against infection. No other kind of contraception (including the Pill) offers any protection at all.

8 The only way of being absolutely certain that a person at risk has or has not got VD is by specialized testing. This is carried out free of charge at any VD clinic. It's particularly important to have this done if you've had any brief, isolated, temporary contact with a stranger, or if your regular partner has had such a contact. Gonorrhoea germs are particularly difficult to detect. A girl may be and remain infected even though a test shows a negative result. For this reason *three tests* are made at intervals; it's important to turn up for *all* of them. If a girl continues to be at risk, *continued tests are essential.*

9 The treatment of VD in its early stages is simple and complete.

10 Untreated VD lies dormant in the body to return in increasingly unpleasant forms. It can cause sterility in both sexes, infect any new partner, affect unborn children and have increasingly serious and damaging consequences.

11 Don't try to cure yourself if you suspect you have VD: *especially, take no antibiotics* – it could mean having repeated checks for over twelve months.

12 VD clinics treat patients in complete confidence, without requiring an initial doctor's letter and without communicating records to GPs. They're there to help, not lecture. To find the address, ring any large hospital or your Public Health department (phone number under your Council or Town Hall), or write to your local Medical Officer of Health: in London, ring 01–928 3401. If you have any difficulty, write to the Ministry of Health, Alexander Fleming House, Elephant and Castle, London SE1.

Most clinics are open 10 am–7 pm, 10 am–1 pm on Saturdays. If you want to make sure, ring and ask first.

Accidents will happen

No one can guard against the pure accident – a tile falling off a roof,

1 *bottle soluble aspirins BP* (means British Pharmacopoeia) *or 1 bottle paracetamol.* Aspirins and paracetamol don't cure, they merely relieve the sensations of pain until your body or your doctor has successfully dealt with the cause. Don't take more than two every four hours, and do this only for a very limited period.

1 *bottle kaolin morphine mixture BP.* Again, a standard medicine available from any chemist. Useful for diarrhoea and mild stomach pains.

1 bottle antiseptic.
Cotton wool
Magnesium sulphate paste
Zinc oxide plaster
Tin Elastoplast and/or Elastoplast strip
Lint
2–3 bandages
1 thermometer

Your medicine box should *not* contain last year's medicines or those prescribed for other people. Many drugs change over a period and become potentially dangerous. Some are suitable for one illness but not at all for another superficially similar. One prescribed for one person may be quite wrong for another. Use only those medicines prescribed by your doctor for you: return to the pharmacy or flush down the lavatory any left over after your illness.

a tree smashing down on a car. But in many accidents the victim is at least one of the causes. If you're ill, in a temper, overtired, depressed, realize that you're in an accident-prone state and take appropriate measures. Make yourself move more slowly. Take extra care. If possible leave everything that's too complex or demanding until you're better able to deal with it. It's too late afterwards to wish that you had.

For practical ways of avoiding accidents at home see pp. 49 to 52. For ways to avoid accidents on the roads see p. 267. If you work in a potentially dangerous job (on building sites, in factories), observe the safety regulations. It's not chicken to take care. Fortunately, most accidents are minor ones.

Here's what to do

Minor cuts, grazes, scratches.

Wash as soon as possible, and apply antiseptic on cotton-wool if you've any handy. (Wash *outwards* from the wound, not across the skin towards it.) Even a minor cut can be painful if it turns septic. It's the potential for infection that matters. A deep cut with a clean knife may heal faster than a scratch from a cat's claw or a gravel-path graze.

If the cut/scratch/graze is somewhere it's going to get rubbed or knocked, then cover it with Elastoplast; otherwise, once cleaned, it's better to leave it exposed to the air.

Septic cut/graze/scratch. If you've been unable to cleanse the wound sufficiently, it may turn septic – that is, instead of forming a hard scab it oozes a yellow-greenish substance. Wash well with dilute antiseptic, pat dry, and put on a little magnesium sulphate paste. Cover with a piece of lint stuck down with zinc oxide plaster. Once the oozing has stopped, leave it uncovered if possible, or put on Elastoplast. If the infection continues, see your doctor.

Scald or burn. Submerge the burn right away in clean water and leave it there until the pain subsides (which could take up to half an hour or even longer). Pat dry with a clean towel or handkerchief and leave it alone.

Sprain. This is a loose term not much liked by doctors. However, for practical purposes, I take it to mean a painful sensation caused by an accidental twisting or pulling of muscles or ligaments. If you've sprained your back, then rest plus getting someone to rub it with a pain-relieving lotion is helpful. If you've sprained your wrist or ankle, try a cold compress. Fold two or three handkerchiefs to form a pad, soak in cold water, lay on the sprain, and tie round firmly but not too tightly with a stretch bandage (or handkerchief if you haven't one).

If your knee is sprained, other than very superficially, you should have it checked by a doctor. If neglected, long-term damage can be caused to the cartilage. You should also see the doctor if any swelling does not go down, or gets more rather than less painful. It may be caused by a cracked or broken bone.

Not-so-minor accidents

With some accidents you need to go either to your doctor or your local hospital. Scalds or burns affecting a large area: suspected fractures: deep cuts which gape apart: a blow on the head followed by either unconsciousness, sickness or fainting; even comparatively minor accidents affecting the ear or eye: all these need expert checking. If you have a hospital near by it generally makes sense to go straight there, as they will have equipment (X-ray facilities and so on) that most GPs haven't. However, some casualty departments, when dealing with a less serious emergency, insist you see your doctor first and attend with a doctor's note.

Where to go

In a large hospital, you'll probably find a separate entrance for accident cases with a sign outside saying 'CASUALTY'. If it's a smaller hospital, go in through the main entrance and ask at the reception desk inside to be directed. In the Casualty Department itself, you will generally find another reception desk. If it's a huge hospital and there are several people behind the desk, look out for a sign saying 'New Patients' and head for that. You'll be asked for your name, address, your own doctor's name and address, and particulars of what happened to you. A card will be made out for you which you need to keep and bring with you for any future appointments. You then have to wait to see the doctor who will decide on any specialist treatment you may need. All treatment and services are, of course, free.

Please note that the hospital casualty departments are for *accidents* – not for illnesses. They are not substitutes for your own personal doctor. If you go to a casualty department because you haven't registered with a GP, you might (a) not receive the treatment you need and (b) be taking time and attention away from other far more urgent cases.

Registering with a doctor is simple. Please make sure you do it (see p. 131).

First Aid to others

Accidents can happen not only to you but to those around you – who will have to rely on your keeping your head just as you, if you have a serious accident, will have to depend on them.

If you're trained, you're likely to be more useful than if you're not. Your local Red Cross Society or St John's or St Andrew's Ambulance Association almost certainly runs a training scheme and will be happy to welcome you.

But even if you have no training whatever, there are a few basic practical steps you can take which might make all the difference. Often, in fact, the most important help you can give is to do as little as possible, and to restrain others equally untrained. *More harm can be done by mishandling after an accident than by the accident itself.*

If the accident's serious, the very first thing (except where you're faced with someone who's stopped breathing, see immediately below) is to dial 999 and call an ambulance, or to get someone else to do this while you're doing what you can.

When breathing's stopped, whatever the cause (drowning, suffocation, drugs, electric shock) the absolute priority is to try to get it started again. Don't waste time phoning for an ambulance: even if it only takes minutes, those minutes may be too long. If your patient has water in his/her lungs, place him/her head downwards to drain it out. Clear out anything in the mouth – weeds, false teeth, vomit. Then place him/her on his/her back, make sure the tongue is forward in the mouth, pull the head as far back as possible (to clear the breathing passages) and pinch his/her nose. Put your mouth over the patient's and blow hard and steadily as though you were trying to blow up a difficult balloon. (If your patient's a small child, cover both nose and mouth with your mouth, and blow more gently.) You'll see the lungs inflate. Remove your mouth and let the chest deflate. (If it doesn't, there must be some obstruction in the breathing passages. Turn your patient on his/her side and hit him/her several times sharply between the shoulder blades.) Give five good puffs like this and then pause to check your patient's colour. You should see the blue tinge starting

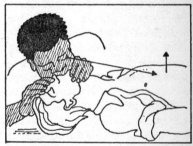

to go from the chin, nose, ear-lobes. Continue until either help arrives or your patient appears to be breathing normally, in which case turn him/her on to the side in the recovery position. Stay close by, watching all the time. Be prepared for the breathing to stop again at any moment, and be ready to start revival techniques once more.

Unconscious person. Lay on his/ her side in the recovery position. Cover with a light blanket or coat. Get help if necessary.

Heavy bleeding. The most important thing is to stop the bleeding *fast*. Lay the victim flat: if the bleeding's in a limb, raise this up (unless there's a suspected fracture). If you've anything clean and handy to use as a pad – handkerchief, scarf, towel – fine: if not, use the palm of your hand or

The Recovery Position

The correct recovery position – this saves lives
Place any unconscious person on their side, *never* on their back. Make sure the tongue is well forward, not lolling back in the throat, and that there's nothing else in the mouth to block the breathing passages. (Many accident victims, when placed on their backs, die from choking on their tongues or from inhaled blood or vomit, not from the original accident at all.)

your thumb; if it's a cut, squeeze the edges together between finger and thumb. Press down and keep pressing until help arrives. If you're using a pad and it becomes saturated, don't take it away, add another padding on top. Often this pressure alone is enough to stop even serious bleeding. *Don't apply a tourniquet even if you think you know how.* First-aid experts advise *very strongly* against it. It's dangerous even in skilled hands, and can be fatal in unskilled.

Serious burns or scalds. For immediate action when a person's on fire, see p. 51. (Yes, well, obviously, you're not going to look it up when the accident's actually happening, but if you *don't* know what to do check now.) If the burn is chemically caused (someone's spilt a bottle of acid or bleach over themselves) remove what burnt or saturated clothing you can (put something over your hands – a towel or thick gloves – while you do it, you won't help anyone by burning yourself too). If any other kind of burn, leave burnt clothing alone – you might remove burnt skin with it. Whatever kind of burn it is, submerge the burnt part *immediately* in cold water. (If the body is affected, if possible, place the person in the bath and fill with tepid water. Don't leave the person alone. Keep the water at a tepid temperature until help arrives.) If

there's no water available, cover the burnt part lightly with any clean dressing (piece of sheet etc.). *Don't put anything else whatever on the burn.* Take off any rings, bracelets, watches, if near the burnt part (swelling might make them irremovable). Don't give the injured person anything to eat or drink.

Suspected internal injuries or fractures. Do as little as possible until skilled help arrives. Don't move the injured person. Give nothing to eat or drink. Cover with a blanket. Except in rare cases (transport across rough country) there's no need to use splints. Handle a broken limb as little as possible. Treat any bleeding with care.

Choking. It may sound comic, but a piece of food or chewing-gum wedged across the throat can choke an adult to death in minutes. The victim is unable to speak or communicate. If you see someone choking, with skin turning grey, and a choking noise from the throat, hit him/her smartly between the shoulders two or three times. (If it's a child, hold it upside down or place over your knees head down and hit it hard between the shoulders in the same way.) This should free the obstruction. If not, and the victim loses consciousness, try to remove any obstruction from the throat with your fingers; if this fails,

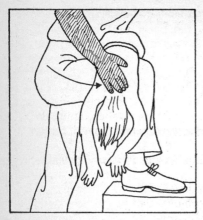

apply the kiss of life – it's sometimes possible to force air past the obstruction.

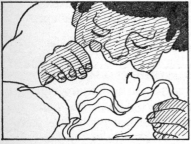

Poisoning. In any case of poisoning or suspected poisoning (which includes any kind of drug overdose), get the person *to hospital as quickly as possible*. Take with you if possible a sample of whatever the person is thought to have taken (or any syringe or container). If the poison is a liquid or acid, wipe it carefully off the lips and face. If the person is conscious, give him/her as much water or milk as possible to dilute the poison. *Do not give salted water* in an attempt to make him/her vomit. Don't attempt to keep him/her awake by walking up and down. Keep him/her quiet; if drowsy, lay flat in the recovery position. In some cases (e.g. a child who has taken a small aspirin overdose)* there may be no signs of discomfort or lethargy, but the person *must go to hospital* just the same. It takes time for the poison to be assimilated into the system, and for signs of poisoning to become apparent, and by then it may be too late for stomach pumping to be effective.

Shock. Anyone suffering from shock will look very pale, be cold and shivering (even on a hot summer's day), feel dizzy, sick and weak, and have a rapid pulse (normally around 72 – up to around 90). Get them to lie down. Cover with a light blanket or coat

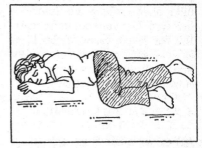

* A large *aspirin overdose – whether accidental or intentional – is agonizingly painful.*

First Aid in fewest words

1 Do *only* what is immediately essential; send for an ambulance.
2 Place anyone unconscious in the recovery position: side *not* back.
3 Apply the kiss of life *immediately*.
4 Plunge burns into water *straightaway*.
5 Stop bleeding by pressure *at once*.
6 For poisons or drug overdoses: give water if conscious.
7 Don't move injured victims.
8 Cover lightly.
9 *Give nothing to eat or drink*. (This could delay hospital treatment: anaesthetics can only be given on an empty stomach.)
10 Reassure as far as possible.

(but only one, not piles). Don't use any hot-water bottles. Don't give anything to drink – no tea, no alcohol. (Except for cases of mild shock where no injury is involved. Use your common sense. But for severe cases of shock, or as a result of accident and/or injury, hospital treatment may subsequently be required.)

4 ALL IN THE MIND?

All of us suffer from attacks of worry and convictions of inadequacy at various times of our lives; and all of us are vulnerable at any moment. Even the most self-confident person can be prey to doubt and depression – especially during that dead hour between three and four in the morning.

To realize this can in itself be a help. You're not abnormal, peculiar or totally inadequate just because at times you feel everything is simply too much for you. Everyone you know would, if they were honest, admit that at times they share your problems.

And when you're starting out on your own, you find yourself at one of the most vulnerable times of your life. Your family, your school, your surroundings, however much at times you may have resented or actively disliked them, were familiar and comprehensible. Now, without them, you find that the world looks different, is stranger and less welcoming than you expected. Everything costs more than you thought. People are impatient, not willing to make allowances. You don't find fantastic experiences waiting round each corner.

So if you get the blues, feel anxious, lethargic, this is not unusual. You can take steps to deal with it.

What to do

Any physical cause? Are your emotional feelings being caused or at least affected by your physical state of health? A poor diet, not enough sleep, inadequate exercise, are quite enough *in themselves* to cause mental depression. Look back to the beginning of this section, and take any necessary action.

Or are you suffering from the tail-end of some illness? A bad attack of flu, for example, can leave you feeling below par and even weepy for weeks afterwards. Patience, rest, and the recognition that this will pass, all help to get over it as quickly as possible.

If you know of no obvious physical reason for your state of mind, and yet don't see any rational motive, either (see below), then go and see your doctor. You could be suffering from something easily diagnosed and quickly remedied, such as anaemia: trust your GP and let him/her do some detective work on your behalf.

Outward circumstances? It's possible to go for weeks or even months feeling tense and worried without realizing that the main cause is not you or your failings, but something about the circumstances in which you're living. Try to think this through, and then take the appropriate steps to put things right. It may not be easy to work this out on your own. A friend, a real friend, who's known you some considerable while, may be the answer (or see below).

If you can pinpoint the main source of your worries, you're on the way to dispersing them. If you're bothered about money – never know you're going to have enough for the rent – perhaps you could try moving somewhere which costs less. If it's about your work – maybe you don't feel you can cope – a talk with your personnel manager or your boss, or your tutor or Careers Officer, might either show that your worries are unfounded or suggest something better suited to your individuality. If it's personal relationships, not so easy – but there *are* people to help (see below).

When you're stuck. When you can't see any physical reasons, or any outside circumstances to account for your feelings, you begin to feel increasingly alienated and on your own.

There are people who can and will help. Start with your doctor. Even if he/she finds no physical reason for your state of mind, he/she may still be able to help you cope emotionally.* Have you a close friend you haven't dared confide in? Try. Most people are more understanding than they're given credit for. Is there any one of your family, or among your relatives, you feel has shown sympathy to you in the past? Then don't assume they're no longer interested – get in touch with them and tell them how you feel. The National Marriage Guidance Council (at present looking for a new name) has counsellors who help with problems quite unconnected with marriage. In many areas of the country, priests and ministers of various denominations have sanctuaries where young people can go to find help. The Samaritans (number in your directory) are there at the end of the phone just to listen and to counsel while you tell them what's wrong – for an hour or longer if

you want. The Youth Advisory Centre, 31 Nottingham Place, London W1 (01–935 8870) has doctors and counsellors available for personal interviews, and will answer letters with problems; you can also ask them for a list of local agencies. The Board for Information on Youth and Community Service, 67 York Place, Edinburgh 1 (031–556 8671) does the same for Scottish residents. Your CAB may also be able to help with suggestions of local groups or individuals to contact.

5 CHOOSING YOUR DOCTOR AND DENTIST

Everyone is entitled to have *their own GP and their own dentist*, and everyone *should*. If you're still within touch of the medical advisers who've looked after you since you were a child, then there's no reason for you to change unless you want to. But if you've moved to a new area, and you're intending to stay for longer than a few weeks, then it's up to you to find and get yourself registered with someone local.

It's a great temptation to put this kind of thing off, especially if you're normally the sort of super-healthy young person who never needs any attention. But do take

---

* *But don't go demanding tablets – these are not necessarily the answer. If you find your GP's response abrupt, this could be part of his/her treatment. Wait a couple of days. If you still feel no better, go back and ask again.*

the trouble. It means that, in an emergency, there's someone you feel you can call on; someone whose business it is to care for you personally, and who will have all relevant medical papers to hand which might affect diagnosis or treatment.

Choosing a doctor

In a completely strange area it's not easy to know how to pick a doctor out of the blue. If you need a doctor in a hurry, telephone operators have a complete list, and can tell you the name and number of one near you. Sometimes – quite unofficially – they can also tell you which one is likely to prove most helpful. If you know no one who can give you advice, look for a partnership (several names on one plate outside a door). Go inside, explain to the receptionist that you're a stranger to the area: ask if there's an appointment system, and what happens if there's an emergency call (an appointment system works well and is to the patient's – your – advantage, but only if it's flexible enough to cope also with emergencies). While you're asking, see if the waiting-room is clean and welcoming, and the receptionist helpful. This won't, of course, tell you whether the doctor is a good diagnostician or not: but a good doctor is unlikely to put up with slovenly surroundings or appoint a brusque, off-putting person. If you're reasonably satisfied, ask if you could join the doctor's list. You'll need to give your medical card or name and address and National Health Number. (If you haven't got one, write to your local area Health Authority – ask at the Town Hall for the address – explaining the situation, and giving your full name and date of birth and where you were last registered with a GP.) If you're from abroad, you can be treated without charge here for any condition contracted since arrival: for up to three months after arrival you will be a temporary patient, after that you will need to be registered as though resident here. (Inquire at your Health Authority as above.)

The advantage of joining a partnership is that, if you can't get on with one doctor, you're likely to get on with another.

Advice from a doctor. When you join a new partnership, ask for an appointment to meet one of your new doctors for the first time and introduce yourself. Don't think up any odd symptoms to interest him/her. Just take a couple of minutes to say who you are, where you've come from, and anything else you think might be relevant.

Choosing a dentist

Choosing a new *dentist*'s panel to join can be even harder. Personal experience shows that dentists vary considerably in their skill and attitudes. Some seem ready to whip teeth out at the drop of a drill; others do their darndest to keep your fangs in your head.

If your teeth are in good nick, and you've already got a tried and trusted dentist in your childhood home, then you'd do best to stick to what you know, even if it means a fair journey every six months or so, until you're happy you've found a good replacement. If your teeth are only so-so, don't wait until they're driving you crazy, look for someone soon. If your teeth have been totally neglected, *don't waste any time*: ask around *urgently*.

Sometimes nurses can be helpful – shop talk can tell them who's reliable and who's not. Sometimes mothers with young children can tell you who at least seems to have a sympathetic approach. If you're really stuck, take my dentist's advice and have your hair done locally. Hairdressers and barbers tend to hear all the inside information.

But one thing you can't do is leave your teeth and hope they'll sort themselves out. They won't. Bad teeth get worse, and smellier. While a good dentist can save and renew even the least promising.

Play fair

Thanks to the National Health, both your doctor and dentist are there to help you whenever you need them. Don't abuse this facility.

If your doctor has an appointment system, use it whenever you can. Most practices ask that surgeries should be contacted before certain times if a home visit seems to be indicated. Try to keep to these hours unless there's an absolutely unforeseen emergency.

When you make an appointment, keep it. If you're late, everyone after you is late. If you're unavoidably prevented, ring up and tell the receptionist. And if you yourself are kept waiting, don't get unreasonably irritated (i.e. unless it happens time and again). Doctors can't measure out their time in precise five-minute lots. Some patient may have problems which unexpectedly take half an hour: if you were that patient, you wouldn't want to feel the doctor was rushing to abide by the clock and push you out through the door.

With dentists, you should pay regular visits at six-monthly intervals – yes, even if you think there's nothing wrong with your teeth at all. This is the way to make sure what needs seeing to gets treated before it turns into something really nasty. If your dentist's efficient you'll get a warning card every half-year: if you know his/her paper work isn't so hot, make a note yourself and stick it up somewhere you'll see it. Six months whizz past in no time.

Keep this up, and you're unlikely ever to find yourself being driven mad with toothache late on Friday evening after surgeries have shut for the week-end.

Costs

Your doctor's care is, of course, free to you. Prescriptions, at the time of writing, are chargeable at 20p per item.

At your dentist's, costs depend on what treatment you need. According to proposed charges to come into force from April 1977, you will pay the cost of each complete course up to a maximum of £6–£7. Under 21's don't have to pay: nor do pregnant women, or those with a baby under one year. Full-time students over 21, anyone unemployed or on social security, or with a particularly low income, will probably be entitled to rebates. Ask at your local Social Security office.

(None of this applies to purely cosmetic dentistry: here costs vary considerably from practice to practice.)

Sickness benefits

If you're not being paid for absence through illness by your employer you can claim sickness benefit. (You won't normally be paid for the first three days off unless you have been receiving benefit within the previous thirteen weeks.) In order to claim you need a form from your doctor after he/she has seen you and diagnosed your illness. It is not enough for you to ring up the doctor and merely say you are ill. Once the form is signed it should be sent immediately to your local Health and Social Security office. If you're not well enough to go out, give it to someone else to take or post. You may lose Social Security benefit if you don't.

Sickness certificate

Some firms insist that you produce a sickness certificate if you're away from work longer than three days. Doctors, for the most part, resent this bitterly. They will sign the certificate. They will not insist on seeing you (you may not in fact have been ill enough to need treatment). They may well add some such phrase as 'X states that he/she has been suffering from flu/cough' etc. And they will make a charge for this document. The medical opposition to this kind of non-form is such that it may have expired by the time of publication.

A particularly good book, which informs you without convincing you that you have every illness going, is A Dictionary of Symptoms, *Joan Gomez (Paladin, 1970).*

Outward Appearances

1 THE WAY YOU LOOK

How we look, how we appear to others, probably bothers us more in our teens and twenties than at any other time. Very few of us have the self-confidence to accept ourselves as what we are. It could help to deal with these very personal feelings if you look at a few objective facts.

You're not the only one who feels the way you do. Virtually everyone has moments of inadequacy, convictions that everyone else around is infinitely more desirable.

No one's perfect. Nature may not have handed out her good-look gifts with total fairness, but the inequalities aren't as marked as we think. Half the trouble is that we insist on comparing ourselves at our worst with superstars at their best. In fact, many of the pictures you see are as much the creations of photographers, visagistes and lighting technicians as of the models themselves.

Don't get stuck with stereotypes. At any given moment many magazines and TV programmes tend to concentrate on the latest fashionable image. It's very easy, under this kind of pressure, to believe that if you don't conform to the pattern you're peculiar; and yet you can see quite clearly that most others don't either. Don't be cowed if you're not identical with the latest fashion photo. Nor is anyone else.

Besides, and fortunately, *beauty is in the eye of the beholder*, which is as true now as it ever was. People like and fall in love with bony men, cuddly men, girls with high cheekbones and girls with square jaws, individuals with long hair, curly hair, ones with rippling muscles and ones without . . . with so many permutations of features and figures, it's not surprising that no one's ever arrived at one absolute standard of ideal beauty.

And, in any case, *you never can tell.* It's not easy to figure out what people are really like from the way they look: and at least as hard to guess how they'll react sexually. Accept this about other people, and give them the chance to accept this about you.

What's more, *things change*. As time goes by, (a) members of the opposite sex care less about whether you've the right kind of shape and more about what you actually are and (b) in any case many start to look their best as they leave their teens well behind.

So don't despair.

Self-help

Which is all very well. But if you're going through one of those stages when you feel yourself ugly and unwanted it's not so easy to believe you're potentially as desirable as anybody else – and certainly we all feel better if we find ourselves moderately attractive.

So let's take steps.

1 Read through the thoughts above.

2 If you're saddled with something which can't be changed (legs too short, rib-cage too broad, eyes too small), then make a positive effort to accept yourself as you are. And if you're acutely conscious of some particular fault, shut up about it. Ten to one it's not nearly as noticeable as *you* think, and people will pay attention only if you insist on harping on about it.

3 If you're bothered about something that *can* be changed (you're too fat, too thin, too flabby) do something about it. There are all sorts of experts around who can help, from doctors to chemists, teachers of fitness classes to exponents of yoga. So don't sit around brooding about your deficiencies, take active steps to mend matters.

4 Basic good health, while it won't transform you into a cover girl/boy, will certainly affect the way you look. A reasonable diet, some exercise, enough sleep, are essential if you're to have and continue to have a clear skin, good teeth, firm muscles. (So you could find it helpful to take a quick look through Chapters III and IV.)

From top to toe

Hair. It can be straightened, curled, bleached, coloured. Are you *sure* yours doesn't suit you the way it is? Or slightly adapted? Drastic changes cost money to keep up, and may not be necessary. If your hair's particularly awkward, find a hairdresser who can cope with it thoroughly (even if you can't afford this very often) rather than someone who dabbles at it every other week. Look around for someone with *hair like yours* and ask where they go, or write to a beauty editor explaining your problem. Wash it frequently; approximately once a week, but this varies depending on how greasy it is and where you live. Get in the habit of combing your hair *before* you wash your face; this helps prevent spots.

Your face. It won't look its best without good skin, sound teeth, clear eyes: all these again depend on good health. If your skin is bad, make sure it's not due to an in-adequate diet (see Chapter III) or to a failure to keep it really clean. If you're sure it's not your fault, it could be the result of some hormonal imbalance or allergy (see your doctor). If your eyes are sore or your vision blurred, you may need glasses. Consult your doctor first and then, if necessary, an

Making up?

Make-up's a changeable but comparatively inexpensive part of fashion. When you feel like using it you'll find plenty of the latest info in any woman's magazine, with more detailed individual advice available from consultants in department stores. A trial and error evening spent swopping cosmetics with friends can be a hilarious (and fruitful) experience.

Always remove all make-up before you go to bed. Water, or soap and water alone, won't do this, though there are some special cosmetic soaps which will. Be particularly careful to take off eye make-up. Leaving this on not only affects the skin round your eyes but can help to cause styes.

No matter how scrupulously careful you are in putting on and taking off make-up, your skin will benefit by having cosmetic-free days, especially when on holiday and in unpolluted air.

Incidentally, where make-up is concerned price is no criterion of value. Ingredients used for cheaper cosmetics are generally as safe for your skin as those in more expensive makes. Dearer cosmetics may offer a wider choice of colours, or a particular texture you prefer, but otherwise you may find yourself as happy with much cheaper kinds.

optician. If your teeth are less than perfect pearls, you may need a dentist (see pp. 109 and 133). Decaying teeth not only make life miserable, they'll certainly make your breath unpleasant whether you realize it or not.

Breasts (female). They vary considerably in shape and size. The way you stand also affects the way you (and they) look, but very few breasts resemble the ones in strip cartoons – and almost all, thanks to gravity, tend to droop slightly. If you've a particularly well-developed figure good bras can help (see p. 148). Good deportment helps too.

Chests (male). Although fashion's turned against the Mr Atlas look, it's hard not to feel puny if you've a narrow chest and skinny biceps. If this bothers you, weightlifting and similar classes at your local institute can help build you up no end – psychologically as well as physically.

Figure generally (both sexes). Again, largely a result of diet and exercise (see Chapters III and IV). You can't change your basic body frame, but you *can* alter the way flesh is distributed round it, train your muscles to do their job.

Sexual organs (male). Letters written to men's magazines and questions put to sex consultants show that most males worry at one time or another about their sexual organs; yet, with rare exceptions, quite unnecessarily. Don't let yourself keep brooding about this. As a first step, see your doctor (see also p. 182).

Sexual organs (female). Girls seem much less inclined to worry; but if you do, again it's a help to know that the odds are that medically you're dead normal. Ask your doctor for reassurance, or write to one of the women's magazines.

And remember that just as people vary in every way – with different ears, fingers, nails – so they differ sexually.

Hands. If you've a dirty job, use barrier creams before you start. (They're invisible, you won't get laughed at.) Dry your hands thoroughly every time you wash them and, if you've a dry skin, use hand-cream afterwards. This isn't just for looks, you save yourself painful chapping.

Nails. Again it's common sense, not vanity, to keep them trimmed. Use very sharp nail scissors (good ones cost money) and/or emery boards. Clean them with orange sticks or a nail-brush. If you use anything metal it scrapes the nails so they pick up and cling on to dirt. Push down the cuticles with a towel as you dry them to keep a good shape.

Legs. You can't make them longer or shorter, but you can to some extent change their shape by the type of exercise you take.

Next to godliness

Keeping clean has nothing to do with not getting dirty. People who work in dirty jobs are bound to get covered in muck, grease, oil, dust: those who do physically arduous work, whether it's belly-dancing or brick-laying, are going to sweat. Keeping clean means removing the dirt and grime at the end of one day and starting the next day fresh.

In any case, everybody sweats at times, particularly when they're rushing around, they're nervous or it's hot. Young people tend to sweat especially easily, partly because their glands function erratically, partly because they're more subject to stress and tension. Fresh sweat is not offensive — indeed it can be positively sexy. But sweat which is left to stale and turn sour does smell, both on the skin and on clothes.

The answer is not to cover it up with deodorants or scent, but to wash it off. The ideal is a bath or shower every day, which I know isn't easy when too many rooms lack access to bathrooms, hot water's expensive, and some landlords/ladies grasping. But do the best you can. Anyone who has a tap, a bowl, and a minimal amount of privacy can keep clean. As a gleaming old lady in a cottage in Islington once told me, 'I fill the bowl and wash from the top down, then I stand in it and wash from the bottom up, until I meet in the middle.' At least wash daily all areas which sweat easily; armpits, groin, feet.

Clothes which touch your skin also need to be changed regularly. Don't buy dry-cleanable clothes unless you can really spare the money and energy to have them cleaned as often as they need it. If you wear the same uncleaned satin shirt day after day you can't be surprised if people start to move away from you.

Once you're clean, if you want to use a deodorant go ahead, but pick ones with none or as little scent as possible. If you like using perfume, don't overdo it – remember that you can become accustomed to it, and that it always smells much stronger to others. Never put scent or eau-de-Cologne on your clothes – it can turn stale and smell unpleasant, and can also stain. *Steer clear of vaginal deodorants.* See the medical note on p. 109. Remember that nature designed the natural you to turn people on, not off.

Swimming, walking, cycling, dancing, all make your leg muscles work. For more specific advice, ask at a local gym or health club.

If you're female and want to defuzz them, an ordinary razor plus soap in the bath a couple of times a week is the quickest, cheapest and (provided you're not ham-fisted) simplest way of doing it.

Feet. Reliable, shapely, walkable-on feet depend more than anything else on well-fitting shoes (see p. 149) and on how you look after them (see p. 109). If you've something wrong already see a chiropodist (look in the Yellow Pages of your phone book), find out why, and get it put right.

2 GLAD RAGS

Some people adore buying clothes. Others resent every penny spent on something they think inessential. How much you want to pay out depends not only on how much cash you've got but on your personal ideas and attitude to life. Don't rely on other people's opinions. You have to know what's appropriate for *you*.

Here are a few pointers to help you decide.

How much money can you spare to spend per month on clothes?

Is this likely to be enough? If you're not used to buying your own clothes, and you've little idea how much things cost, investigate various shops and note prices.

What if it won't be? Are you going to:
– take a part-time job to earn more?
– cut down on your requirements?
– buy cheaper clothes?

– buy on credit? (tricky – see p. 332)

– change your way of life?

Don't just hope you'll miraculously acquire enough cash because you won't. You'll end up cutting down on essentials like food.

How do you feel about fashion? You can adopt it wholeheartedly because it's fun; you've got the money; you won't be young long; you're in with people who expect you to. You can ignore it because you can't afford it; it's wrong to spend money on it; you're saving up for something which matters more; you've got your own ideas; you're not interested anyway. Or you can take up some kind of position halfway between being committed and bored.

What you decide is up to you. But unless you're one of the very few with a large private income you'll have to end up making a *choice*. You can't do everything. You're not likely to be able to afford new clothes every week *and* a month abroad, or a new guitar, or deposits in a building society.

What kind of clothes are your *priorities?* They could be heavy boots or elegant coats. This depends entirely on you and your kind of life. If you have to do a lot of walking, several pairs of well-fitting (probably expensive) shoes could be essential. If you're a girl with an awkward figure, beautifully fitting (and perhaps sadly pricey) bras might cheer you up more than the classiest sweaters.

Can you tell when you're getting value for money? Prices for clothes aren't entirely a good guide for what you get. Here are some of the variables which affect what you pay.

– The cost of the basic raw materials (of cotton, wool etc.) which reflect world commodity prices.

– How they're treated. Different dyes, patterns, textures, all affect the final cost.

– How each garment's designed and cut. Clothes with more separate pieces, darts, tucks, or made in a large range of fittings, are bound to be more expensive. (Items like collars etc. add considerably to the cost.)

– The finish. Linings, seam-bindings, hand-sewing of buttons, all cost more. (Yet, oddly enough, some of the more expensive clothes are among the worst finished.)

– Whether there are expensive extras like unusual buttons or buckles.

– The name of the manufacturer or designer. Often you pay more just for the label.

How to pick and choose

Make up your mind beforehand what you have to get, and stick to

Why manners matter

It's what you are and how you behave, rather than how you look, that makes others find you likeable or otherwise. First appearances can attract, and further acquaintance repel.

A greater politeness and an easy manner to others makes social intercourse less stressful and life generally more tolerable. (Apart from anything else, if you're not generally well mannered, how can anyone tell when you positively intend to be rude?) Politeness today means not a rigid etiquette but the sort of manners which spring from a consideration for others and a disinclination to wound or snub. There are few rules. You can work out yourself what seems important to you — think what, in the past, has annoyed you in others' behaviour, and resolve not to do the same.

Here are some suggestions to start you thinking.

Politeness is:

not taking other people for granted

not shouting others down

exercising patience: not expecting others to jump around just because you want them to

not talking in public at the top of your voice so that all around are forced to hear you

taking the trouble to listen

trying to understand other people's points of view

and so on.

If you consider the feelings of those with whom you come into contact, your manners are not likely to let you down. If you don't, no amount of polish will conceal your basic contempt.

it. If you need a thick sweater to spend a winter week in the High-lands, there's no earthly point in coming back instead with two bargain cheesecloth shirts. If you know you're open to temptation, head straight for the appropriate shops or departments and save the window-gazing for later.

Have some idea too of what colours and materials are possible, how much you're prepared to pay, and what your absolute maximum is. Unless you've bags of time, work out where you're most likely to find clothes in your price bracket, and head straight there.

Practical point: if you're carrying *cash* on you, or one of the more vulnerable credit cards (see p. 335), make sure you're not going to be pick-pocketed or have your hand-bag snatched. It's too easy for a thief to wait until you're totally preoccupied looking at coats. Keep a purse zipped up in a shopping-bag you never put down, a wallet in your inside breast pocket. (A wallet in a hip-pocket is just asking to be lifted.)

Where you go for your clothes depends very largely on your *figure*, your *tastes* and your *money*.

If you've a *standard* shape, you can shop virtually anywhere. If you haven't, you'll need to con-concentrate on the stores or boutiques which stock your kind of fitting. (If you find a particular manufacturer whose figure stan-dards happen to coincide with yours, you're in luck.) If you can't find clothes to fit, you could try making them yourself (see p. 147), having them made (expensive, but could be worth it), or made-to-measure through direct mail (chancy, you can only send things back because they're badly or wrongly made, not because you don't like them).

Your *tastes* help to dictate where you go. However individual your ideas, don't overlook the chain stores. They often – especi-ally in city centres – try out experimental batches with adven-turous designs. Keep your eyes open: these are often in and out of a store within three days. Even run-of-the-mill lines are often very well designed, and excellent value.

More than anything else your *money* – or lack of it – dictates where you shop. However, it can be worth going round high-priced stores, even if you can't afford to buy there or don't think you'd want to anyway, just to see what ideas you can get. In any case, money and clothes value don't necessarily always go together (see p. 141).

You can't beat *surplus clothing stores* for sheer warmth per pence. You never know what you're going to find, which is half the charm. Check through though for holes and other sizeable blemishes. *Jumble sales* and *second-hand shops* are also great places for bargains. Look out especially for things which new cost a lot of money –

coats, jackets. Some clothes are worth buying for the material, or buttons, or zips. Check vulnerable parts – zips, elbows, underarm seams. Allow for any necessary washing or cleaning costs. *Street markets* are good hunting-grounds, provided you can resist being pressured into buying unwanted rubbish.

What to go for. Faced with rows and rows of clothes it sometimes seems impossible to make a decision. When you find yourself dithering, try checking these three points.

1 Does it fit?

2 Do you positively like what it's made from, its colour, weight and texture?

3 Can you afford the initial cost, and how expensive is maintenance going to be?

Ideally, your choice should score on all three points. Sometimes you may be forced to settle for two. But if your selection only rates one, give it a miss.

1 *Does it fit?* Have you tried it on? If not, are you buying from somewhere which will refund money if it doesn't fit? If you have, did you get a good look at it in a mirror (preferably set at an angle with others, so you could see all sides)? Does it fit well at all the points it needs to? Across the shoulders? hips? waist? chest? collar? If not, could you alter it yourself or get it altered? You can

often take in seams and turn up hems, but letting them out or down is always difficult and often impossible. Don't buy anything pulled so tightly across tricky parts (your top or bottom) that the seams strain. It's generally also a mistake to buy something so large you rattle inside. Badly fitting clothes get more annoying, not less.

2 *Do you like what it's made from?* Do you like the look of the material? The way it feels? Is it warm enough or cool enough? Does it hang well? Will it crease? Do you like the colour? If you don't, do you positively dislike it, or is it simply a colour you haven't worn before?

3 *Can you afford its cost; and upkeep?* Is it about what you expected to pay? Do you know what the material is, how good the quality? (See p. 146.) How well made is it? Check weak points: look inside at the width of seams, particularly where they're under strain, under the arms, and at the crotch of trousers. Are they bound or oversewn? Is it completely washable? If not, remember you'll have to pay dry-cleaning costs maybe every time you wear it.

If you still can't decide, it can be useful to work out what it's going to cost per wearing – i.e. the price divided by the number of times you'll put it on.

A pair of shoes might cost £12,

Fitting feathers

Society is much freer and easier than it used to be. There's more freedom over how people dress, and less inclination to grade them by their clothes. However, it would be rash to conclude from this that you can wear what you want when you want to. Some circumstances suggest, more or less strongly, the kind of clothes you should choose.

If you're applying for a job, choose clothes which both reflect your personality and match the kind of job you'll be doing. (If you haven't any which do both, then maybe that kind of job's not right for you anyway.)

If you're being taken out by an elderly relative, it's civil to choose an outfit which won't give him/her heart-failure.

If you're invited by someone to a festive occasion (a birthday, an end-of-exam celebration) turn up looking fairly festive yourself. Arriving in your gutter-cleaning outfit suggests that you don't think it/him/her worth sprucing up for.

If you're starting a new job, turn up in the kind of clothes you can do it in. Don't wear trailing sleeves if you're going to be washing up, or high heels if you'll need to run up and down ladders.

If you're going walking, climbing etc. wear practical shoes, warm clothes, really water-proof top clothing. Take advice. Platform shoes for fell-walking can cripple or kill.

There's no need to feel your personality's been got at because you have to adapt slightly to circumstance, nor do you need a colossal wardrobe. A very basic minimum of clothes in various categories (warm, cool; elegant, tatty; zany, conventional) should see you through.

Note: Keep one set of old clothes for cleaning, painting, etc. Otherwise, give to jumble sales anything you've kept without wearing for a year; or you'll find your drawers stuffed with mounds of unworn outdated tat.

but if you wore them every other day for eighteen months they'd cost (not counting any repairs) around 4½p a wearing; while a partyish dress for £20 you might only wear half a dozen times, working out at a pretty pricey £3 + a go. Which might be worth it, or might not – but an analysis like this can help you decide what you think it's worth spending most on.

Look at the label

Before you buy anything to wear, look at the label (not the brand name, the one that gives you information). You may find it attached to the collar or waistband, or concealed in a side-seam. This ought to tell you what the garment's made of, whether it should be washed or dry-cleaned, and whether there's anything else you need to know. Sometimes there are two separate labels.

If there is no label at all, you may be able to find an assistant who can supply the missing information. If you can't, then you have to weigh up the fact that you don't know whether it will shrink, run, lose colour – or even fall to pieces – against its desirability.

Here's what labels ought to say

What something's made of. Whether it's wool, cotton, acrylic, polyester, nylon and so on. All pure natural fibres have un-

matchable qualities: wool is warmer than any synthetic, linen cool and absorbent, and so on. Most man-made fibres are easily washable (but get dirty very quickly), but many are non-absorbent and can be less comfortable to wear.

Often mixtures of natural and synthetic fibres give you the best of both worlds. Wool/nylon gives you the warmth of wool and the toughness of nylon; linen/Terylene gives you the texture of linen plus the resistance to creasing of Terylene. You should find the label gives the proportions of each fibre. If not, by law the one first mentioned is the one there's more of – so if you buy a coat labelled polyester/wool it's largely polyester.

Note. Assistants will often tell you something is made of crêpe, poplin, velvet etc. These are names of *weaves*, not of materials. For example, velvet can be made of cotton (often washable) or rayon (which never is).

*Whether it's washable.** Good labelling should not only tell you whether it's washable, but how it should be washed, in what temperature water, and, if ironing's needed, what temperature the iron should be.

However, *woollens* (especially

* *For a translation of the latest clothes care symbols see page 359.*

knitted woollens) described as machine-washable certainly aren't in the average automatic washer you'll find in your launderette. So you'll need to continue to wash these by hand.

Whether it's dry-clean only. If it is, make sure you can afford the bills for upkeep (see p. 144).

Whether it's colour-fast. If it isn't, and it's marked 'Always Wash Separately', decide whether you want to risk the bother of washing it forever by hand. Although some clothes lose all their loose dye in the first few washes, and can thereafter be stuck in the washing-machine, others – especially cheap clothes – keep losing colour until they fall to bits. Very bright or strong colours (especially reds), hand-blocked prints, Madras cottons, are always risky.

Whether it's pre-shrunk. This usually applies only to cottons and some woollens. If a garment isn't so labelled, and it only just fits you, then beware. Cotton jersey (T-shirts etc.) almost always shrinks: corduroy often does: so do (though not always) cheap woollens. Styles loosely woven or knitted are always trickier to wash.

Warning. Some labels are deceptive. 'Shrink-resistant', 'shower-resistant','crease-resistant' mean only what they say, but no more. Some process has been applied which means the fabric is *less* *likely* to shrink, let in rain, crease – not that it won't.

Sew-it-yourself?

Whether making your own clothes is feasible, pleasurable, profitable or plain impossible depends on a number of things.

(a) Whether you're male or female. Male clothes are much harder to make. Even shirts incorporate tricky sewing points.

(b) How skilled you already are. Making even simple clothes well takes a certain amount of knowledge and trouble. If you're even more ambitious, you *can* learn as you go along, but it might make more sense to join an evening class and get expert help.

(c) Whether you find a stock pattern size to fit you. If you do, half your troubles are over. If you don't, and you have unstandard proportions, you do need skill to adapt even simple patterns. Patterns are mathematical. Add or subtract, and everything affected by your alteration has to alter too.

(d) Whether you've someone to help you with fittings. Fitting clothes on yourself is difficult and time-consuming. Someone who's ready to help you (perhaps on reciprocal terms) can save a lot of bad temper.

(e) Whether you've the use of a sewing-machine. If you haven't, you need to off-set what even a second-hand machine's going to

Tricky fitting problems

You all over. If you're unusually tall, short or broad, it's hard to find clothes to fit you can stand the sight of. Small non-specialist shops rarely carry more than a few items in non-standard sizes. In department stores, policies vary. It's simply a question of heading for your nearest large centre and tacking from one shop to the next. Or, less tiringly, you could start by making a list of the largest from your local Yellow Pages and writing to explain your problem and ask what stocks they carry in your size.

When you're desperate, there are shops which specialize in unusual sizes and will supply them mail order. Among these are:

(for large males) High and Mighty, 164 Edgware Road, London W 2.

(for tall females) Tall Girls, 32a Grosvenor Street, London W 1.

Bras. If you're one of nature's luscious larger ladies you're unlikely to want to go bra-less, but you can find it surprisingly difficult to find ones which fit, are comfortable, and do you justice. Manufacturers do in fact make a much bigger variety of bras than you might have realized, with four or even five fittings in each size. Again, only the largest specialist shops and department stores carry anything like an adequate range, but it can be worth the journey to get what you need. Ideally, the more difficult you find it to get bras which fit, the more particular you should be to try them on before buying: but if you're completely stuck, mail order can help. Write to D. H.

Evans & Co. Ltd, 318 Oxford Street, London W1, who keep large stocks of less usual sizes.

Shoes. If you've corns on your feet, little toes bent under, large toes pushed well out of the straight, then you're almost certainly wearing shoes that don't fit.

Feet like this make you self-conscious by the beach or swimming-pool: and though it may seem remote to think of this now, ignoring signs like these leads at least to discomfort, at worst to real pain and the possibility of operations later on. So if you suspect your shoes may be wrong (a great many people's are) check these points.

(a) Are they too short? Are your toes jammed against the end? You need a half-size or size larger.

(b) Are they too tight across the foot? Do you have corns on your toes? You need a broader fitting.

(c) Do they fall off at the heel? You need a smaller size or (more likely) a narrower fitting.

(d) Does your foot slide forward so your toes buckle under together at the end? You need a lower heel or better support for your foot at the instep.

It's one thing to decide that in the Save Our Feet cause you need better fitting shoes; it can, alas, be quite another to find them. Trousers come in different lengths, bras come in different cups, but too many shoe manufacturers believe all feet come in the same width. So if you, like many of us, have not-quite standard feet, you'll need to concentrate on the (probably very few) shops in your area that do stock shoes in separate fittings. Some shoe departments of large stores do: so do branches of Peter Lord Ltd. Elliots sell narrow shoes; the Narrow Foot League (57 Abbey Lodge, Park Road, London NW8), will supply to members the addresses of other retailers. Lilley & Skinner, 358 Oxford Street, London W1, sell mail-order shoes in several widths and also in unusually small and large sizes. Selfridges, Oxford Street, London W1, sell mail-order broad and narrow shoes. K Shoe Shops with a 'Blue Ribbon' sign in the window have trained fitters and sell a wide range of fittings.

It does mean, inevitably, that you have far less choice over colours and styles, with broader feet on the whole coming out even worse than narrow. If you can't find what you want, consider having shoes made for you. It's not cheap, but a hand-made pair should outlast any number of ones which are badly fitting and shoddily made. (A retailer recently said that he did not expect those he sold to last longer than three months — pretty poor value for money at £7 + per pair.)

Don't abuse your feet. One day they'll start shouting back.

cost you against how seriously you mean to use it. Some people find it worth joining evening classes for the use of the machines alone.

(f) How much free time you have. The less skilled you are, the longer everything takes. Don't under-estimate how long even a simple article takes to finish. I'm convinced practically every house in the UK has at least one cut-up garment languishing in its cup-boards.

(g) How much space you have. If you've nowhere you can leave things between sessions it makes life difficult.

(h) Whether you like sewing or do it as a chore. Some people find clothes-making soothing. Others, the sort who always find them-selves cutting two right sleeves, loathe it.

(i) Perhaps the most important, what your main motive is.

If you want to make clothes *because you're forced to* (you can't get clothes to fit or afford to have them made), then sheer necessity will probably drive you into over-coming other obstacles.

If you want to make clothes because *you've original ideas* you want to carry out, then this again can inspire you to overcome problems.

If you want to make clothes *to save money*, then whether you succeed depends on how you rate your time, what kind of clothes you want, how high your standards are. It's not that easy to undercut the cheapest bought clothes, once you've paid for material, pattern, interlining, zip, buttons etc. — even if you entirely discount your time. On the other hand, once you've acquired the necessary skills you can make the equivalent of very expensive clothes for a fraction of the price.

Knitting and crocheting?

Knitting and crocheting take up less room than sewing. You can pick them up and put them down, keep going while reading or talking (though having to listen to the clackety-click drives some people mad). Because knitteds are more adaptable than fabrics, you don't have to be as fussy over fitting, but most people find knitting patterns harder to adapt. It's less easy, without special training, to carry out original ideas through knitting and crocheting. Even without taking your time into account, you can often end up saving only shillings by doing-it-yourself. But if you enjoy it, you can make yourself, relatively effortlessly, woollens which are unusual and individual because of the colours and textures you choose.

There are some excellent books to help you, among them:

Patons Book of Knitting and Crochet, Patience Horne and Stephen Bowden, Heinemann, 1973.
Streamlined Dressmaking, Renée and Julian Robinson, The Bodley Head, 1966.

3 SIMPLE SEWING

Buttons pop off, zips break, hems fall down. You don't have to wait until your garments fall un-anchored from you; a stitch in time *does* save nine. (And for most rescue operations you don't have to have a sewing-machine.)

Your rescue kit

1 packet of assorted needles. (If you're not used to sewing, look for long thin ones with long thin eyes.)
Pins (long, sharp, non-rusty).
Thimble.
Seam-ripper (easier than scissors for cutting open machine-stitching – e.g. when you need to

Invest in underwear

Set yourself up. Buy lots. It's much easier to shove 7 pairs of machine-washable socks and pants into the launderette once a week than dabble away every now and again in a basin – and far more agreeable for all around you than keeping the same lot going. After all, it costs no more in the long run.

ASSORTED NEEDLES

PINS

THIMBLE

SEAM RIPPER

REELS OF THREAD

MULTI-COLOURED SEWING PLAIT

TAPE MEASURE

take out a broken zip).

Reels of thread (1 black, 1 white to start with, also 1 reel heavy-weight button thread).

1 multi-coloured sewing plait. (Look for these in big department stores. You get a selection of sewing-length threads in around thirty colours, so you have the right one handy for sewing on odd buttons etc. without the expense of buying a whole reel.)

Tape measure.

Threading a needle. Pick the right needle. If you're sewing on buttons, see it's fine enough to go through the holes. If you're sewing thick material, see it's long enough to go through and be gripped the other side. If you're sewing delicate material, see it's thin enough not to pull holes through it.

Cut your thread with a really sharp pair of scissors, at an oblique angle, so it won't have a whiskery end. Hold it between the thumb and first finger of your left hand with 2 cm. showing. Lick the first finger of your right hand and pinch upwards the end of the thread. This makes it compact and slightly rigid. Close your left finger and thumb more tightly so that now only the tip of the thread projects. Place the eye of the needle over it. Release the pressure of your left finger and thumb and simultaneously push the eye of the needle down. The thread will slide in. (Thread the needle as

THREADING A NEEDLE

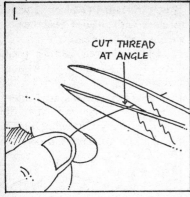

1.

CUT THREAD
AT ANGLE

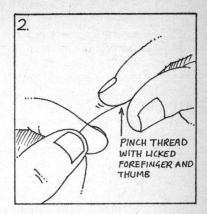

2.

PINCH THREAD
WITH LICKED
FOREFINGER AND
THUMB

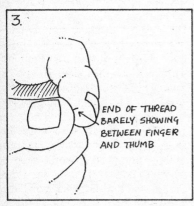

3.

END OF THREAD
BARELY SHOWING
BETWEEN FINGER
AND THUMB

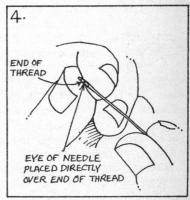

4.

END OF
THREAD

EYE OF NEEDLE
PLACED DIRECTLY
OVER END OF THREAD

the thread comes off the reel to cut down the chance of knotting.)

If you're threading wool, double the end over into a loop. Hold this between your left finger and thumb. Push the needle through it and then upwards, to force the loop into a tight shape. Pinch this tightened loop, and bring the eye of the needle down on top of the doubled wool.

Reverse if you're left-handed.

This all sounds a song and dance about nothing, but if you've never sewn before you can give up before you start.

How long is a piece of thread? If you're going to sew with a single thread, cut it a few centimetres longer than your needle to your elbow. If you're using a doubled thread (for button-sewing etc.) cut it twice as long.

Mending a gaping seam

Turn the garment inside out. Pin the two pieces of material together, making sure that the original stitching lines are exactly opposite each other. If you're mending a curved seam (armhole, trouser crotch) tack (sewing with big stitches in different coloured thread) along the stitching line to make sure that the material is not pulling away on either side.

Thread your needle with appropriate coloured thread. You can use it doubled if the material is heavy and the seam likely to come under strain. Knot the thread(s) firmly at one end.

Start beyond the point where the seam has burst. Sew either with running stitch if the seam isn't under strain, or back stitch if it is.

You sew *from right to left* (left to right, if you're left-handed).

Running stitch. Pull tightly enough for the stitches to lie flat, but without puckering the cloth.

Back stitch. This makes a much stronger seam.

Finish off firmly (on the wrong side) when you get to the end, or the whole lot will pull out again. One way is to push the needle through the next to last stitch, pull the thread through a couple of times, then push the needle through the final loop to make a knot. Then push the needle in and out of a few stitches and cut the thread off close to the material.

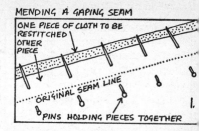

MENDING A GAPING SEAM

ONE PIECE OF CLOTH TO BE RESTITCHED
OTHER PIECE
ORIGINAL SEAM LINE
PINS HOLDING PIECES TOGETHER
1.

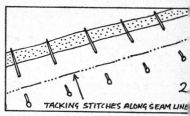

TACKING STITCHES ALONG SEAM LINE
2

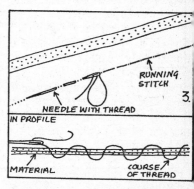

RUNNING STITCH
3.
NEEDLE WITH THREAD
IN PROFILE
MATERIAL
COURSE OF THREAD

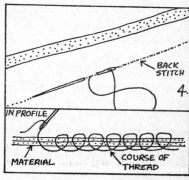

BACK STITCH
4.
IN PROFILE
MATERIAL
COURSE OF THREAD

Resewing on buttons

Of course sewing on buttons is child's play – provided you remember to make allowances for the thickness of the buttonholed material which will come between the button and the material it's sewn to. It's no good ignoring this and smugly sewing your buttons tightly down. If the material's more than cotton-thin either you won't be able to do them up at all or they'll immediately pop undone again.

If your material is very thick, and the buttons have no shank of their own, you'll have to provide them with one of tough thread.

If the buttons have come off because they've pulled a hole in the material, you'll need to provide a new, firmer base. The simplest way is to stitch a length of strong tape or petersham ribbon to the underneath of the material (tack it down around the torn holes) and sew the buttons to this.

Use doubled thread. If the material is heavy, use button-thread. Knot the ends firmly. Sew the button on, using four or five sets of stitching. If the material is thick, and you're using a button without a shank, place one or two matchsticks between the button and the material to keep the stitches evenly tensioned. Take out the matchsticks. On the right side of the material, wind the thread round and round the loose

SEWING ON BUTTON

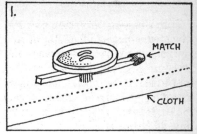

1.

MATCH

CLOTH

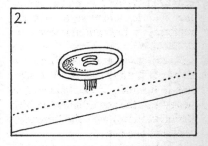

2.

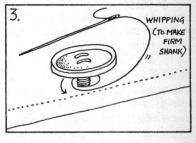

3.

WHIPPING (TO MAKE FIRM SHANK)

vertical threads to make a tough shank. Finish off firmly on the wrong side. Check to make sure you haven't sewn the button on either too tightly (you won't be able to do it up) or too loosely (it'll droop).

Replacing a zip

Take out the broken zip. Use your stitch ripper if you have one,

REPLACING A ZIP

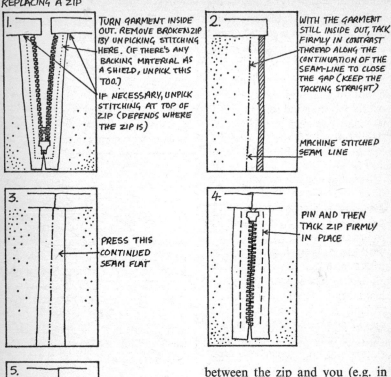

1. TURN GARMENT INSIDE OUT. REMOVE BROKEN ZIP BY UNPICKING STITCHING HERE. (IF THERE'S ANY BACKING MATERIAL AS A SHIELD, UNPICK THIS TOO.)

IF NECESSARY, UNPICK STITCHING AT TOP OF ZIP (DEPENDS WHERE THE ZIP IS)

2. WITH THE GARMENT STILL INSIDE OUT, TACK FIRMLY IN CONTRAST THREAD ALONG THE CONTINUATION OF THE SEAM-LINE TO CLOSE THE GAP (KEEP THE TACKING STRAIGHT)

MACHINE STITCHED SEAM LINE

3. PRESS THIS CONTINUED SEAM FLAT

4. PIN AND THEN TACK ZIP FIRMLY IN PLACE

5. ADJUST TOP ENDS OF ZIP MATERIAL ENDS AS NECESSARY. RESTITCH WAIST-BAND ETC. IF YOU HAD TO UNPICK EARLIER

BACKSTITCH FIRMLY IN POSITION

DO DOUBLE LINE OF STITCHING HERE

otherwise a small sharp pair of scissors. Cut along the stitching, not along the zip. If you find other odd flaps of material around between the zip and you (e.g. in trousers) take these out too. If you're not used to sewing, they're too fiddly to deal with. You'll simply have to take extra care in future.

So you'll be left with, basically, two pieces of material which come together in a seam which is open where the old zip was and your new zip will go.

Check that you have the right length and weight of zip. You can get light-weight zips for cotton shirts and dresses, medium-weight for skirts, heavy-weight for coats, curved for trouser flies. If you're replacing a zip in e.g. an anorak, you need one that's open-ended. I personally prefer metal zips.

With the garment inside out, tack with a different-coloured thread along what would be the continuation of the seam if the zip weren't going there. If you're feeling thorough, press this 'seam' down flat.

Take the zip and pin it into place. Make sure the pull-tag bit comes at the right level and that you've got the zip the right way round (horribly easy to sew it with the pull-tag facing inwards). Make sure that the centre of the zip lies along the seam line you've just tacked. Now tack the zip.

Using a firm back stitch (see above) sew along both sides of the zip. (You'll probably need a thimble to help push the needle through.) Make sure you stitch through both the narrow seam allowance and the main piece of material: you should see your stitches on the right side. Carry your line of stitching about half-way between the teeth and the edge of the zip. (If you stitch too close to the teeth the pull-tag will catch, if you stitch too close to the edge of the zip (a) you'll miss the seam allowance and (b) the done-up zip will gape.) Fasten off firmly. Pull out the tacking threads. You've done it.

Fixing a hem

If a hem's come unstuck, whether at the bottom of a shirt or skirt or coat, how you fix it back depends on what the material is and how it was fixed before.

If the material's fine, ordinary hem-stitch (felling) will do. Press the hem into place. Pin down. Sew with a single thread. Hold the material as shown, with the thumb of the left hand holding down the hem as you sew. (It's easiest, particularly with heavy material, to put the garment on a table so its weight doesn't drag while you sew.) Sewing from right to left, take tiny stitches into the main material (though you make quite large stitches in between). Keep the tension loose. You shouldn't be able to see a thick stitched hem-line to give the game away. Often bad sewers make the best hemmers!

HEMMING

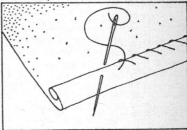

If the material's middling thick, or it has a raw edge, or it's jersey or some similarly stretchy fabric, herringbone stitch is better than

Glue-it-yourself

If you can't bear the thought of sewing, there are various adhesives for materials, iron-on patches, hem-bindings etc. which you can find at most large haberdashery counters or Woolworth's. These can be particularly useful if you have to turn up a hem in very thick material. (The conventional way demands hem-binding, which takes a sewing-machine or plenty of patience.) However, these repairs won't stand up to repeated washing or dry-cleaning, so whether you find them useful or not depends on what you're fixing and your own temperament.

plain felling. Press down the hem as before. (Use a damp cloth if necessary – see ironing, p. 162.) Pin into place. Herringbone *from left to right* as shown. Again, keep the tension loose. The stitches going through to the right side of the material should be kept very small.

HERRINGBONING

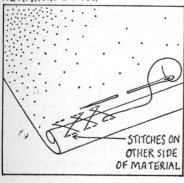

STITCHES ON
OTHER SIDE
OF MATERIAL

Mending rips

If you've a fairly straight tear in not-too-thick material, and you don't care passionately if the mend shows, the simplest thing is to turn the garment inside out and either use a line of running-stitch or oversew the torn edges to pull the two sides of the tear together.

If the material is thick, or the fitting isn't slack enough to allow for this kind of darn-effect, or you want to try something more invisible, you can try cobbling it together like this.

Choose a thread as near the colour and kind of material as possible. You can use invisible (nylon or Terylene) thread, but remember it will melt if you iron it. Working on the right side of the material, sew in and out, in a kind of fish-bone pattern, to draw the edges of the tear together. How invisible you get this mend depends on how patient you are and how frayable the material is.

Darning

There are lovely fancy ways of darning for those who have the patience and the clothes to justify it. But if all you want to know is how to keep your toes from sticking out at the end of your socks or your elbows out of your favourite sweater, the simplest way will do.

(You will, incidentally, do away with a lot of mending if you only buy socks reinforced with nylon, wash them daily, and keep your toenails short.)

If your socks or sweaters are thin all over before they need darning it's hardly worth doing unless you're absolutely broke. The darns superimposed on the thin material will pull away in no time.

Choose a thread or wool as near as possible to what you're darning (i.e. same type and weight as well as colour. If you have trouble matching the yarn, look out for those sold for tapestry work. They come in a wide range of colours, and are sold mainly in needlework shops or large department stores.) Going to and fro in one direction, make a kind of mini-loom. Then go from side to side in the opposite direction, passing under and over alternate

threads, until you have woven a neat(ish) patch.

4 KEEPING CLOTHES CLEAN

Various helpful councils have worked out eight different washing processes you can subject your clothes to, which must be invaluable if you're running a family or laundry, but is less practical when it comes to you and your little mouldy heap.

What you want to know is what you can take to the launderette; what has to be washed by hand; what has to be dry-cleaned. See p. 359 for the symbols on clothes care labels, *and*:

– look at your heap

– remove anything with a 'dry-clean only' label, and which is new enough or loved enough not to be entrusted to water

– remove anything woollen (even if it says 'machine-washable')

– remove anything which you know or suspect may not be colour-fast

– remove anything which might be harmed by brisk spinning – e.g. boned bras or tights.

What's left is very unlikely to make up more than one machine-load. (The average commercial machine takes 5 kg or 7 kg – large ones take more.) Most launderettes only offer two washing programmes: hot and warm. Very basically: you can only put into

Before you take your clothes to the launderette, squeeze a little liquid detergent on extra dirty parts (collars, cuffs, stains) and scrub gently.

the *hot* wash white and colour-fast cottons and linens without any special treatments and sometimes, depending on how hot the water actually is, white nylon. Everything else machine-washable needs a warm wash only. If you wash something at too hot a temperature you risk damaging it (Orlon, for example, creases badly). If you wash something at a cooler than ideal temperature it might turn out minimally less clean, but that's all.

So unless you end up with a machine-wash composed *entirely* of hot-wash articles (towels, fast-coloured cotton shirts etc.) you'll need to stick to a *warm* wash only.

At the launderette

Launderettes have would-be helpful notices around which tend to terrify the novice. Don't panic. What they mostly boil down to is that you shove your clothes in the machine (do up any zips first), spread them around evenly if it's a top-loading kind, pour in the detergent, shut the lid, put the money in the slot and set it going. Don't overload it. You'll get gritty bits of dirt sticking to your clothes.

In some launderettes you have the chance to use an extractor (large spin-dryer) after the wash is over. This is worth it, especially if you're going to put your wash in a tumble-dryer, but don't put in anything which creases easily and which you don't want to have to iron (e.g. Orlon sweaters).

If your launderette has tumble-dryers, they may be set at hot for cottons etc. only, or one may have a gentler heat for man-made fibres. If you only have a hot tumble-dryer, don't put in anything other than cottons or things you don't mind getting creased. Heat-impressed creases (in e.g. Courtelle) can be tiresome to remove. There's no point in getting bone-dry things you're going to iron. Ideally, take them out while they're ironing damp.

How much detergent? The launderette notices will instruct you to put in a large cup of detergent. Detergent packets may say much the same thing. Detergent is expensive, and my own experience leads me to conclude that you don't need as much as recommended. Obviously, it depends on how dirty your clothes are and how efficient your launderette's machines are, but I'd suggest you take your own detergent along and experiment by cutting down a spoonful or so a time.

Hand washing

Keep out until last anything which loses colour.

Put warm (not hot) water in your sink. Add some soap powder or detergent. (Detergent is better in hard water.) Again, my experience is that you don't need as much as it says. Something like $\frac{1}{2}$–2 tablespoons per sinkful is usually ample. (Don't forget, the more you put in, the more you have to rinse out.) Dissolve the powder. Put in the garments, swoosh them gently about and leave them to soak.

When you come back (in, say, 30–60 minutes), swoosh them round gently again. If there are still dirty patches, rub into them a little dry detergent or liquid detergent and squeeze gently. If the clothes are very dirty, run out the dirty water and leave them soaking in a fresh lot of detergent-water.

Most clothes that need hand-washing won't stand hard rubbing. Exceptions are colour-running jeans, shirts etc.

Rinse the clothes thoroughly in at least two rinses of water, three or four if necessary, until the water runs clean. It's cheaper to use cold water, sometimes better for clothes, and rarely harms them.* Spin-dry if you can and if the clothes will stand it, otherwise hang up wet to drip if drip-dry, wring and hang up if not; or, if wool, roll in a towel, pat as dry as possible, pull into shape and dry flat.

Worry-free woollens. You can wash most woollens successfully for months and years (but see p. 146), provided that you remember:
– always use *tepid* water, never hot
– handle gently when wet, don't rub or scrub
– never wring
– dry flat unless spun-dried (and even then, hang up with care).

A spin-dryer of your own? Buying your own spin-dryer may seem ridiculously extravagant, but it can sometimes make good sense. You can buy a second-hand one for about as much as it would cost you to use the launderette once a week for a year. If you haven't a handy launderette, or you've a lot of hand-washing, or you don't mind the washing part but it's the wringing that gets you down, then a spin-dryer of your own could help. Spun-dried clothes dry quickly, so take up less space and heat; spun-dried woollens keep their shape and texture. (But don't over-spin them, 15–30 seconds or so is generally enough.)

Drying clothes

This is often more of a problem

* *But if you use soap, not detergent, you may need to rinse in warm water.*

than washing them. If you have a tumble-dryer at your launderette, a communal drying-room, or handy radiators, you're in luck. If not, you have to resort to clothes-lines, either inside or out, or a clothes-horse. Even a piece of string over a bath or sink is better than nothing; but Woolworth's or any local ironmonger's can sell you something a little dearer but more efficient.

Don't leave things too close to open or electric bar or gas fires; never hang things over fires or cookers; don't obstruct or leave clothes dripping onto fan-heaters.

If you take a couple of extra minutes at the drying stage, you can save yourself work later. When you're hanging up things which shouldn't need ironing – T-shirts, sweaters etc. – take care to pull them into shape, peg them evenly, pull collars and cuffs into shape. Don't stretch ribbing: either put the whole garment over the line or rod (which may leave a mark) or peg it upside-down just below the unstretched rib. Hang cotton shirts upside-down. As far as possible, hang garments singly and without touching each other – it's annoying to have something completely dry except for one patch where it was jammed against something else.

Pre-ironing

If you handle things with fore-thought at the washing/drying stage, you'll find many things today won't need ironing. Among those that *do* are:

Ordinary cottons. Aim to catch these while they're still damp and before they're dry. They should feel barely moist, certainly not wet. If they do get too dry, you'll need to damp them down. There's no point whatever in trying to iron bone-dry cottons, it doesn't work. Use a bottle of water with a few holes pricked into the lid and sprinkle. You can roll them up and leave them in a polythene bag until you're ready.

Fiddly things like *crêpes*, *silks*, *rayons*. Follow the instructions on the label carefully. Some need to be damp, some almost dry.

Woollens. Dried carefully, most sweaters etc. won't need ironing. If they do, you'll have to press them with a damp cloth (unless you have a steam-iron – see p. 164).

How hot an iron?

New irons are marked from 1–5 on the dial, with 1 the coolest and 5 the hottest. Older irons are marked in various ways: some with the names of the materials at the appropriate heat; others with very hot/hot/medium/cool etc. After you've switched on the iron to the correct setting, leave it for from 5–10 minutes (the time depends on the age and type of iron). Many irons overheat considerably to start with and take time to adjust.

If what you're ironing is new and correctly labelled, you'll find the right temperature marked on the label.

If it isn't, and you're not sure, here's some guidance.

Pure linen (you're not likely to have much) needs a very hot iron (5).

Pure cottons need a hot iron (4).

Pure woollens need a warm iron (3).

Most silks need a cool iron (2).

Most man-made fibres need a cool or very cool iron (1 or 2). Some man-made fibres are very tricky or impossible to iron. They melt or permanently crease. If what you're ironing is a mixture of fibres, set the iron for the one needing the coolest temperature, e.g. for Terylene/linen, set the iron for 2 not 5. If you're in any doubt, set the iron to a cool temperature, and try that first. If it doesn't seem to work, and you know the material is damp enough, raise the heat a little.

If, when you're ironing, the iron refuses to glide over the material, and starts sticking, take it off immediately. The iron's too hot. If you smell scorching, ditto.

By following these simple suggestions, you're less likely to end up with iron-shaped holes in skirts or slacks. (*Note:* some colours, especially reds and pinks, change colour as you're ironing them, but revert to normal as the material cools down.)

Melted-on goo. If you have a disaster, and cover your iron with melted, burnt-on goo, you can sometimes get it off by turning the iron to the lowest heat and then rubbing the hot-plate on a pad of soft rags. There's also a special iron-cleaning paste, but not easy to get outside large department stores. Otherwise, in desperation, you can try acetone, Polyclens or meths, depending on what you've got handy. Don't try anything abrasive which will scratch the hot-plate.

Warning. Nylon zips are often fitted into clothes (e.g. cotton dresses) which need to be ironed with a hot iron. Don't let the iron stray near these zips or you'll melt them.

Sometimes, too, nylon or Terylene thread is used for sewing non-nylon or Terylene clothes (e.g. wool trousers). Again, you need to steer clear of this when you're pressing, or you'll melt this too. (Manufacturers oughtn't to do this sort of thing, but they do, so watch out.) Some plastic buttons are also sensitive, but as long as you don't actually rest the iron on the buttons, you should be all right.

Never walk out of the room leaving the iron on – even if it's only to answer the door or telephone. It's fatally easy to forget all about it. A friend of mine came back to find her iron had burnt through the ironing board, fallen on to the carpet and burnt through that, and was in the process of burning through the floorboards.

Dashing away with your smoothing iron

Ironing is a lot easier than it looks. If you've never tried before you'll find yourself slow to start with, but you'll soon speed up remarkably. You'll see it's worth learning how if you study the prices at your local laundry.

You can iron on a table, provided you pad it well with e.g. old sheets. An *ironing-board* is easier. It makes manipulating clothes simpler, and you can iron one side of a skirt or shirt without doing the other simultaneously. If you're buying one for yourself, look out for one with a wooden frame – it's much easier to anchor down ironing-board covers with drawing-pins. Covers which slide with you when you're ironing are infuriating.

On the other hand, most people can live quite happily without a *sleeve-board*.

A *light iron* is quite as successful as a heavier one for most materials except, perhaps, the heaviest tweeds. It's also less tiring and quicker to handle. A *steam-iron* cuts out the damping-down pro-cess and does away with the cloth method when pressing woollens. On the other hand, it's generally heavier and less manoeuvrable.

A *flex-holder* is an optional extra which speeds things up considerably. You can concentrate on ironing away briskly without bothering whether the flex is rucking up what you've already done.

The only secrets in ironing are (a) ironing things of the right dampness (see p. 162), (b) using the right heat (see p. 162) and (c) pulling the different sections into shape and laying them down as smoothly as possible on the ironing-board or table (see p. 165). If you try to rush at it and lay things down crookedly, you'll iron creases in instead of out.

Iron *into* gathers. Pull pleats into shape and iron on top. Keep the most conspicuous bits (collars, cuffs, shirt-edges) until last.

Hang up to air

Anything you've finished ironing will almost certainly be damp. Hang it up to let the steam evaporate. Put shirts and dresses on hangers, flat things over a clothes-horse if you have one or chair backs if you haven't. Don't put them away until they're thoroughly aired (an hour or so). If you do, you trap the damp inside so they crease again – and you may get a mouldy smell too.

Two good ways to iron a shirt

(For a right-handed person. Reverse suggestions 1–5 if you're left-handed.)

Even with lots of polyester and nylons around, some of the most interesting shirts still come in cottons and wools that need to be ironed to look their best. Once you know how, ironing a shirt isn't nearly such a hoo-ha as it feels. And, after all, it takes no longer to iron a shirt well than to iron it badly.

So here goes . . .

Set the iron correctly according to the fabric (see p. 163).

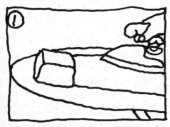 

1 Lay one of the shirt sleeves, open cuff side upwards, flat on the board with the shoulder-end next to the ironing-stand. Pull it into shape with your hands, so that the top seam lies straight along the top and the bottom seam straight along the bottom. Pull the open ends of the cuff towards each other so that the sleeve pleats (or gathers) take their natural shape. Hold the cuff end of the sleeve taut with the left hand, and iron from the shoulder down into the pleats and gathers with the right hand.

2 Turn the sleeve over and lay it flat again, making sure the open edges of the cuff (now underneath) stay close to each other. Holding the sleeve taut again, iron once more from the shoulder to the cuff.

3 Moving the sleeve as little as possible, open the cuff and lay it flat on the board, right side down. Iron on the wrong side.

4 Turn the cuff over. Now iron it on the right side.
5 Repeat the other sleeve in exactly the same way.

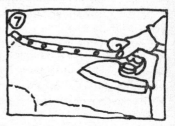

6 Place the yoke of the shirt, wrong side down, over the nose of the ironing board. Iron first one half of it, then move it across and iron the other half.

7 With the collar-end of the shirt at the nose-end of the board, lay the right front on the board and smooth it into shape. Iron this from tail to collar.

8 Move the ironed front over the far side of the board, and smooth out the right side of the back. Iron this from tail to collar.

9 Move the shirt round some more so the newly ironed bit is dangling over the edge of the board, and now iron the left side of the back.

10 Move this ironed part over. Smooth out the left front. Iron this.

11 Spread the collar out as flat as possible on the board, right side down, and iron it on the wrong side.

12 Turn the shirt over, carefully, lay the collar out again, wrong side down, and iron the right side *from* the points *towards* the centre. (This makes sure the looseness of the bias-cut doesn't end up as puckers in the most conspicuous part of the collar.)

13 Do up the shirt at the top. If you crease it slightly doing this, lay it down for a moment on the board, still done up, and just touch it up round the top button.

14 Ease it on to a hanger. Do up another button further down (or you'll get creases appearing as the shirt fronts drag away from the top button).

If you're using an ordinary table because you haven't got an ironing-board, here's a second method.

Do the sleeves exactly the same way, until you get to the end of stage 5, then go straight to 11 and 12 and tackle the collar.

Now lay the back of the shirt, right side down, on the table, and iron this on the wrong side. (Keep the shirt fronts pushed aside out of the way.)

Do up the shirt, keep it flat on the table with the fronts on top, and iron these fronts on the right side.

You can iron a shirt on a table perfectly well this way, especially if the back isn't too fully pleated and the double-material on the yoke isn't too thick.

If you've never ironed shirts before you may find it takes ages. Don't worry. Soon you'll be dashing them off in 3-4 minutes.

How to press a perfect pair of pants

If they're made of something that needs to be ironed damp (cotton, linen/Terylene) see they're evenly dampened and rolled up well before you need to iron them.

If they're made of something which needs to be pressed (wool mixture) have ready a pressing cloth – could be a large handkerchief – and a basin of water.

If you've a steam iron, fill it.

You can iron pants equally well on an ironing board or table.

On an ironing-board

1 Do up the pants. Pull them roughly into shape. Lay them down flat, with the side seams at the side and the centre seam or fly in the middle. Iron or press. Be careful near the zip. Don't go right up to the side seams, or you'll leave a crease where you don't want one.

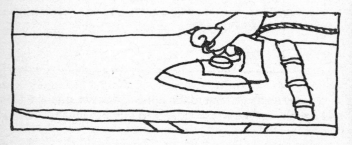

2 Shift the pants round, and iron first one leg and then the other, again being careful to go close to the side seam but not right over it. Make sure as you do this that the legs are stretched as flat as possible, to avoid ironing creases in the underneath bit.

3 Turn the pants over and do the same the other side.

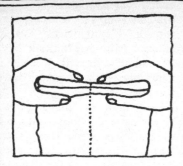
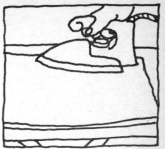

4 Take the trousers and hold them upside-down. Place both legs together with the seams exactly opposite. Shake briskly so the legs fall into place all the way down.

5 Put the folded legs together flat along the ironing-board. Feel with your fingers to check that the seams are directly underneath each other all the way along. Press firmly along both edges. Turn the pants over and do the other side.

N.B. If your pants aren't badly creased and need freshening-up rather than really ironing then skip stages 1–3.

On a table
Follow the same method, except that since you'll probably be short of space you'll have to iron both the legs at the same time and push the top of the pants gradually over the table. Otherwise, since all the ironing's done flat, there's no problem.

Skirts and dresses too
Skirts are usually simpler than trousers. You can either iron them *flat* (if they're straight or gored) or going *round* the ironing board (if they're pleated or gathered).

Most dresses can be ironed round the ironing-board if it's no fatter than you are; or flat if it is; or tackled as combined shirts-and-skirts, depending on the cut and style.

Dry-cleaning

If you've clothes which can't be washed, it's cheaper to take them to a dry-cleaning machine in a launderette than to a specialist cleaner's. Some machines are less efficient than others, and you won't get individual care, but if you're stuck with non-washable clothes this is one way out. Some launderettes insist you take along a full load (3·5–5·5 kg) but others let you take in one garment at a time. You pay by weight.

Remember that after taking these clothes from the dry-cleaning machine you must *hang them to air in a well-ventilated room.* The fluids used are *poisonous* and also *highly inflammable*, so don't drop off to sleep in a room draped with just-cleaned garments, or hang them near any source of heat.

Stowaways

Rolling sweaters in bundles or dumping shirts in piles over chair backs makes them look creased and tatty before you've even put them on.

Hang up on hangers anything that hangs up (shirts, dresses, trousers, jackets – but not knitted woollens, which tend to stretch and drag). For tailored clothes with shaped shoulders and high collars you need the more expensive kind of hanger with shaped shoulders to match.

Keep skirts in better shape by using a proper skirt-hanger. Slip pants, folded, over the rod of a triangular hanger. If you haven't enough of the right sort of hangers (who has?) think big – buy some more. It won't cost much and will vastly simplify these petty details.

If you're short of hanging-space you could get a plastic packaway wardrobe; or a mail-order metal pole on supports (wobbly, but it functions); or even hang a clothes-line or fix a broomstick on brackets from one wall to another if this seems practicable. (Clothes weigh plenty, so you can only do this if your walls and supports will take the weight and your landlord/lady doesn't object.)

Clothes kept in drawers take up less room folded flat. Here's how to do it: use the same principle for woollens, shirts, T-shirts.

1 Fasten up three of any buttons present (top, bottom, middle). Lay the garment flat, face down. Smooth out any creases, and check the collar's not too rucked.

2 Fold the two sides over parallel to each other.

3 Fold the arms back on themselves.

4 Fold the garment across once or twice, depending on its length.

Packing it up

If you're taking away several pairs of shoes or a whole stack of books, put these – and anything

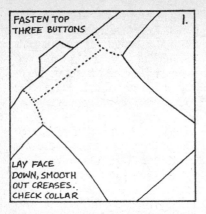

1.

FASTEN TOP
THREE BUTTONS

LAY FACE
DOWN, SMOOTH
OUT CREASES.
CHECK COLLAR

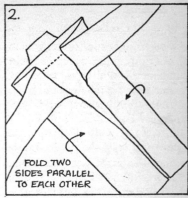

2.

FOLD TWO
SIDES PARALLEL
TO EACH OTHER

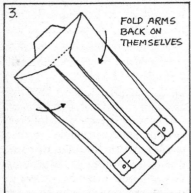

3.

FOLD ARMS
BACK ON
THEMSELVES

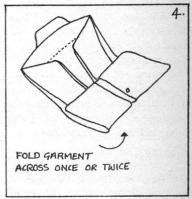

4.

FOLD GARMENT
ACROSS ONCE OR TWICE

else which is heavy – at the bottom of your case before you start packing. Otherwise, you'll generally have enough room round the sides to add these later.

Fold your clothes to fit the case as efficiently as possible, using the least number of folds (see above). If you're feeling particularly fussy, or taking away easily creasable clothes, it helps to lay sheets of tissue paper on garments as you fold them – folding the tissue in

with them, sandwich-wise. Put the heavier clothes (jackets, skirts, woollens) at the bottom, with lighter stuff on the top. Push all the extras (make-up, razor, socks) round the edges. Roll up underclothes to fill in gaps. If you're short of space, put things inside things – e.g. films inside shoes.

Your case should have a stick-on label with your name and address inside the lid, just in case it ends up as Lost Property.

Friends and Lovers

1 JUST GOOD FRIENDS

Moving out on your own's an ideal opportunity for meeting new people and making new friends – or it should be. Unfortunately, it doesn't always work that way.

Not long ago I saw a card in a window offering a room in a flat 'at a really low rent to some young guy who's lonely as I am at the moment' and ending 'Call round and see it any time. Or just drop in for a chat.'

If you're still within reach of childhood friends, breaking in to adult life can follow a much smoother path: but if you're really out on your own, in a new district or new job or new college, loneliness can begin to threaten. Yet, unless you live in the middle of the moors, all around you are people waiting to be met and known.

Whether you meet this challenge successfully depends more than anything else on your ability to recognize that neither friends nor lovers are delivered gift-wrapped to your door. You have to take initiatives, to respond to others, and to understand that most close friendships (and loves) take time and nurturing to grow.

New acquaintances

Almost all friends start by being acquaintances – people we meet casually, pass the odd word to. Then, with time, some acquaintances become friends, others we decide we don't want to know better, others again we enjoy meeting but from force of circumstances are never likely to know any better.

So to start with, be prepared to make (and accept) easy, unintense, friendly approaches to people as you come across them. Be open-minded. Aiming to meet only those who are like yourself is like wanting to talk only to yourself. It's possible to make acquaintances (and maybe later friends) of people who are older, or younger, or poorer, or better off, or of a different colour or background to yourself. Wanting to be exclusive restricts your horizons, and makes you yourself a less interesting and stimulating person to know.

At the same time, there's no rule that says you'll like everyone. If you don't get on with someone, or don't like the way they carry on, there's no point in forcing yourself to put on a false face. (And by the way, don't expect yourself to be loved and admired by one and all, and you'll be less upset when you're not.)

So being ready to say hello to the bloke in the bookshop, the girl in the baker's, the old man who hands out the tennis rackets, is all good practice. It helps you to learn to consider people, and to respond to their individual personalities. It's a first stage to friendship.

Friendly meetings

But what if your acquaintanceships never seem to develop? You feel that you never meet people often enough or long enough or in the right kind of circumstances to turn them into friends?

First take a look at yourself: are you sure you're not being offputting? Deliberately snubbing friendly approaches? Are you too shy to recognize that welcome gestures are being made? Or are you, on the other hand, so desperate that you frighten people away by over-reacting to casual remarks?

If you're positive none of these possibilities is true, but believe you never meet potential friends, look around for methods to enlarge your circle.

Many people make friends through work. If all those you meet are totally uncongenial, then it could even be an indication that you're in the wrong kind of job. I mean, if you're working for the Inland Revenue and everyone else goes for chess problems and crosswords and you want to spend your free time discussing the cinema, then you might do better to change your job and your circle of acquaintances at the same time.

Others meet friends because of where they live – through flatmates, people in the same hostel, or acquaintances they run into on the communal staircases. If you don't share, or don't like the people you're with, or never run into anyone because you're in a self-contained lift-served block, then moving somewhere else could make sense.

Yet others meet people quite casually, and this is probably the area where you can do most, most simply, to start enlarging your circle of could-be friends. The most obvious places are not the best. Pubs and dance-halls are not necessarily good starting-points for friendships. Other far less likely places can be. Launderettes are tops, especially in bedsitter or student areas. Everyone has to wash their clothes sometime, and Sunday, a lazy do-nothing day, is an obvious choice. Another first-class spot is any public art gallery or museum. So is waiting in a queue for tickets for pop concerts, or soccer matches, or the Royal Ballet, or even the No. 11 bus.

Another first-class rendezvous for potential friends is evening classes. Again, it's no good joining one simply because you want to see new faces. This won't work. But if you take a class because you're positively interested, and you're joining it along with (presumably) a number of kindred spirits, then it would be very surprising if sooner or later you didn't connect. If you have in the back of your mind the thought that it

would be nice to meet new people then, when choosing between two otherwise equally attractive topics, pick the one which involves most discussion or student involvement. A writers' group, not a lecture on English literature: folk guitar, not analysis of symphonic structure. If you feel particularly short of companionship of the opposite sex, pick classes which you might expect to be bi-sexual or ones which you might reasonably suppose would attract plenty of the desired species. But again, what counts is your genuine interest in what you've chosen to do.

Depending on your age and tastes, there are also in most towns various clubs and groups – youth clubs, sports clubs, professional groups – through which you could meet others of similar interests. If you're in London, London Village is a loosely knit organization which aims to help small groups of people contact each other. (Ring 01–731 4366.) The Centre, Adelaide Street, London WC2, welcomes young adults 16+ several evenings a week. The National Federation of Eighteen Plus Clubs (16–18 High Street, Dartford, Kent) may be able to put you in touch with a local independent centre with facilities for acting, dancing, debates and so on. Several other social groups advertise regularly in *Time Out*.

Or you could offer your services to a charity, and help others as well as yourself. Ring up the local branch of any which interests you, or contact organizations like Task Force.

Section VII, on 'Liking your Leisure' (p. 204), has other suggestions which might prove inspiring.

The other sex

It is perfectly possible to make *friends* of both sexes. Pointing this out might seem absurd, if it weren't for the strong emphasis in fiction in many magazine stories and on some TV programmes on showing all inter-sex relationships as sexual or potentially sexual. This is partly an attitude of mind and partly the demands of the medium used – if the writer's tell-ing a story in only 2,500 words there isn't room to describe any but the main characters – but you're not living in a fictional world and there's plenty of room in your life for a cast of both sexes. It's quite on the cards to find both casual acquaintances and good friends among members of the opposite sex. A close friendship may develop into a sexual relationship: but it's quite possible to enjoy a number which never would or could develop into anything else.

Too many people today, especially in big cities, lack companionship. Seeing members of the opposite sex always in terms of potential mates, potential trophies, potential threats, can't help. So risk a smile, or a passing comment, without fearing that it's going to lead to a lifelong commitment.

(At the same time, if you're fairly clear in your mind that you don't want any romantic/sexual developments, then steer clear of situations which could encourage these. Sharing flats (see p. 14) or holidays with members of the opposite sex on a purely friendly basis can work but often doesn't, depending on personality, maturity, and simple chance; situations like these can also be misinterpreted by less understanding observers.)

Talking to people comes much

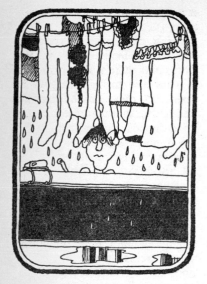

harder to some than to others. If words don't spring to your lips as easily as you'd like, turn to p. 239.

Cementing friendships

Meeting people is only a beginning. It takes time, thought and genuine interest on your part to turn them into friends.

Some people seem to have the gift of making and keeping friends from an early age. Others find that it's only in adulthood that they seem to meet those to whom they can feel really close. Some are naturally more solitary than others: some like to feel surrounded. Life is not a popularity contest, and since we are all individuals we're bound to develop individually. One thing to remember too is that it's not possible to have a really close relationship with more than a handful of people. If you have as many as three or four you can rely on and call friends, you're fortunate.

What turns someone from an acquaintance into friend? First, obviously, an initial liking between the two of you: sometimes you feel this spontaneously, sometimes it grows slowly. From this grows an imaginative care and concern for the other person, a willingness to listen to each other's point of view, a readiness to help and participate, even if it means putting yourself out, a feeling of mutual trust, a conviction that you can be yourself without disguises, that you can rely on the other for support and understanding.

Some friendships ripen quickly, but most take time to mature. They take time too to keep in good running order. You can't expect to forget people for six months, ring them up because you want something, and to find them ready to jump at your whistle. (Though a long-held and well-tried friendship can endure for years with only minimal contact, provided the concern and affection are still there and alive.) Those most ready to give of themselves are most likely to gain in friendship.

Personality pitfalls

By the time you have reached

your mid or late teens you have probably had plenty of experience and some success in making and keeping friends. Those who still keep having problems most often fall into two extreme groups – on the one hand those who happily make friend after friend and then find disillusionment sets in and their friendships languish, and those who eagerly want friends and try hard to make them, but discover that in practice none of their relationships seems to progress from first base.

If you think you fall into one of these groups, try to look objectively at yourself.

Are you one of those outward-going, amiable, charming people always on the go? Who find it easy to turn acquaintances into friends, soon exchange confidences, maybe even force the pace? Then make a deliberate effort to take things more calmly. Everyone can't be your friend. Let things progress at their own pace.

Or do you on the contrary basically distrust yourself? Feel sure no one will find you worth knowing, so that in your efforts to interest people you're over-intense? Force yourself to relax. Not easy, I know. Some find encounter groups or classes in yoga helpful. Others gain confidence by becoming absorbed and skilled in something quite outside themselves, whether it's orienteering or lacemaking or boxing.

Real friendship exists only between people who at heart feel themselves equals. If you regularly turn yourself into either the pusher or the pushed, your relationships with others can't help but suffer.

2 SEX AND CONSEQUENCES

It's almost impossible to struggle through to adulthood without having been advised, exhorted, warned, cajoled and harassed about sex: yet too often the torrent of words confuses rather than enlightens. Some advice is factually incorrect. Some is misleading. Some is so narrow that it ignores immensely important considerations. Much is obviously biased. If you sometimes feel simultaneously deafened and baffled, you're one of many.

Without for one moment suggesting that all you want to know is here, I've tried to clear the decks a little. To look at how attitudes take shape. To begin to separate observable facts from theories. To suggest how far the two sexes differ from and reflect each other. To take a look at some undeniable realities. To offer various ways of considering personal relationships. To give you something solid to chew over while you work out your own approach.

1. Changing attitudes

Sex has, obviously, been with us as long as mankind's been on earth. What has changed, and is still changing, is people's attitudes, which have varied dramatically with – among other factors – nationality, race, class, education, religious teachings, financial security, age expectations, the role of women, medical knowledge.

One reason why so much advice about sex at the moment is conflicting is that society itself is in a state of flux. Life, together with people's expectations, is very different from what it was fifty or even twenty years ago. It's changing all the time, in many different ways, and often changes apparently unconnected with sex and with personal relationships can still have a profound effect.

Much of what your hear about sex, morality, hopes, fears, is bound to vary and often to be contradictory, because people's opinions vary with their backgrounds, education, ideals, age, with how all the different factors involved affect their own particular views.

Only you can work out what the essential you thinks, feels and believes. It may help you to understand yourself and others if you take a look at some of the recent and continuing changes which shape the way people think – the way *you* think – about sex.

It's much easier to get informed and sympathetic advice about birth control (see p. 193). In particular, thanks to the Pill, it's much easier for the girl to take the responsibility for preventing unwanted pregnancies.

This may mean you feel freer to have sexual relations without fear of practical consequences; or that you think you know about contraception without actually putting it into practice; or that you feel a greater sense of personal liberation; or that you think you're being pressured towards sexual involvements you don't want; or that in your conviction that you can control physical results you overlook the ones you can't – VD and the less obvious psychological consequences.

Women's role and status has changed and is still changing. These improved birth-control techniques, combined with the conviction that over-population is a serious and immediate threat, have made perhaps the most radical changes in what women expect from sex, marriage and life, and to the attitudes of their men towards them.

This may mean, if you're female, that you look forward to a life with wider horizons and greater potential than your mother probably had, or that you shrink from the prospect and wish you could turn back the clock. Or, if you're male, that you enjoy the stimulus of an independent mate and welcome the increased burden-sharing, or that you feel threatened and diminished.

Different people have different attitudes to marriage. Many couples expect more from marriage than ever before – a real partnership, a positive sharing of sex and life, total commitment. On the other hand, others listen to those psychologists and sociologists who look critically at the structure of marriage itself, and believe that it can stifle as well as give security. What you read and hear, and your own experiences of your parents' or relatives' marriages, is obviously bound to affect your own views, and this will in turn affect any sexual relationships you may have.

Families are less tightly knit: people are moving around more – to new jobs, new places to live. This may bring you a detachment, a feeling of personal and individual freedom you cherish (in which case you may find yourself increasingly able to distinguish between what really matters to you and what doesn't, or you may simply move from one meaningless encounter to another); or you may look for someone you can grasp at to provide a centre for your life (in which case you may be searching for a genuinely deep and meaningful attachment, or merely clutching a relationship around you to keep out the world).

Many expect better living stan- *dards* than their parents did. Your hopes may still be modest – running water and your own bathroom – or positively grandiose – a penthouse bachelor flat – but in either case it can make a vital difference to your sex life. It may involve you in longer education, harder work, less free time, mean you deliberately put off marriage, determine not to have children, or simply shy away from any close involvement.

Many are dissatisfied with material values. At the same time, many are becoming increasingly dissatisfied with what they see as an over-emphasis on material progress. You may express this dissatisfaction through intellectual protest, meditation, social help, community concern: and you may in the process see sex either as non-essential and disruptive, or the one basic life-enriching element.

People are less ready to do things just because they are told, whether by their parents, religious leaders or the State.

As a result you may find yourself striving for independent thought and the acceptance of personal responsibility; or you may end up convinced that nothing matters much; or, in reaction, you may search for someone to impose restrictions on you.

These are only some of many recent changes. Among others are changing attitudes of religious

Where you're at now

Some are fascinated by sex in their early teens, others remain cool and detached until much later. Some go in for practice, others are content with theory. Some are much concerned by morals, others dismiss these out of hand. Some dream of love, others aim for uncluttered sex. Some boast, others keep quiet. Some want to get married, others dread the thought. Yet most people want or hope for a good and satisfactory relationship with someone of the opposite sex. If by any chance you're among those who are frightened at the prospect and are worried by the whole idea (possibly because of something which happened in your past) then it could be sensible to look for help. Your doctor might be a good place to start: or write to the Youth Advisory Centre, 31 Nottingham Place, London W1 (see also p. 129).

If you're not frightened, but don't at the moment feel particularly interested either, that's perfectly normal. People's sexual feelings vary anyway, so do the ages at which they become involved. Young adults, especially if they're wrapped up in their work, or study, or craft, often tend to postpone their sexual development. There's no reason why not, and every reason why you shouldn't feel pressured into sexual relationships before you're ready for them: which is particularly true if you're a girl. Many girls, partly because of their physiological differences, partly because of their upbringing develop sexually more slowly (often much more slowly) than boys. There's no need to rush. (Please note that despite much publicity and pressure to the contrary, there's nothing abnormal about keeping one's virginity.)

Many people pass through a stage when they become closely involved with members of their own sex. Most move beyond this point well before they leave their teens: if you haven't, and it bothers you, then you may find it a help to talk it over. Again, your doctor may be able to help: or write to the Campaign for Homosexual Equality, 28 Kennedy Street, Manchester, M2S 4BG, or to Mrs Robertson at Parents' Enquiry, 16 Honley Road, Catford, SE6 2HZ. In London the CHE London Information Centre, 22 Great Windmill Street, W1 (01–437 7363) is open six days a week.

leaders, new abortion and divorce laws, the impact of higher teenage earnings, the increase of sex-ploitation films and magazines. Indeed, the sheer volume of words and pictures put out about sex is enough to create consider-able pressure on its own.

All societies have to cope with changes. But the past few years have seen so many and such rapid ones, that the result – people ex-pressing many different and often opposing opinions – can be bewildering. It isn't easy, but it's very important, to try to work out what *you* think, what *you* feel, what *you* want. Be ready to listen to others, talk to others, argue with others, but don't forget that it's *your* life, and what you make of it is your responsibility.

Living involves choosing. And where sex is concerned some of those choices may affect you for the rest of your life.

2. What's it all about?

'I thought I could manage him,' said one pregnant unmarried girl.

'I never dreamed how much I'd want to, too.'

At its most elemental, sex is a powerful force which impels male and female together and urges them into intercourse. A scientist has observed that 'nature cares for the species, not for the individual': which means that the impulse to mate can exist whether those con-cerned care for each other or not, whether children are wanted or not, whether intercourse is planned and desired or not.

What this means in practical terms is that you can't afford to take liberties with sex. You can't turn people (others, or yourself) on and off like taps. Get yourself into a situation where you are sexually stimulated (and/or stimu-lating) and there's the time and opportunity for intercourse, and it's extremely likely to take place, though you may neither have planned it, wanted it, nor have had the opportunity to take any kind of contraceptive measures.

Don't overestimate your powers of resistance, and remember that both drink and drugs blur caution and weaken self-control. The cries for help that go to women's magazines after the office party are no joke. A too careless, unguarded attitude to sex can create havoc.

Facts first

Biologically speaking, intercourse exists to bring about an opportunity for one of the male sperms to fuse with a female egg and thus create new life. Hundreds of millions of male sperms are constantly being created in the testicles (balls), ready at any moment for ejaculation. In comparison, the average female produces only one egg a month (though sometimes more than one is released at the same time, and sometimes more than one at different times of the month). This egg (or eggs), no bigger than a full stop, at the right moment in the girl's cycle moves slowly down one of the Fallopian tubes towards the womb. If at this point there is intercourse, and a male sperm unites with it, conception takes place and a baby is on the way. If there is no intercourse, or no sperms arrive, at the end of the monthly cycle the normal menstrual period follows as the womb sheds its prepared lining and the unfertilized egg-cell, and the new cycle starts.

In order for intercourse to take place, the man has to actively want it. He has an erection: his normal soft penis (cock) becomes rigid as though stiffened by wire and stands erect, reaching an average length of just over 15 cm. (Although unerect penises vary considerably in size, erect ones don't.) If the woman is aroused and ready for intercourse, her vagina (cunt) becomes slippery with a special lubricant, so that there'll be no hurtful rubbing and the vagina can provide a welcoming moist channel for the sperms. (But intercourse remains perfectly possible whether she wants it or not – this is one of the basic physiological differences between the sexes: see p. 185.)

At the moment of intercourse the man inserts the tip of his penis inside her vagina and then slides the whole length of it inside. As he thrusts inside excitement and tension build up until he reaches orgasm. At this moment a rush of fluid (semen – whitish, thickish, slightly sticky) spurts from the tip of the penis, carrying with it from 200 million to 500 million sperms, which set off on their journey towards the one egg. If it's the right time of month, and there's nothing to stop them, or there's a gap in the defences and just one of the sperms makes it, then a child has been conceived.

Whether conception has taken place or not, the penis now returns to its normal limp state and slides out of the woman's body.

This is a clinical explanation which tells you what happens, but nothing at all about what either of you feels, or thinks, or wants, what happened before or what happens next. It simply seemed like a helpful place to start: and here are some other basic questions which can worry or perplex.

Questions

(a) *Is it possible for a woman to be literally 'torn' inside by a man's penis?* No. The vagina of an adult woman, past puberty, can accommodate any size of penis (they don't vary all that much anyway, see above). A virgin, or recent virgin, may feel some soreness, but there is no question of tearing or damage.

(b) *Is first intercourse ('deflowering', 'breaking the hymen' or 'maidenhead') the painful and bloody business it oftens seems to be in novels?* Highly unlikely. Many girls have no hymen anyway. Some were born that way: in others, the use of tampons has weakened or done away with it long before first intercourse. Even where there still is a hymen it's normally thin and stretchy, and bleeding, if any, is not likely to amount to more than a teaspoon. Very rarely, the hymen is thicker than normal. If you're a girl who's had difficulties inserting a tampon, or you have any other doubts, consult your doctor.

(c) *Can a man tell whether a girl is a virgin or not?* No. Because many girls today don't have hymens, not having one is no proof of non-virginity.

(d) *Does frequent intercourse make you physically ill?* No.

(e) *Does masturbation make you physically ill?* No.

(f) *Does refraining from frequent intercourse make you physically ill?* No.

(g) *Can a girl get pregnant 'the first time'?* Yes.

(h) *Can she if she's standing up?* Yes.

(i) *Can she if she doesn't have an orgasm?* Yes.

(j) *Can a virgin get pregnant?* Yes. If there's close contact of the sexual organs at the time of emission (or even before) sperms can swim into the vagina if they've landed anywhere near it.

3. Not-so-simple sex

What any one act of sexual intercourse means to you, what you feel, before, during, after, depends on a great many things: why you wanted to, what you feel about your partner, how physically sensitive you are, what your personality is, even what ideals and ambitions you have for the future.

This may seem complicated, but that's the way it is. People *are* complicated. The last few years have seen what feels sometimes

like a PR campaign for sex. Magazines, true-life confessions, stories, songs, all often seem to promise that sex is straightforward, sex in itself is marvellous, and that any sexual experience is almost bound to be fantastic.

This simply isn't true, and realizing that it isn't true can save you a lot of heartbreak and disillusionment. A sexual relationship can be physically exhilarating or spiritually unifying, or both – or it can be meaningless, embarrassing, frightening, unpleasant or just plain boring. You can have a perfect relationship with someone one day and feel alienated the next. Or one of you feel intensely while the other fails to react at all. What started off

unpromisingly can develop into something vital. What began well can become meaningless.

What matters is to realize that sex will not *automatically* bring you ecstasy, satisfaction, or even mild pleasure. This is particularly true if you're a girl. Quite apart from the other, more complex factors which concern you whether you want them to or not (see ahead) you're directly affected by physiological responses which are natural to you and only partly under your control. Males and females are not only physically different, which is obvious, they are physiologically different – which means that how they're made affects the way they feel and react.

These are less obvious differences and less widely known than they ought to be, but knowing they exist can save a lot of unhappiness, in marriage as well as out. For example, a girl who discovers she feels nothing sexually may conclude unhappily that she's frigid, but the reason is far more likely to be her partner's failure to understand her different sexual make-up.

Playing consequences

Any relationship with another brings with it the possibility of repercussions. A relationship which includes sex carries with it the implications of more conse-

What's the difference?

Experts are still arguing about physiological differences between males and females, and about how far these are innate and how far formed by upbringing and education, but here are some of those which seem to be generally valid.

(I'm not, obviously, implying either that you're in the middle of a sexual relationship, or that you ought to be, merely pointing out that these differences do exist and that it can help to know about them.)

He can be rapidly aroused and ready for intercourse within a very short space of time. From cold to hot may take only minutes.

She may need a lot of love-play – kissing, caressing – before she even begins to feel like intercourse. If she has intercourse before she's ready for it, she's likely to find the whole thing a disappointment.

He can't have intercourse without an erection – that is, he has to actively participate. Uncertainty, nervousness, ridicule, coolness, could all make him lose his erection.

She can take part in intercourse whether she's passionate and involved – or bored and resentful.

Normal sexual activity culminates in climax and emission. This is true even when young and inexperienced.

Intercourse may or may not result in orgasm – most likely not, if she and her partner are young and inexperienced. (Which may matter to her – or may not.)

He will probably be in some degree sexually satisfied even if his partner is totally passive.

She is unlikely to achieve any kind of satisfaction without her partner's active cooperation. She generally needs much more than this: imagination, understanding and the desire to please.

He can function sexually whether he has warm feelings for his partner or none at all.

She may fail to feel any sexual response if she has no personal feelings for her partner, although this does depend very much on her individual personality.

♂ *cont.*

He can enjoy the sexual side of a relationship even if it's on an insecure basis.

His sexual reactions tend to be narrowly centred around the penis. Male sexual activity, especially young male sexual activity, tends to be short, brisk and to the point.

He can feel sexually aroused at any time of the month or year.

He's likely to react sexually to visual stimuli – blue films, nudes etc.

He will probably, especially if young, tend to consider the physical side of sex as pre-eminent, and detached from any spiritual considerations.

♀ *cont.*

Without confidence in the security of her relationship, she may be unable to respond sexually.

Her reactions are more diffused over her whole body. Female sexual activity tends to be searching, indeterminate.

She's likely to be affected by her monthly cycle. Most girls feel much more sexually aware at some times than others (though these times vary from individual to individual).

She's less likely to react sexually to pornography or near-pornography – but this could be because traditionally it's produced by men for men.

She's likely to see sex as part of a whole, wanting to achieve a mental and spiritual rapport as well, and find these expectations reacting on her purely physical responses.

---

quences than most, and the only thing you can say for sure is that it's impossible to know beforehand what these will be. Sometimes the most far-reaching are the least obvious.

You might gather from some fiction that about the only motives for wanting sex were lust or love. Far from it. You can make love to someone to prove you're grown up, or from spite – to prove to an ex that there's nothing wrong with *you* – or because it's a lovely summer's day, or it's raining, because you're bored, or you've lost your job, or you think it's time you got married, or you're homeless, or you fancy a baby. Or, of course, just because you feel like it or because you're deeply in love.

To some extent, the more trivial your motives the less likely you, at least, are to suffer from a psychological backlash. (Though even there you can't be sure. Spite, for example, has a nasty habit of provoking unpleasant results.)

The more deeply you're involved, the more likely you are to discover that certain consequences can have a long-term effect. And no one can accurately forecast physical results.

Not always happy happenings

The chance of pregnancy. Any sexual episode involving intercourse or near-intercourse (see p. 183), however meaningless or casual, may produce a pregnancy *unless contraceptive measures are taken.* (And sometimes even then.) Helpful, professional advice is available (see p. 193). What matters is to remember that no form of contraception is effective unless used, and unless used *every single time.* It's very human to think you're so much in love it just doesn't matter, but unless you're truly able to face the consequences of a real pregnancy, which will end unless interrupted in a real baby (see p. 198), then it does. It matters to you, to your partner, and most of all to the potential infant.

Catching VD is another highly possible consequence – yes, even if your partner is nice, clean and you're thoroughly in love. The one *guarantee* that you won't catch it is if you were both previously virgins. Using French letters cuts down the risk of infection, but it doesn't remove it. Unrecognized or untreated VD has serious consequences. (*And you won't always know you've got it:* see p. 118 for how you can tell and what to do.)

Psychological consequences are much harder to pin down, but can be at least as far-reaching. A pregnant girl whose boyfriend is standing by her may suffer less than another who appears to have escaped physical consequences, but who's been abruptly abandoned. Most of us are vulnerable, and can be damaged more easily than we like to think: entering into a sexual relationship enlarges the possibilities for wounding.

When you settle for *short-term relationships* you may seem to be avoiding deeper consequences. Even here, though, you can't be sure. Something which started as a game may suddenly develop, possibly on one side only, into something much deeper: or you may find yourself tied up, against your will, with someone you don't even like. Another risk is that going for a series of brief encounters can establish a personality pattern you can't break away from even when you want. It can mean that you never

Sex and the law

It is illegal for a male of any age to have any kind of sexual contact with any girl under sixteen. This is so whatever the degree of contact and whether or not she agreed to or even encouraged it.

There is no age beneath which it is illegal for a boy to have sexual contact with a girl over sixteen. (In law, it is presumed that a boy under fourteen is incapable of sexual intercourse.)

There are no laws restricting lesbian behaviour between girls over sixteen.

It is an offence for a man to take an unmarried girl under eighteen away from her parents without their consent in order to have sexual intercourse without marriage. So a boy may be prosecuted if he urges a girl of seventeen to leave home and move in with him, even though sexual intercourse between them is in itself legal.

It is illegal for a youth under twenty-one to have homosexual contact with another male of any age. Over twenty-one, homosexual contact is not against the law as long as it is in private, between only two people, and with the consent of both; but this *does not apply* to members of the armed forces, merchant seamen, or to men 'soliciting or importuning in a public place'. The 1967 Sexual Offences Act does not apply to Scotland or Northern Ireland: here any kind of homosexual contact is still illegal.

develop the possibilities – sexual or otherwise – of any relationship. It can even lead to intense loneliness and dissatisfaction with yourself.

Research indicates that the majority of young adults enter into stable, *semi-permanent relationships*. If this applies to you – or is what you're aiming at – then what happens to you because of it depends on you, your partner, and the circumstances. A long-term loving relationship can teach you about yourself, about your partner, about your desires and ambitions. You can grow in imagination, understanding, compassion. It may even develop into a deeply satisfying life-long commitment. Or it can be a trap. You may find yourself locked into a relationship which is hard to break away from when you want to. Or you may find yourself lured by security into prolonging something which no longer has anything going for it.

4. Could you, should you?

So far, not a word about moral considerations. Which means they don't exist? Hardly. Although there are people who think, or say they think, that moral considerations not only shouldn't exist but don't exist, there are far more who do believe there are standards of right and wrong, and who try – even if only intermittently – to find out what they are and to follow them.

There are books and books on morality (see p. 190 for suggestions); it's clearly impossible to give you a brisk run-down in two pages. However, without going into abstractions, here are three basic approaches to moral questions which you'll probably recognize, remembering that few of us are consistent, and that all of us switch from one attitude to another as our experiences and beliefs shape us. (Incidentally, to hear some people talk you'd gather there was no morality or immorality outside sexual relationships, which is clearly rubbish, and worth bearing in mind. We're all of us faced with moral choices all the time in our dealings with others, whether sexual or not.)

Do as you please. This pleasure principle approach seeks to bypass moral considerations. Aiming consistently to please yourself does seem at first sight to be both attractive and straightforward, but when you examine it more closely it often turns out to be neither. When it comes to the point we're often not certain what we want today: we're even hazier about what we might want tomorrow: and the more experienced we get the more painfully clear it often becomes that present pleasures can destroy future ones. Moreover, few of us are capable of being as consistently single-minded and ruthless as this approach demands.

Do what you want as long as it doesn't hurt anyone else. This is obviously more involved, and the closer you look at it the more complex you discover it to be. In practice it's not possible to work out beforehand the consequences of any particular action or set of actions, so decisions often come down to 'It won't hurt anyone – as long as he/she/they don't find out.' All too often he/she/they do, and the damage is done whether it was planned or not.

Do as you would be done by. This is an approach which requires imagination, consideration, and empathy – qualities which all of us are short of some of the time, and sometimes more often than others. It demands for a start that you consider others as equally important human beings. The moment you begin thinking of others as objects, without ideals and hopes of their own, the less possible it becomes to treat them seriously or as having equal value with yourself. The same is true if you let yourself be treated as an object: you become devalued.

It's never been easy to decide what's right and what's wrong: and you're not likely to find it any easier than anyone else.

If you follow an organized religion you'll have priests and teachers to help with guidelines for you to follow – though even here you'll find disagreement and controversy. Unless you're willing to sign your conscience away to someone else's care, you're unlikely totally to be able to escape the need to work out your own moral standards. If you're an agnostic, your problem is in some ways even harder. But part of the difficulty of being out on your own is to accept that some problems are difficult to work out, that there may be no clear-cut answers, and yet accept that you have to try to find them.

A final warning: at a time when personality is still fluid it's easy to deceive yourself and others without even meaning to. It's even easier to do it on purpose. Lying to others – or yourself – is generally one of the quickest ways to cut short a relationship. Pretending to feelings or beliefs or intentions that you haven't, or denying ones you have, is, except from the narrowest and most immediate point of view, a recipe for unhappiness or worse.

The FPA stock (and publish) books on sex and personal relationships. *Family Doctor* also publish informative booklets. Send a sae for booklists and prices to FPA, Margaret Pyke House, 27 Mortimer Street, London W1; *Family Doctor*, 47–51 Chalton Street, London NW1.

5. What is love?

Since you've got so far without more than a passing reference to love, you might reasonably begin to assume that it doesn't exist. Which of course is rubbish. Love, stripped of sentimentality, is as essential to human beings as food and drink. Scientists have shown that unloved children don't develop; while children formerly thought backward have, with love, made remarkable advances. We all need love. From childhood to death, we never have enough.

A baby's love is totally demanding, giving nothing. A mature adult's (a wholly mature adult probably doesn't exist) is giving, totally undemanding. Somewhere along the line we slot in, sometimes giving, sometimes grasping, changing from one day to the next.

But whatever we are, whoever we are, we need love – and not just, incidentally, from our sexual partner(s), but from our friends, our relatives, those much younger and much older than we are.

It's easy to say what love's not. Not flattering, or giving in, or bribing, or fearing, or concealing. It's not so simple to say what it is – especially when it's lit up and to some degree distorted by sex – and I'm certainly not going to be bold enough to try. However, here are a few possible clues.

Would you put his/her happiness before your own?

Would you want to care for him/her if he/she were ill?

Do you like him/her more when actually *there* than in your imagination?

Would it worry you if he/she were unhappy?

Do you care what happens to him/her next week? next month? next year?

If the answer to all these is 'yes', then perhaps you love him/her: and if not, not: but there's no sure rule or test.

Love isn't something that can be summarized in ten easy words, and you (and I) are likely to die still knowing little about it.

But it does exist. It's important. You can't ignore it – only appear to ignore it.

What is dangerous is tying yourself – especially in marriage – to someone who is at a different stage of adulthood; or sees love in a different light; or even laughs at the whole idea.

6. Being careful's not enough

Any act of sexual intercourse, or near sexual intercourse (see also p. 183) may result in pregnancy unless contraceptive measures are taken beforehand to prevent it. So never tell yourself 'it won't matter this once' or 'I'm so much in love I won't think about it': and if you're a girl be on your guard against psychological pressures which urge you to take a chance. Beware of feelings like these:

– Gambling like this puts some interest into life

– It might be fun to have a baby

– Being pregnant would show the world you're grown up

– It would make people be nice to you

– It'd stop you being bored

– It'd force your boy to take you seriously

– You'd have something to love

– You'd have something to love you

– It'd make a change.

None of these is an adequate

More than just a piece of paper

It's popular to say that 'marriage is only a piece of paper', but this doesn't make it true. Leaving aside for the moment all the legal and financial implications, being married is not the same as having a brief sexual episode, or even a long-term partnership. It's an affirmation (even if it not subsequently lived up to) that you intend a *permanent* relationship. It carries with it implications of fidelity, probably parenthood, an acceptance of the possibility of problems as well as joys, even ultimately of death. A relationship outside marriage doesn't necessarily convey any of these. On the contrary, there's quite possibly an understanding, even if only on one side of the partnership, that this relationship probably isn't permanent and isn't intended to be.

What this difference means to you depends on your personality. You may like the liberty of an unmarried relationship, and feel that it gives you liberty and spontaneity, or you may feel that the temporariness is threatening and destructive. The implied permanence of marriage may frighten you, feel like prison, or it may release you – and perhaps this needs stressing as it's so rarely said – offering you a sexual freedom, an opportunity to give yourself without restraint or fear.

Quite apart from abstract and sexual considerations there is one basic and absolutely concrete difference between marriage and other relationships. Marriage is a package deal. When you get married, you enter into a contract which society supervises and for which rules are laid down; you may also enter into a religious pact; you take on pre-stated legal and financial obligations; personal choice and freedom is curtailed not only by the relationship itself but by law. (Which is not to be taken as an attack on marriage, but a suggestion that you should at least consider possible implications before you enter into it; until very recently, for example, a British girl marrying an alien or Commonwealth citizen could be deported.) Marriage is not just wedding bells and happy-ever-after, but tax allowances, maintenance, property rights, and guardianship of children.

A long-term relationship, because it has (except occasionally in Scotland) no status in law, carries with it virtually none of these obligations. Nor, of course, does it necessarily offer security, help with children, a stable family background, religious blessing, or the incentive to keep the relationship going through difficulties.

reason for bringing a new person into the world, and yet just the hint of these or similar notions can be enough to make you ready (perhaps even eager) to risk pregnancy and all that follows – which is a much longer, more complex and demanding business than you can possibly imagine (see p. 198).

Unfortunately, all reliable birth-control methods need forethought. Psychologically, it can be difficult for someone young, inexperienced, and perhaps very much in love, to admit to their partner that they were so certain of intercourse that they had come prepared. This is something you have to face up to and be prepared to think about. Knowing that there's often a point when it seems simpler, more spontaneous not to use birth control, or admit to having considered it, may help you to deal

with that moment when it comes. The fact is – and it can be a harsh fact – that when you decide on sexual intercourse you're entering into an adult world with adult responsibilities. For your own sake, and your partner's, never forget that a potential baby is always only nine months away.

Get good advice

There's no one birth control method which is 100 per cent reliable and suits everyone. Personal advice is better than reading about it. Your own GP may be able to help, but not all doctors give contraceptive advice, and some patients in any case prefer to consult someone else. All Family Planning clinics will help both married and unmarried people: the Brook Advisory Centres (London and some provincial towns only) give advice almost entirely to the young. For addresses of clinics or centres near you, write to FPA, Margaret Pyke House, 27 Mortimer Street, London W1; Brook Advisory Centre for Young People, 233 Tottenham Court Road, London W1.

You can now get contraception on prescription *free* through the NHS, whether through your GP or through any of the clinics mentioned above.

Here is some preliminary information on the more reliable (and some less reliable) methods.

French letters (sheath). Easily obtainable, moderately effective when used properly. (Especially important is that a sheath should be put on before there is any genital contact at all.) Safer when used with a spermicide; even so, not fool-proof. A disadvantage from the man's point of view is that it dulls sensation, from the girl's that she has to rely on the man to provide it and use it sensibly.

The Pill. Extremely effective. At present has to be prescribed. Many different varieties; it may take time to find one which is suitable. Some girls continue to have unpleasant side-effects – headaches, sickness, tendency to put on weight. There's still little knowledge of really long-term effects, but it has been used widely for fifteen years.

IUD (loop – various designs – inserted in womb). Cheap, very effective and doesn't interfere at all with intercourse. Available only through a clinic or some GPs. But it produces heavier periods for some months after insertion; some women can't tolerate them. Generally more suitable for women who've already had a child. A new mini-device is now available which is suitable for girls who haven't.

Dutch cap (diaphragm). To be effective, it has to be prescribed and the right size chosen by a doctor, and used with a chemical cream. Efficient, has no health side-effects; the girl is responsible for her own security. (But she has to remember to put it in beforehand and remove it afterwards.)

Aerosol foam. Easily obtainable and pretty effective. Using it can be inhibiting.

Warning. Vasectomies are, with rare exceptions, performed *only* on married men over thirty with two children. Anyone who does not fit into this category but claims to have had a vasectomy should therefore be regarded with distinct scepticism.

Other chemical contraceptives. Tablets, pessaries, jellies etc. Easily obtainable, but not reliable when used on their own.

Rhythm method ('safe period'). Recommended by the Roman Catholic Church (and others) as the only natural method. Possible only when menstrual cycles are regular, but only relatively reliable even then (though temperature-taking over a period considerably increases reliability). Depends on mutual cooperation of both partners: removes spontaneity and can make the calendar more important than feelings.

'Being careful'. Withdrawal of penis before orgasm. Needs no forethought. But unreliable even when man has complete self-control, as some sperms may be released at any stage of intercourse from the first moment the penis is hard. Can be frustrating and unsatisfying.

Douche. Washing out the vagina, with or without a syringe, immediately after intercourse. Totally unreliable, and where chemicals are used may even be dangerous.

For further detailed information, see *Family Planning* by Paul Vaughan from the FPA (address opposite), which also provides free information leaflets.

7. Unplanned pregnancy

Although I'm directing this piece primarily to the potential mother, naturally an unplanned pregnancy should and generally does affect the potential father too. Because she's left holding the baby doesn't mean that you – the male – are not implicated. You are. And the more mature you are the more closely you'll know yourself involved.

When, after intercourse, a girl's period is late, by far the most likely reason is that she's pregnant.

If this happens to you (or your girlfriend) the important thing is to find out for sure as soon as possible. You can have a pregnancy test done by consulting your GP, or Family Planning clinic, or contacting one of the advisory services (list on p. 198). At present this can only be carried out fourteen days after the start of your missed period (i.e. six weeks after the start of the last one). These tests aren't always 100 per cent accurate: if one shows that you're pregnant, you probably are, but if the result is negative you still may be and you must have the test repeated a week later.

Warning. Apply for a test *only* through a reputable medical source, as above: *don't* attempt to get in touch yourself with organizations advertising pregnancy tests. Some of these are reputable, but standards vary considerably. Even when scrupulously carried out, these tests are not infallible. There is considerable evidence that in some commercial laboratories the margin of error is so large that the test results are virtually meaningless.

If you find out you're pregnant you have to make up your mind what course you want to take. (Depending on your temperament and all the circumstances, a sensible first step could be to tell your parents and discuss possibilities with them.)

Marriage. Particularly in a small community, there may be a lot of pressure put on both potential parents to marry. It's unwise to let yourself be pushed into marriage in this way. A marriage of two people who resent each other and the baby which forced it is unlikely to be happy for any concerned. However, research shows that many of what look like shotgun marriages do in fact turn out perfectly happily: what matters is the true relationship between those concerned, their attitudes and outlook.

Keeping the baby, without marrying the father, but staying in a stable relationship with him. Here again, it depends on the relationship between you whether this seems to be a viable possibility. Is your man likely to change his mind when the baby arrives and the pressure starts? What about the practical side – can he earn enough for two, at the very least

for the first few months? Where will you live? How will you cope? Have you money put by? Most important, how will he react to sharing you with a baby?

Keeping the baby, but on your own, without the active help or support of its father. This can be done, but it's not easy, especially in the child's first few months and in the early pre-school years. *Before* the baby arrives it's very vital to realize as far as possible (you can't really, you have to live through it) everything that's involved. Child-care, money, housing, health, your own attitude, all matter (see p. 198 for details).

Many children born to unmarried mothers live happy and fruitful lives, but research shows that many others do suffer, not necessarily because of their illegitimacy or their mother's upbringing but because of the sheer pressure of social disabilities – from lack of money, space, care.

Having the baby, but offering it for adoption. Emotionally, it's very difficult to go through a pregnancy, have a healthy baby, and then give it away – very often after caring for it for several weeks yourself. It is true that there are many childless wives who badly want to adopt, and true, too, that research shows that adopted children tend to do better than illegitimate children cared for by unmarried mothers, better even than legitimate children in their own families, but this won't necessarily make your decision any less painful.

Having the baby, and having it fostered. The same disadvantages mentioned above, plus the possible problem for the child of not knowing where he/she belongs. It depends partly on how short-term you intend the fostering to be. If you contemplate handing your child over to a foster-mother for months or even years, you have to face the possibility that from the child's point of view she will become far more of a mother than you will be.

Having the baby, and letting your mother or some other relative care for it. This may seem like a good solution, especially if your mother has offered. However, there may well be problems. You and your mother may disagree on child-care: she may in practice resent being tied down once more, she may not have the necessary physical energy to cope with a growing child. Whether this could work depends on the relationship between the two of you, your age, your future plans.

Having the baby, and handing it over to the father (or more likely the father's family) to care for. An unlikely solution, but it does happen. Most of the disadvantages mentioned above, with the added one that you're possibly even less likely to agree with the ideas of your child's paternal grandmother.

Terminating the pregnancy. If you decide you don't want the baby, you need reliable advice about abortion as soon as possible.

Medically, the earlier you have the abortion the simpler it is. With the extraction technique, now being increasingly introduced into out-patients' clinics, you don't even have to go into hospital. The longer you leave your decision, or the longer it takes to get medical approval, the more complex and potentially dangerous it becomes.

Psychologically, some women remain unscathed by the operation; some are immensely relieved by it; others are affected deeply, some immediately afterwards, others months or even years later.

Legally, the Abortion Law of 1967 made it simpler in some circumstances to get an abortion. However, it still remains difficult for a single childless woman, and in some areas – especially for those without money – virtually impossible.

Because of the different standards between different parts of the country, and even between different hospitals in the same part, you need good advice fast. It's best, if you feel you can, to consult your GP. If he/she agrees an abortion is the right decision, he/she can refer you either to your local hospital, one of the non-profit-making charities, or a private clinic. If you don't want to consult your GP, then get in touch with one of these:

The British Pregnancy Advisory Service (branches in Birmingham, Brighton, Coventry, Leeds, Liverpool; phone numbers in your directory).

Pregnancy Advisory Service (London only: 01–409 0281; Manchester and Liverpool: 061–228 1887)

The Family Planning Association

Brook Advisory Centre

A welfare officer in your local Medical Office of Health's department.

Remember that none of the traditional methods – tablets, gin, hot-baths, jumping up and down – is in the least likely to work: and *illegal abortions remain extremely dangerous.*

For advice, you can turn to the National Council for One Parent Families (formerly the National Council for the Unmarried Mother and her Child) at 255 Kentish Town Road, London NW5 (01–267 1361); and Gingerbread, 9 Poland Street, London W1. Lifeline (01–222 6392) is concerned to avert abortions and will offer moral support and sometimes material help. Let Live (01–231 0271) does much the same.

8. And baby makes two

It's not easy to think rationally about what having a child means, and for many – especially those without younger brothers and sisters – it's almost impossible even to try. So I thought it would be helpful to try to give some idea of what's entailed. If it makes it all sound too frightening and exhausting, I'm sorry. There are many joys and pleasure in having children: but you're more likely to experience them if you're not bowled over by problems and sheer hard work.

TLC as the hospitals put it – tender loving care. A baby and small child needs a great deal of personal love and attention, and preferably to a large extent from one individual and the same individual (this is particularly important in the first few months). It's undoubtedly better for the child if that person is either the mother or an equally single-minded devoted mother substitute.

A new-born baby spends much of its time sleeping and the rest feeding. If you breast-feed the baby – best for both of you – you can reckon on spending between 5 and 6 hours a day (perhaps less, perhaps more) doing nothing but feeding and changing your child. As the child gets bigger it spends less time at feeds, less time sleeping, but more time awake and eventually moving around, until by the time it's two, say (but children vary), you'll be spending 10–12 hours a day with your child. You can't safely leave a toddler for longer than a minute without risk of its causing damage to itself or property. Caring for a child is quite literally a full-time job. The more conscientious a mother you are, the truer this is: it takes more time to walk slowly with a child than dump it in a push-chair, to listen to its talking and talk back than shove it in front of the television.

Then there's the *extra physical work* a baby soon-to-be-a-child brings. Even if you're not the fussy type, there are still extra clothes, nappies, sheets to wash, food to prepare and cook: even dressing, lifting, carrying a baby is hard work.

Yet many mothers find the extra physical work nothing beside *the mental strain*. Knowing that this infant is totally dependent on you both for his whole progress and indeed his very life can make demands on you unlike any you have previously known.

Cash. This is a problem for all but mothers of professional standing or independent means. Even small babies cost money (the cost of necessary equipment adds up even if you sensibly buy what you can second-hand). As they grow they eat more, need more clothes, want shoes, books, sports kits. The putative father has a duty to contribute to the support of your child, but the sum obtainable is rarely anywhere near the actual cost. (The National Council for One Parent Families will help you here: also the Child Poverty Action Group, 1 Macklin Street, London WC2.) You are also entitled to Supplementary Benefit if you're not in full-time work. Ask for the form SB1 at your local post office and post it to your nearest Social Security office. You may also earn a small sum without losing benefit: but in order to return to even part-time work you have either to be able to take your child with you or have somewhere to leave it, or someone to leave it with.

Even with cash, it can be hard to find *somewhere to live*. A baby can sleep in your room if you have one, and if your landlord/lady allows it. The older it gets, the more of a strain this becomes. Even the best child snuffles and snorts at night, and most wake early in the morning. This can be a strain on sleep and health. Yet it may be difficult or quite impossible to get even barely adequate accommodation. Facilities for single parents with children are very limited, and the less money you have the harder it gets.

A residential job is very often the only solution for those lacking accommodation, private means, and/or a highly paid professional job. It can work out, but all too often it's merely the best of a number of even worse choices. There are too many opportunities for exploitation, plus generally cramped accommodation, plus the lack of privacy.

Some organizations now have well-run *crèches* attached: if this is a possibility it could work well, at least until your child is old enough to go to school. Some areas (but very few) have *day nurseries* which provide full-time care: these are usually heavily overbooked. *Nursery schools* and *play-groups* help with older children, generally from $2\frac{1}{2}$ or 3, generally with $2\frac{1}{2}$–$3\frac{1}{2}$ hour sessions.

Lacking suitable relatives, the only other solution is *child-minders*. Some registered child-minders are conscientious child-loving people who only take one or two children at a time and give individual care: most, alas, are not registered and profit by illegally herding the maximum of babies and toddlers they can cram in their premises. Children brought up like this grow up stunted mentally and often physically too, arriving at primary school unable even to talk.

For many mothers, lack of any social life plus enforced *loneliness* becomes a major problem. Depending on where you live and who's around, your new life with a baby can be very solitary. It's not easy to meet new people, especially men, not easy to go out alone (unless you're lucky enough to have built-in baby-sitters), not easy to bring people back if you live in one small room.

The important thing to grasp is that your pattern of life will change completely once your child is born. You can't go out as you please, eat when you please, work as and when you please. No matter how determined you are beforehand to fit your baby into your way of life, the fact is that you are far more likely to find yourself adapting to your baby.

It's not just you, plus a baby, but you-and-a-baby, which for most people involves a whole new way of life.

All these disadvantages and difficulties can be overcome, and are by many mothers. Each individual will find some aspects more menacing than others. But if you want to keep your baby the time to think about these problems is beforehand. It's not easy, because there's often physical lethargy plus a psychological unwillingness to make plans. Unfortunately, if you leave it until after the baby's born, you'll find everything much much harder. You're likely to find yourself physically weak, mentally low, and handicapped by having to carry the baby with you wherever you want to go. So don't give in to the temptation to put everything off. Look ahead. Get all possible advice and help. Be prepared to be flexible. Make all the positive plans you can.

9. Towards long-term relationships

Research plus the experience of, for example, consultants in the Brook Clinics, indicates that many young adults take their relationships with each other at least as seriously, and perhaps more so, as any previous generations. Many young people, if not most, aim at a deep, loving, non-temporary relationship. This ambition may and generally does make itself felt later on the male side (for some attitudes see p. 178), but doesn't seem to be confined to one sex, or one standard of education, or one kind of upbringing. Most young adults want a relationship in which each partner is equal to and complementary to each other, where each matches the other sexually, intellectually, emotionally. They aim to take themselves and their partners seriously – and pleasurably – sometimes with, sometimes without marriage.

Yet far more young marriages break up than older ones, and many would-be long-term relationships dissolve in bitterness.

So what goes wrong? Many of the problems spring directly from the personalities of those concerned. Here are some of the possible causes . . .

Negatives

Too changeable. In your late teens and twenties you're likely to change and develop rapidly and radically – so much that someone of twenty-two can seem almost unrecognizable to those who knew him/her at seventeen. And yet it's just at this volatile period that people look for companionship, love, sex. Not surprisingly, many young people quite naturally grow out of each other; the younger, the less formed their personalities are when their relationship starts, the more likely this is to happen. If Romeo and Juliet hadn't died they might well have ended up at each other's throats.

Too one-track-minded. There's been so much emphasis over the past few years on sex as a powerful, liberating force, that it's sometimes been made to seem almost *the* main point to life. This can have unfortunate consequences. Some commit themselves to a long-term relationship – often marriage – in the belief that the sexual relationship will in itself provide a meaning to their lives which is otherwise lacking. Since sex is only one of many elements in a relationship, this is rarely possible.

Too intolerant. For any relationship to thrive you need a certain tolerance. It's impossible to agree with anyone 100 per cent of the time. Tolerance, true respect for another's point of view, takes time to grow.

Too insecure. Some relationships are negative from the start. People cling together in fear of the outside world or because they dread being on their own, rather than because they want to spend their lives and leisure with each other. This kind of relationship all too soon becomes a trap.

Too unreal. Day-dreams have great power. Sometimes they mislead. When the fantasies stirred up by heart-throb fiction, or men's magazines, or pop music, or pub jokes, spill over into real life and are mistaken for reality, they become dangerous. Girls expect men to be what they aren't and can't be (romantic heroes, or supermen, or father-figures), men see girls as something quite inhuman (dolls or dream-goddesses or second mothers). Trying to force others to fit pre-imagined roles can cause damage and heart-ache.

Too real. The realities of marriage or a similarly close relationship are often too different from what was hoped and pictured to be tolerated. No relationship between two people, except the most trivial, could possibly be all fun, all joy, all sweetness and light. When the inevitable collisions occur, there is neither the ability

nor the determination to cope with them. Often, too, the realities of an unplanned pregnancy finally shatter illusions.

Positives

Make a mistake in a relationship outside marriage, and you can find yourself facing heart-ache, bitterness, possibly pregnancy. Make the same mistake within marriage, and you have the same problems with others added.

Since marriage can have the more serious consequences, let's assume – for the sake of argument – that that's the way you see your long-term relationship ending up. What guidelines are there to ensure that it turns out a happy one?

Enjoying. It's not easy for a marriage, especially a young marriage, to keep going without a good sexual relationship. This doesn't necessarily mean that you have to have proof of weeks of steady ecstasy, because in any case a good sexual relationship may take months or years to develop fully. What it does mean is that you enjoy what physical contact you have and look forward to more and better of the same; and that if you positively don't enjoy it, or are even repelled, then you need to stop and take a good look at where you're heading.

On the other hand, you may know that sexually you've got everything going for you and still be shaping up for disaster. Make sure you're not being swept overboard by sex itself, rather than by your particular exponent of it; and don't let it blind you to your partner's total personality.

Liking. Kindness, patience, a sense of humour can be as important in marriage as sexual compatibility. Do you *like* your partner as a person? To talk to, laugh with, go out with, as well as be in bed with? Is he/she a friend as well as a lover?

Sharing. Do you share at least some of the same ideas – specially about matters which are going to be important to you both? About spending money, children, holidays, living styles? You don't want someone who's your mirror image, but you must have *something* in common or your marriage can never be more than a half-baked beginning. If your ideas differ very basically over matters which are extremely important to you both, such as religion or education, then you need to think deeply and be confident of your own maturity to be able to handle the problems which will arise.

Fair-dealing. Are you being as honest as you know how – and is your partner? This is the time when it's absolutely vital neither to deceive nor be deceived. It's one thing to make an attempt to share someone else's interests and ideas, quite another to pretend

you already hold them. Deceit ultimately defeats itself.

Accepting. Remember that it's potentially disastrous to marry someone with the intention of changing them. Novels and the divorce courts are full of those who have tried and failed. I'm not saying it's impossible to alter someone's character, only that it's extremely difficult.

Living. Have you considered the practical aspects? Where you'll live, what jobs you'll have, what'll happen if children come along? Do you want to marry because you want to share your life, love, home with this one particular person – or to get away from home, have someone to do the work/earn the money?

Loving. Finally, and very importantly, do you begin to share the same ideas about love; and do you agree whether or not you anticipate a spiritual side to your relationship?

PS

It's very easy when you're out on your own to let slip contact with your family. This seems a shame. If you've got on with them in the past (parents, siblings, uncles, aunts), don't ignore them now. Keep in touch. Write to them, or ring them up, or just send postcards, but send them often. Close family ties do count, even in this changing world.

Liking your Leisure

From time to time you may find yourself at a loose end. When you do, maybe some of these suggestions will inspire you.

Keep an open mind, not forgetting that how bored (and boring) people are depends to a large extent on their own attitude. Some seem to go through life defying others to interest or amuse them. It's hardly surprising that they find everywhere, everything and everyone to be as boring as they've clearly made up their mind it's going to be. You'll enjoy yourself more if you avoid this determinedly down-beat attitude.

Some of these suggestions you can follow on your own. Others involve joining in classes, or clubs, or groups. Don't rush to proclaim 'I'm the non-joining type'. All you mean is you haven't joined the groups etc. you haven't joined, which is obvious: what's less obvious is that you could very well enjoy joining others. Don't cut yourself off from activities you might go for by taking up a preconceived stand.

And if you do want to join, go ahead and do it. By all means take someone along to give you moral courage, but if there's no one handy don't give up the idea. Take the necessary steps on your own. Write, phone or just turn up. Most secretaries and organizers will be only too happy to see you.

If you've come straight from the kind of school or background where most of your time has been organized for you, then it's not always easy to switch to making the decisions, planning your leisure, yourself; to go out and involve yourself with others rather than wait for others to involve you. Make a start as soon as you can. The longer you put off the first move, the harder, in your imagination, it becomes.

It really isn't. Prove it for yourself.

1 PAUSE FOR REFLECTION

You'll never have so much free time again. So make the most of this period of non-commitment, of ample leisure. Use it. Go out, see things, travel. Don't waste it sitting around twiddling your thumbs: particularly if you're on your own and sometimes lonely.

Look outwards, not always inwards. We are all passionately interested in ourselves. This is understandable, and even desirable, but not when we're so busy with what we think, want and do that everyone else becomes virtually invisible.

Don't let yourself become totally self-absorbed. Turn your eyes outwards. Look at and listen to others. No matter where you live and work, you're surrounded by people who have their own interests and passions as you have. Every day you see incidents which are funny, pathetic, bizarre. Keep yourself alert. Observing the world around you is not only interesting and entertaining – it helps you to understand yourself.

Look inwards, not always outwards. Many of us are basically deeply introspective, and never more so than in our teens and twenties, but if you're one of those who's always out and about, always busy with others, always involved, then take time off every now and again to sit and listen to yourself. Do you really like what you do, how you spend your time? Or are you just going along with others? Have you talents you're not using, interests you're not following up? Were there sub-

jects you enjoyed at school you've not yet had a chance to develop? Are you following a pattern of life which started maybe months or years ago, but without any longer much enthusiasm? Ideas and interests change. Pausing every now and again to reflect helps prevent yourself getting fossilized at an early age.

2 GET UP AND GO

Wherever you are, and however poverty-stricken, you can *walk*. Walking is just about the cheapest and one of the best forms of exercise there is. (Yes, all right, it's tough on shoe leather, but you can always use stick-on soles from Woolworth's: though, for serious walking, you need proper boots.) If you're bored with your own neighbourhood, take a short bus or train ride to somewhere else. The more you know about your area, the more interesting you'll find it. Find old maps (ask your local library) to see how roads have taken shape, buildings changed. If you're interested in the country, invest in large-scale Ordnance Survey maps: or your library may have some you can borrow free. If you want to walk further afield, both the Ramblers Association, 1–4 Crawford Mews, London W1, and the Youth Hostel Association, Trevelyan House, 8 St Stephen's Hill, St Albans, Herts, will help you with suggestions and semi-organized groups both here and abroad. There are now several long-distance footpaths, some fairly easy, some tough, throughout Britain (the Pennine Way is one, the North Cornish another) which provide a challenge, stimulus, and solitude if you want.

Almost as cheap is *cycling*. If you haven't a bike, you may be able to hire one locally to see how cycling suits you. If you decide to buy, see p. 211 for full details and practical suggestions.

Other *active sports* depend very much on your local facilities, which vary a lot from place to place. (If your area is particularly short of sports opportunities, how about trying to put pressure on your local authority? Start by writing to your local paper.)

If you have a *swimming-pool* close by, you'll often find that, as well as being open for the general public, there's a swimming club where you'll get coaching, usually with vacancies in the late teens and twenties group. Some also have *diving* and *aqualung clubs*.

Local authorities generally have also *tennis* courts, often surprisingly under-used, and sometimes *golf-courses*, though you have to be up at the crack of dawn for these. Bigger authorities also have *gymnasia*, *athletic clubs*, and *squash* and *badminton* courts. Local private clubs can also offer

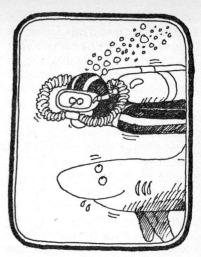

tennis, squash, badminton etc., but these are generally pretty expensive and beyond the reach of the average young adult. However, you can often find that your local education authority provides facilities through evening classes for sports – like *fencing* – which could otherwise be prohibitively expensive.

Skating or *riding* are usually within reach, though again on the pricey side. (How about cutting down on cigarettes, booze, or hairdressers' bills?) Or if you want to try something like *gliding*, *potholing*, *parachuting*, *rock-climbing*, *under-water swimming*, this is perfectly possible too, though obviously you'll have to be prepared to travel further afield. Send for the booklet *Take Part in Sport*, from the Sports Council, 70

Brompton Road, London, SW3. Many industries and individual firms subsidize *sports centres*, often with excellent facilities. (This could even influence your choice of job.) *Youth clubs* vary from district to district, but some do cater for older age groups and provide both space and coaching. Ask at your library for particulars, or at your Town Hall. (There may be a Youth Officer who can help.) The YHA not only have inexpensive hostels, they also run *adventure* holidays of all kinds, from boating to gliding, and individual hostels frequently arrange special week-end events. Write to YHA, address as above. The National Trust has local branches, some with special under-thirties groups, which arrange long walks plus excursions to places as different as breweries and opera houses. Write to 42 Queen Anne's Gate, London SW1.

3 SIT DOWN AND START

When you've had enough of walking, cycling, diving, there's no lack of more tranquil activities around, though again your opportunities depend on where you live. You'd have to be pretty remote, though, to be out of reach of a *library*, even if it's only a book-lined twice-weekly van. A television has only three channels, a library has 300, 3,000, more than you can imagine. Through books you can travel in time and space, find out how other people live and cope. You can find books to make you laugh and books to make you think, books to soothe you and books to upset you. It doesn't matter what you're interested in, there's a book or books about it, and if the library can't help you there then it'll order what you want for only a modest sum (plus stamp). You'll find trained librarians to help you. Some libraries have also records, tapes, even pictures you can borrow: all *free*.

Many in areas with a high immigrant population have books and newspapers in Indian and Pakistani languages; some have books in European languages and all can obtain them if you want them. They've also got masses of information about pretty well everything, including local councils, welfare centres, cinema clubs, drama groups etc.

Never think a library's just for others. It's for you too. (Take your books back on time and don't let fines accumulate. But if you do – shh! – some libraries have amnesties when you sneak books back without paying.)

Evening classes may sound stuffy, but they're not. The people who go aren't either. Among the students of the last classes I went to were a barman, a bricklayer, a

Japanese revolutionary, a poet, an actor and several assorted trendies, mums and grannies. The larger your local institute, the more choice. Get a booklet and find out. (If you've any trouble finding the necessary information, ring your local education authority.) Mine offers, as well as subjects like French, photography, woodwork, guitar, more unconventional topics like black experience, environment, civil liberties. The cost is subsidized: you pay remarkably little. Some of the more popular courses (among them yoga, pottery, jewellery) usually have more would-be students than spaces. To be sure of a place you have to be there early on the first enrolment day. (An alternative: even popular classes often have a vacancy or two in the summer term; people fall ill, move, or just give up. Join a class in this last term, and, provided you attend regularly and show that you're serious about it, you may then be able to claim a former student's privilege of re-enrolling early. See also p. 174.)

If you enjoy music, do you go to *concerts*? There's no need to pay a fortune. The cheapest seats cost surprisingly little: you can hear just as well. Try out different kinds of music: choral and chamber as well as orchestral, Tippett and Scarlatti as well as Beethoven. You may find you enjoy the kind of music you've hardly even heard of yet. For news of modern *jazz* or *pop groups*, try your local paper. If you're in a university town you can usually get to sessions even though you're not a student. Local BBC studios will supply tickets (generally free) on request to BBC concerts.

If you want to *sing* or *play yourself* you'll find most local groups – from light operatic to Bach choirs – very happy to welcome you. Ask your local library if they know names and addresses, or look out for advertisements, especially around September, when choirs and orchestras are recruiting with Christmas ahead.

Most towns of any size boast at least one *museum* and *art gallery*: lots have more. If you haven't visited these, give them a go. Don't go with the grim determination to be interested. Walk around until you find something which does strike a reaction in you. If nothing happens, and you're not involved, never mind – leave and try again another day.

If you're hooked on museums already, there could be a local *historical club* you could join. And though it's hardly a regular pastime, in many areas archaeological societies are in desperate need of volunteers prepared to come and join digs, often at a moment's notice. If you want to know if there's anything locally, write and ask the Council for British Archaeology, 7 Marylebone Road, London NW1.

Local *theatres, reps, fringe groups, pub entertainments* all have plenty to offer. If you're stuck for ideas, again, get your local paper. And you may not know that many areas have local *cinema clubs* – not the flash and porn variety, but showing films of all ages, kinds and backgrounds. To find out if there's one near you, write to the British Film Institute, 81 Dean Street, London W1.

Some of these suggestions are easier to follow in or near towns and cities than in the remote countryside. But if you do find yourself isolated, you have opportunities denied to many others. Not only is it easier to walk, ride,

cycle with less danger of instant death, but you have scope for a different range of pursuits: you can *keep goats or bees, make wine from local fruit and veg., trace back local history.* Not everyone can write another *Akenfield* or discover how to create a new cheese, but you certainly don't know what you can do until you actually try.

4 HOP OFF AND HELP

You can get a great deal of satisfaction in using part of your free time to help others. Again, opportunities vary from district to district, with some organizations and areas being better equipped to make the most of volunteers than others.

In London, try Task Force, Clifford House, Edith Villas, London W14. Outside, the Young Volunteer Force do much the same job: ask your local council if there's a branch near by. Most local social service departments and hospitals welcome volunteers. So do most charities (Oxfam, War on Want, Age Concern, Samaritans) and practically all the agencies dealing with young people mentioned throughout HELP! – plus many of those that aren't. Just ring up or write, and ask. Only apply to one or two at a time; you won't want to be swamped with suggestions.

Giving blood is not precisely a leisure-time activity, but it's so socially valuable that, if you can help, do. Anyone of normal health and not anaemic can be a donor. The body makes up the blood taken very rapidly, and there are no ill effects. Inquire at your local hospital where you should go; or write to the National Blood Transfusion Service (City Centre), Moor House, London Wall, London EC2.

Don't expect the work to be glamorous, or people to fall over themselves with thanks and praise. To start with, until you know the ropes, you're likely to find yourself with mundane tasks like envelope-opening and addressing, filing, answering telephone calls.

But as you get more experienced, and show yourself willing and ready to take on more demanding and responsible work, you'll get it all right. In my experience there are simply never enough *reliable* volunteers to go round. Incidentally, most organizations much prefer one hour a week of definite and never-fail commitment to four hours of enthusiasm followed by five weeks' silence.

Some areas are more open to suggestions than others; but keep looking, and you'll find someone who needs the help you offer.

5 FEED YOUR FUTURE

Let yourself be open, be interested, ready to try new experiences. Not only will you enrich your day-to-day life, you can never tell where what starts as a part-time interest may lead. I knew someone heading for agricultural college who was led by her hobby of model-painting first to a study of heraldry, then to an arts course, and who ended up as designer to a famous Italian film director. (Someone else could have taken the opposite route – from art school to farmer, and it would have been equally right for him/her.)

How you use your free time now determines not only who you are but who you are going to be – in ten years, in twenty, when you're sixty-five. So don't yawn time away. In later years you'll wonder how you could.

About and Away

1 GETTING AROUND

Beat the traffic with a bike

Cycling is the cheapest and simplest way of getting around. You can pay anything from £10–£45 for a second-hand basic bike to a three-figure sum for one hand-built to your measurements. If you buy second-hand, check the bike thoroughly first, particularly if you're buying from a private individual. Remember that every deficiency (worn brake blocks, bent pedals, broken spokes) will need to be put right and that repairs will add to the total cost. (However, spare parts for bikes cost little, especially when compared to e.g. parts for cars.) Get a privately bought, second-hand bike overhauled by a bike shop. Rickety bikes can kill you as efficiently as decrepit cars.

If you buy new, go to a cycling specialist shop, and take their advice. To make the most of your purchase, you'll need in the future someone who will listen to your problems and be able to help.

The simpler your bike, the cheaper its upkeep, but in any case, unless you go in for something really elaborate, the cost over a period will be very little.

For practical advice on buying, see *Richard's Bicycle Book* (p. 215).

Taking your bike with you on holiday. This is dearer than it should be, unless you're going abroad. If you want to take it by British Rail you pay at present half the single fare (there's considerable pressure from cycling organizations to have this reduced). You have to label it, take

---

Wear bright, light clothes when you're cycling
Flexible shoes. Cycle clips if you've got trousers, even if there's a chain guard. No trailing skirts. And warm gloves whenever there's a wind – your hands feel it first.

Mending a puncture

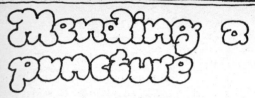

You need to know how to fix a punctured tyre. It may happen miles from anywhere. Here's how to fix one at the back. (The front wheel's similar, but easier, because removing the wheel's more straightforward.)

Get out your puncture repair outfit.

Look at the wheel on the bike and try to trace where the puncture is. If you find what's caused it (a piece of glass, a nail), remove it. If you leave something fixed in the tyre you'll repuncture it the moment you re-insert the inner tube.

Remove the wheel. Turn the nuts at each side of the wheel anti-clockwise. Turn them gradually, giving each only one or two turns a time.

Remove the nuts. Place each, the same way up, on its own side of the bike.

Remove the rings and place on the nuts, the same way up as removed.

Remove the chain.

Remove the wheel.

Remove the ring and valve and place in your puncture repair box.

Take three tyre levers and insert them in the wheel at 7–10 cm intervals.

Persuade the rim of the tyre to leave the wheel.

Pull out the inner tube. If you know where the puncture is, mark the spot with chalk.

Put back the valve in the inner tube.

Pump up the inner tube.

If you don't know where the puncture is, push the inner tube bit by bit into a bowl of water. At some point you'll see air bubbles rising. This indicates the exact spot of the puncture.

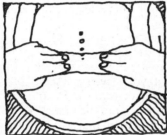

Feel over the puncture area to make sure there are no bits of glass etc. still in the tube.

Place the inner tube on the tyre with the valve against the valve hole. Now recheck the place in the outer tyre corresponding with the inner tube puncture to make sure there's no glass or gravel left there either.

Dry the inner tube.

Lightly sandpaper the area round the hole. Apply the solution supplied with the kit over an area larger than the patch you need. If the inner tube is non-rubber Butol, let the adhesive dry, then apply a second coat and leave to get tacky.

Tear off a strip with the right-sized patch. Press the patch firmly on the puncture solution. Leave it a minute. Then re-

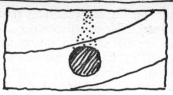

move the paper backing.

Dust the sticky surround with powdered chalk or talc.

Blow up the tube again to check that no air is escaping.

Remove the ring and valve and put in the puncture outfit box.

Place the tube in its correct position on the tyre. Push the valve-holder through the hole in the rim. Put in a couple of pumps-ful of air.

Push the inner tube back inside the tyre.

Use the levers again to push the tyre + inner tube back inside the rim. *Take care not to pinch.* Use all three levers, moving the back one ahead (leaving the other two in place), then moving the new back one ahead, and so on. You'll find this gets tricky towards the end, as the tautened tyre fights against the rim, but provided you move the levers in small steps you'll succeed.

Replace the valve and ring.

Blow up the tyre.

Place the wheel in position, making sure the cog is on the correct side. You may have to persuade the brake blocks apart.

Replace the chain.

Make sure the flat pieces on the wheel axle screw are parallel to the forks. Push the wheel down the forks until the chain is tight.

Slide on the rings and nuts.

Tighten the nuts *gently* with your fingers. Then tighten them with your spanner, still doing it gently, and doing a *turn a time each side.* (Otherwise you'll end up with your wheel off-centre.)

Now try out your bike somewhere safe—not the main road—to make sure all's fixed and all's well.

it down to the guard's van on the train by which you're travelling, and put it in yourself. Theoretically, the guard should put it off again at the right station, but if you're the worrying kind (I am) you rush down when you get off to make sure it's been done. Costs for travelling by boat and train to other countries vary, depending on the countries concerned. Check with the appropriate tourist offices. Transporting your bike to the Continent by hovercraft or ferry costs a fairly modest sum. By air, a bike counts as and is weighed as luggage.

The Cyclists' Touring Club, 69 Meadrow, Godalming, Surrey, can give you plenty of practical help and advice on all cycling topics: also information sheets, cycling maps and reduced insurance rates. A very practical book is a Reader's Digest Basic Guide, *The Maintenance of Bicycles and Mopeds* (50p), which explains with clear illustrations all you need to know to keep your bike on the road. *Richard's Bicycle Book* by Richard Ballantine (Pan, 1975, £1.25) is not only a workshop manual but tells you how to stay alive and get the most out of your bike.

Safety First, see p. 274.

Count the cost of cars

Socially and environmentally – in terms of energy used, pollution caused, and the high cost to the community of every accident – cars are costly objects. For the individual, buying and running a car can often swallow up far more money than ever anticipated.

In a city, driving a short distance and finding somewhere to park may take longer than either public transport, cycling, or even walking: it will certainly cost more. On the other hand, if you live in rural districts or your work involves a great deal of travel or cross-country trips, or you have large loads to transport, a car may be essential.

Owning and running a car is the average person's largest single expense after housing: in many cases, *the* largest single expense. So don't rush into it without thinking about it. You may be able to recoup if you change your mind, but it's rather more likely you'll lose out heavily.

If you decide you do need a car, *what kind* depends on what you want it for and how much you can afford to pay. It involves weighing up price, reliability, repair costs, petrol consumption, and so on. You can start by sending for information from manufacturers. *Autocar* and the AA can both supply detailed road tests for individual makes. Your library will have copies of *Motoring Which?*, also general books on cars and driving. One very detailed and comprehensive book is *Money-Saving Motoring*, published by the AA.

If, like most young adults, you'll be buying *secondhand*, you can start to get a fair idea of current prices by reading the ads in your local paper. *The Motorist's Guide to New and Used Car Prices* can be helpful; so can *How to Beat the Secondhand Car Game* (Topper and Macdonald, Paperfront, 35p).

Unless you're mechanically expert, your best bet is to buy through a reputable *dealer*, who is *legally* bound to supply you with a roadworthy vehicle: some in addition offer worthwhile guarantees. Read any documents, papers, carefully, particularly the small print. Get expert help (from e.g. the CAB) if necessary. Check also if you're buying on HP that you're not signing a promissory note by mistake (see p. 335). It can be sensible to take along a friend to act as a witness in case of future legal action.

If you buy *privately*, remember that you get no legal protection whatever. This is why some shady dealers regularly make apparently 'private' sales from a house rather than a garage forecourt. Beware of someone advertising different cars from the same phone no., either on the same day or on several days in succession; also if you see more cars than you would expect parked at or near the seller's house.

When you feel you've made up your mind, it can be a wise precaution, especially if you're buying privately, to ask the AA or RAC to carry out an inspection before you agree to buy. (You have to

be a member to ask for this: often a good reason for joining.) It can take an expert to spot, not only more straightforward faults, but, for example, disguised accident damage.

Check too – through your CAB – that your prospective purchase is the *property* of the vendor – i.e. not subject to any HP deals.

Incidentally, don't forget to ask for the manufacturer's handbook which should come with every car. You'll need this, and – particularly if it's an old model – you may find it hard to get a copy later. Get the car registration papers as well, and add your name and address.

Inescapable expenses

In the first flush of enthusiasm you can overlook future expenses. This is unwise. You could find yourself with a white elephant you can't afford to ride. Here are some of the individual items.

Annual Road Tax. This is the money you pay to get the round tax disc to put on your windscreen. It is illegal (and a fineable offence) to have your car on public roads without this clearly displayed on the windscreen (bottom nearside). You apply on a form which you get from any post office. You can pay either for twelve months or for four in advance. Paying annually works out cheaper.

Insurance. The minimum *compulsory* insurance is cover against *third-party risks*. This, the cheapest form of insurance, covers you *only* against personal injury caused by your negligence to other people, whether they're passengers or others on the road. It does *not* cover you against damage to other people's cars, or to property; you may still be legally liable for this, and thus risk bills of several hundred pounds. It is not sensible to take out only this minimum cover, and most insurers will only issue these policies in very exceptional circumstances.

You need pay only slightly higher premiums to get a much wider form of cover (third party, fire and theft) which includes also damage to other people's property and loss of your own car due to fire or theft.

Comprehensive insurance covers third-party risks, fire and theft, as above, and also all damage to your car, virtually however caused: it also, by arrangement, covers articles in the car (including radios) and other drivers using your car with your permission.*

* *Please note that you have this kind of cover only if you specifically ask for it and it's included in your policy. Without this, if you allow someone else to drive your car, and that someone has an accident, you could find yourself faced with unfortunate legal and financial consequences.*

Note also that if you drive someone else's car *without* their permission *you are driving uninsured*. (Even with permission you could be driving uninsured if the car's covered by a named-driver policy only and you're not on it.)

The cost of whichever cover you choose depends on a number of factors:
– the insurance company
– where your car is kept
– what make it is, its age and value
– your age
– your driving record
– your job.

Cars kept in cities cost more than those in rural areas; sports cars cost more than family-type cars; young drivers pay heavier premiums than experienced drivers (because statistically they're worse risks). You can't change your age, driving experience, where you live: about the only factor you have any control over is the kind of car you want to insure – so make sure *before* you buy it that it falls into a category you're going to be able to afford.

If your parents have regularly taken out insurance with the same company or through the same insurance broker, it makes sense to follow in their footsteps. Or approach the AA or the RAC, who will provide you with an individual policy tailor-made to suit your circumstances.

Wherever you get your insurance, *read the actual policy carefully*. If you have any worries at all, consult your Neighbourhood Law Centre or CAB.

Don't be tempted to tell lies on a form applying for insurance. If you ever need the cover, you'll find out that even minor inaccuracies can make your insurance null and void.

Repairs. How much repairs cost you depends partly on the age and reliability of your car, partly on whether you can do some maintenance jobs yourself or are totally dependent on garages (see also p. 267), but also to a large extent on its actual construction and the cost of its spare parts. (Parts for foreign cars cost more: so repairs cost more: so insurance costs more.) On some cars, a minor fault can involve the replacement of a major item; cars of similar cost and size can have similar spare parts costing very different amounts. Try to find out about this before you settle on your make of car. Read the motoring magazines, check with friends, ask your friendly neighbourhood garage if you have one.

Generally speaking, the older the car the more you can expect to have going wrong. (Though an elderly car, regularly maintained by one owner, will be a better bet than a newer one which has passed through several hands and had little maintenance.) Don't buy a car if the only way you can afford it is to assume that nothing will ever go wrong. It will.

Petrol and oil. How much petrol and oil you need depends partly on your make of car, partly on your type of driving, but obviously mostly on how much you use your car. If you're buying secondhand, be reasonably sceptical about the previous owner's estimate of miles-per-gallon consumption. Check this against published figures. High-performance cars need high-performance petrol: increasingly expensive the further you get from city centres.

Depreciation. This is a hidden cost, and one that most of us are only too happy to overlook. It certainly exists. This is the rate at which your car loses its value during the time you own it. It isn't easy to calculate. At its simplest, if you buy a car for £900 cash and sell it one year later for £750, during that time its value has depreciated by £150; i.e. it has cost you £3 a week simply to own it. If, as is usually the case, you borrow money to buy the car, the *real* cost is considerably higher. (Of course age is not the only thing which affects the value of a car. Mileage and maintenance do too. And very occasionally, with vintage cars, age actually increases the value. Generally, though, this dwindles with every month that passes.)

The newer the car, the faster the depreciation. By the time it's ten or fifteen years old depreciation becomes almost a negligible item.

Extras. Parking fees. Garage charges. Fines. Contributions to motoring organizations. Paying for tolls. Buying maps. These can amount to virtually nothing to pounds per week, depending on your driving pattern.

It all adds up

The AA regularly issues figures for the average weekly cost of running a middle-sized family car, but like most averages this figure conceals big differences at both extremes. A new, powerful car, with maximum cover, owned and driven by an inexperienced driver and maintained by garage mechanics, will cost far more than a small, sound, ten-year-old veteran maintained by its owner and with insurance cover benefiting from several years' claim-free driving.

You can at least work out your potential *minimum* costs by adding together road tax, insurance premiums, depreciation, fuel costs, and extras, and setting aside a calculated sum for maintenance.

If the result horrifies you, think again. A car that spends most of its time in pieces because you can't afford to repair it, or in a garage because you can't afford to license it or pay for petrol, is useless. You'd be better off without it.

Don't make life easy for car thieves/'borrowers'

Don't leave windows open. Don't leave the keys in the car. Don't leave stealable objects temptingly visible. *And don't leave your car registration papers in the car.*

Day-to-day demands

You may decide to leave periodic maintenance to trained mechanics, but you'll need to be able to attend to day-to-day running yourself. Keep your handbook with you in the car.

These are the absolutely basic chores.

Filling up. Know what grade petrol you need. Using a higher grade is a waste of money. Make sure the pump-gauge is set to zero to start with. If you use a self-service station, read the instructions one at a time, and act on them: don't assume all pumps work the same.

You feel pretty daft if you run out of petrol, so find out how accurate your gauge is, and never drop below the danger mark. Keep a pound for emergencies sellotaped to the inside of the glove box. (It can be a wise safety precaution to have a lockable filler-cap fitted. Non-lockable ones sporadically get pinched and petrol can be siphoned off.)

Checking the oil. The oil sump is generally an oblong box-like looking thing at the bottom of the engine with a removable metal rod (the dipstick) poking out at an angle. It needs to be kept supplied with enough oil to keep the engine lubricated. You have to check the oil level at regular intervals – how often depends on how far you drive and your individual car's consumption. Always check *only* after the car has been standing for some time on the level. Open the bonnet. Take out the dipstick. Wipe off the oil on a piece of rag. Replace the dipstick, pushing it down as far as it will go. Take it out again, and see how much oil is left clinging to the end of the stick. You'll notice two marks at the bottom of the stick. If the oil level is below the bottom one, it's dangerously low and you must put in more oil immediately. If it's above the second one, you have plenty. If it's between the marks, you need more some time soon. Multigrade oil suits most cars. If yours needs something different your handbook will tell you.

Radiator. Check the radiator *before* you start out. (Never take off the cap when the engine has been running and is hot. You risk having steam or boiling water spurting in your face.) Untwist the cap. If you see no water level visible, then you need to top it up. Gently pour in ordinary tap water until you see the level rise. Switch on for a minute or two: then switch off. Wait a few seconds and then if necessary top up again. In autumn, you'll need to drain the radiator (the handbook will tell you how), put in anti-freeze, and top up with fresh water to within 5 cm of the filter level.

Tyres. Your tyres must be the right kind, correctly matched, with an adequate tread, and inflated to the right pressure. Don't mismatch cross-ply and radial tyres.* (If you buy re-cut tyres, get them only from a reputable company and make sure they're suitable for cars. Recently, cheap substandard imported tyres only fit for light agricultural use have been wrongly and dangerously sold for cars, so beware.) How often you need to reinflate your tyres depends on what loads you carry and how far you travel. If in doubt, always check. You can keep and use a foot pump of your own, but most motorists use garages. (Air is free, but it's tactful to buy petrol at the same time.) The correct pressure

* *You can have cross-ply on the front and radial on the back, not the other way round. Never mix the two types on the same axle. Radials are a better buy.*

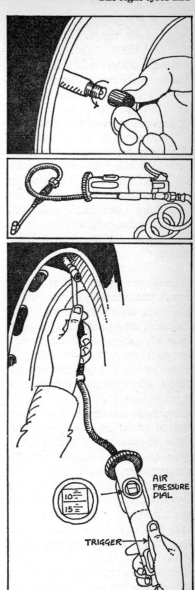

for your tyres depends on the make of car, the type of tyre, and whether they're rear or front. Your handbook will tell you: if you've left it behind, garages keep a list near the air pump of pressures needed by most common makes. Always over-inflate by 1 kg for long high-speed motorway driving before you set out.

Unscrew the little valve cap on the tyre. (This is just to keep dirt out, not air in.) Place the nozzle of the pump against the valve and push. The gauge will now register. (There are different types of gauges – some have vertical scales, some clock faces.) Wait until the indicating line is at rest. This shows the present air pressure of the tyre. If it's below the level required, now press the trigger to start the pump working. As you do this, the indicator line will probably drop as the gauge ceases to register while the pump is actually working; so take it carefully, press the trigger for only a second or so, then stop pumping; leave the nozzle pressed against the valve, and wait until the indicator reaches its new level. If this still isn't enough, repeat the process. (If you go slowly like this you shouldn't exceed the correct pressure, but if you do, remove the pump, and press the valve down with your thumb-nail to let a little air escape.) Replace the valve cap. Do the same for the

other three tyres. Occasionally check the pressure in your spare tyre too.

Battery. The battery is the large oblong box with wires going into it/coming out of it and a number (usually eight) of screw-down caps on top. It's generally in the engine compartment, under the bonnet, but is sometimes stored somewhere less get-at-able. It needs to be kept clean and topped up with distilled water. The water *must* be distilled. Recent tests have

TOPPING UP BATTERY

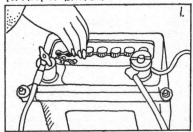

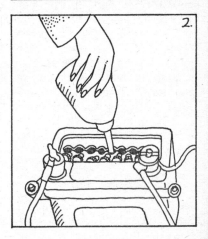

shown that the water kept in unsealed containers on garage forecourts can be contaminated, and occasionally is not even distilled water. So, except for emergencies, you'd be better advised to buy your own distilled water and keep it in the car to use as you need it. You'll find yourself topping up the battery more often in summer than winter. To check, unscrew the caps on top and look inside. The water should be covering the surface of the horizontal metal plate you can see. If not, gently pour in more water until it does by 5 mm or so.

Brakes. Your brakes and clutch will gradually fade unless the hydraulic fluid is kept topped up. You shouldn't need to do this often, but take a look every now and again. The fluid is kept in two vertical cylinders looking rather like large taps. Unscrew the top of each in turn: if the level has dropped below the recommended level top up with more. (You can buy this from any garage.) *Always* clean the outside of the cylinders before you unscrew the tops: before you replace them check that the tiny pinhole in each top is unblocked.

Lights. Check all lights regularly, not forgetting the indicator and brake lights, and replace defective bulbs immediately.

Apart from these regular chores which you see to yourself, your

TOPPING UP BRAKE AND CLUTCH FLUIDS

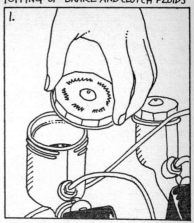

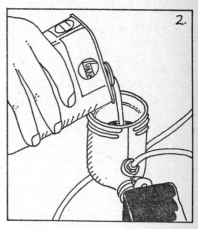

car must have periodic overhauls at fixed intervals as recommended by its manufacturers. Don't skip these, even if your car seems to be running fine. The whole point of regular maintenance is to pick up small deficiencies before they turn into major ones. Thorough over-

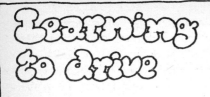 

The earliest age to hold a provisional licence (for learning to drive on public roads) is seventeen. The best way of learning is undoubtedly from a patient, unruffled, expert driver, who understands both theoretical mechanics and practical techniques. There are people like this in some driving schools: unfortunately, not enough. Again, as with garages, personal recommendation is best. Failing this, head for an RAC-registered school. These employ largely RAC-registered instructors who have passed both theoretical and practical exams.

It doesn't generally work out to try to learn from family or friends. Many beautiful relationships are ruined, and many bad driving habits get passed on. Think hard before you do this. The money saved is rarely worth the anguish caused.

(If you've already passed the driving test, and are asked to sit in with a learner driver, think twice before you agree. You will be legally in charge of the car, and could find yourself legally responsible for any offence caused by your 'pupil' and possibly even liable for any consequent accidental damage. Whether your insurance covers this depends on your policy. Check first.)

Passing a driving test is only a beginning. Newly fledged drivers cause a high proportion of all accidents. For *how to drive better,* and *what causes accidents*, see pp. 268 and 269.

Remember too that learning to handle your car properly will not only, most importantly, help to keep you and others alive, it will also save you money. Bad driving ruins engines: good basic driving techniques – like cutting out hard revving-up and avoiding last-minute braking – reduce wear and cut costs.

Map-reading

You can make driving pleasanter and often easier for yourself by buying a good set of road-maps and using them to keep off high-traffic roads at busy times. For really complicated cross-country routes you'll need a navigator. Allow yourself sufficient time. On a cross-country trip, if you average 30 m.p.h. you'll be doing well. Unnumbered white roads are quite adequately surfaced, but they'll probably be narrow and twisting – you won't be able to keep up high speeds and you certainly shouldn't try. There are many unexpected hazards on rural roads, from children to sheep to tractors, but if you want to see more of the country you're living in, instead of heading straight from A to B, this is the way. The petrol companies' maps are good and clear. Ordnance Survey maps are excellent if you want to know a small area well. *The Reader's Digest AA New Book of the Road*, based on OS maps, is excellent for touring, with handy continuity flaps which prevent you from falling off the edge of the page.

hauls can save you breakdowns, money, even your life.

(See also p. 267.)

Taking your car abroad

Taking your car abroad is not cheap. Naturally, the bigger it is the more it costs. Petrol prices abroad vary. Sometimes it's possible to get tourist rebates: often these have to be applied for here before you go. Ask at the individual tourist offices. Be sure to take out extra insurance. Although you can generally travel in Common Market countries on your ordinary insurance, you'll only be covered there for *local* basic third-party risks, no matter what your cover is here. For anywhere outside these countries, and for better cover within them, you'll need extra insurance. (Even a minor accident could find you up against extra hotel bills, transport costs, hiring expenses, and so on: don't risk it.) You can also face unanticipated expenses. For example, many motorways are paid for by tolls – travelling from north to south of Italy on these could add pounds and pounds to your bills. In some countries, minor road traffic infringements are met by arbitrary on-the-spot fines. You're unlikely to be able to be in a position to argue the toss.

Motoring abroad can be an interesting and stimulating experience, especially out of season, enabling you to get to places you might never see by public transport. It can also be exhausting, expensive, disappointing, even frightening. Thinking ahead can save a lot of hassle.

P.S. Motoring regulations are not the same abroad as they are here. For example, the famous French *priorité à droite*, giving precedence to traffic entering main roads from minor roads to the right, however fitfully observed it actually is, does exist. Rights of way on roundabouts are different too. When you're in another country, the local cops expect you to abide by that country's laws and regulations. Find out first.

Moped or Motorbike

Cycles, for healthy people and in dry weather, are the simplest way to cover short distances in towns, but once you have to go more than say two or three kilometres the effort and time involved may be too much each end of a day's work. A *moped* could be the answer. These are basically bicycles with a small engine to do the hard labour instead of you. Most of them have only a single gear, but some models (designed to appeal to sixteen-year-olds, who aren't allowed to drive motorbikes with more powerful engines) have several gears and a motorbike type frame. Mopeds are light, nippy, quick on short journeys. Running-costs, insurance, tax, are all low. On the other hand, you get cold in cold weather, you have to buy some wet-weather clothing, you can't carry much, and many people find them uncomfortable over long distances.

Motorcycles are less manoeuvrable than mopeds in heavy town traffic, but faster and more comfortable over long distances. Prices vary between different makes and sizes just as with cars, and as with cars the true price of riding may be much higher than you realize. (Check with p. 219 for comments on depreciation etc.) Servicing is

Both the AA (Fanum House, Basingstoke, Hants) and the RAC (83–5 Pall Mall, London SW1) offer many advantages to both drivers and motor-cyclists: help in case of breakdown, special arrangements for foreign travel, insurance packages (which include bringing your car back from abroad). Opting for extra services (of course at extra fees) can also bring help with hotel bills, garage fees, additional transport, incurred through breakdown or accident. Write for details.

Moped or motorbike?

Warning. People riding scooters or motorbikes are much more likely to have accidents than pedestrians, cyclists or car-drivers; in particular, the *death and serious injury risk* for young motorcyclists is very high (see p. 266). If you're set on a motorbike this probably won't deter you, but if you're hesitating between that and a car it's worth remembering that, while cars aren't accident-proof – far from it – you are inevitably more vulnerable on a bike, and more at the mercy of other drivers' mistakes.

Evidence shows that many motorcyclists get involved in accidents because other drivers never see them at all. You can help keep yourself in one piece by making yourself as visible as possible, with white helmet, fluorescent jacket (or at least a light-coloured overshirt) and reflective strips. (And see p. 267.)

cheaper than with cars – many motorcyclists do their own – and the running costs of fuel, tyres etc. are much lower. Road tax too is much lower: on the other hand, insurance, especially comprehensive insurance, can be very high. The younger and less experienced you are the more you'll have to pay. (This reflects the company's statistical conviction that you're likely to damage yourself and vehicle.) You'll also have to spend on good wet-weather clothing: you may also want to spend on garaging – motorcycles are more vulnerable than cars to theft and casual damage. (If you store motorbikes or mopeds inside, remember that they could be a fire hazard because of the petrol tank.)

You're more likely to keep yourself alive if you learn to handle your machine well. A recommended way is through a properly organized course. If you're near one of the RAC and ACU's 175 centres, you can take advantage of their standard twenty-four-hour course (split into one-hour lessons) for a very modest fee. Write for details to the National Organizer, RAC/ACU Training Scheme, 83–5 Pall Mall, London SW1. An invaluable guide is *Motor Cycle Roadcraft*, HMSO, 1973, 33p.

Going abroad. Taking a moped, motorcycle or scooter abroad is simpler and much cheaper than taking a car. However, all the comments on p. 225 on insurance, expenses and complications apply as much to two wheels as four. If you're a member, the AA or RAC will give detailed advice.

Economize with coaches

Coach travel is generally slower but cheaper than trains. It may be less adventurous, but it's more reliable and certainly a great deal safer than hitch-hiking (see p. 275). Some find it restful and interesting: others find it makes them tired or even sick. You're inevitably more cooped up than in a train. Don't go on twelve-hour trips until you find how it affects you.

Coaches run to all parts of the country. Some of the express coaches, using motorways, compare very favourably in time with trains. Others, which make many stops and with timetables often designed to fit in with local buses, can provide the only public transport method of getting at out-of-the-way villages.

Fares are often surprisingly reasonable, with day returns little more than the single fare. They vary depending on the time of year and day. There are so many schedules, special offers, special trips, that the best way of finding out what's available is by calling at your local coach station. (In London, contact National Travel (NBC) Ltd, Victoria Coach Station, Buckingham Palace Road, London SW1, 01–730 0202.)

Relax by rail

Travelling by train, except in commuter rush-hours, can be a civilized and restful way of getting from place to place. You can stretch your legs, watch the scenery, catch up on your reading. If you want to make sure of a seat, you can reserve one. (It costs only a little extra.) If you travel to the West Country in the summer season, you *have* to reserve one by buying a supplementary ticket.

There are all kinds of special rail offers which don't seem to get much publicity. You get very considerable reductions if you book three weeks in advance and travel midweek. Weekend returns and seventeen-day returns are cheaper than ordinary returns. Special day returns are very economical. There are also many Awayday trips, often combining reduced fares with entrance fees: also special packages, including hotels, for bargain holidays.

Your local station or travel agent will probably have details of many of these, but much of the latest information seems to turn up only at main-line stations. You can book rail tickets at any travel agent; seat reservations can also usually be made through agents, but not always.

Play the planes

The air travel world seems to be in a constant state of upheaval, with prices and conditions changing almost from day to day, and no two agents agreeing on the cheapest way to where you want to go. Keep your ears open for the latest reports, visit more than one booking agent if necessary, and read all the small print, especially where terms of cancellation are concerned.

This appears to be the situation at the time of writing.

Scheduled flights, run by the big international companies, are both

the most expensive and the most reliable.

Advanced Booking Charters (ABC's) are much cheaper, but run only to the USA, Canada, or the Caribbean. You book up to 60–90 days in advance (times keep changing, and vary with different countries). The return fare is very much cheaper, but you have to stay a minimum of 10–14 days, and any cancellation is penalized. Prices are not controlled, and rates vary.

APEX flights are similar. The timing is more reliable, but prices are higher.

If you're not over-committed to time schedules, you may be able to use *short notice flights* (at present to Amsterdam, Brussels and Paris). You book the day before you want to travel, and the booking is only accepted if there

If you're a *full-time student*, holding an international student identity card, you can get not only cheap air fares (up to the age of thirty) but also cheap train and coach fares here and abroad. For details, contact NUS Travel, 117 Euston Road, London NW1.

are spare seats on the plane.

On some routes you can find cheap *youth flights*. The upper age limit varies depending on where you're going – can be up to 23 or even as high as 30. Check at your travel agent.

Many *package tours* cost less than the scheduled fares. Thomson Holidays have recently introduced new low-price package deals which they hope to develop in several countries, offering air travel plus simple accommodation at even more modest prices.

2 HAPPY HOLS

What kind of holiday you plan, where you want to go, how much you're going to spend, depends on:
  When you go
  How far you go
  Your living conditions
  How much pre-planned fun/ tuition you have
  Whether you need/want a working holiday.

When you go

No matter where you want to go, both travel and accommodation cost much more at certain times of the year than others. If you're not forced to take your holiday in peak periods (July/August, Christmas, Easter) then you'll save pounds if you don't. City holidays here and abroad are much more agreeable out of season: fewer crowds, less competition for all you want to see. (On the other hand, 'Special Attractions' are often shut then, and holiday resorts without personalities of their own can be dreary.) Trust House Forte run off-season Bargain Breaks for weekends and sometimes longer which offer excellent value: write to THF Reservations Centre, 71–5 Uxbridge Road, Ealing, London W5. Interchange Hotels do much the same: 1 Victoria Road, London W8. British Rail and other individual hotels also advertise special off-season terms. Off-season package holidays abroad are very much cheaper indeed than in season: collect brochures from the various agents. (The best bargains get booked up early.) If you can go away for longer than a couple of weeks, you can rent holiday cottages for very low rates: see the classified columns in national papers. (You often need to be hardy to enjoy these. They're usually equipped for summer tenants, and standards of heating, electricity, sanitation and even water can be a distinct challenge in mid-winter.)

How far you go

On the whole, the further you go, the more you have to pay. There are sometimes odd anomalies, but none the less it's generally true that it costs more to go to Bolivia than Birmingham. Travelling always costs money, and is probably going to go on getting more expensive. Apart from the various booking suggestions mentioned above, the only cheaper way to travel is to get someone else to pay for it. This is sometimes possible. Families wanting au pairs/nannies/tutors or managers wanting barmen/dancers/waitresses are sometimes willing to contribute to your fares for the privilege of employing you. However (and it's a pretty sizeable however) you need to scrutinize all such propositions carefully to make sure you won't be paying through the nose in other ways – through minute wages, bad conditions, or sheer fraud.

One unusual way of covering big distances and seeing many places for a comparatively low price is through the educational cruises run by British India. These visit many countries in the Mediterranean and Scandinavia from spring to autumn. They have dormitory accommodation at modest sums for around 1,000 passengers: these places are mostly taken up by pre-arranged bookings from schools, colleges, youth clubs etc., but there are occasional berths vacant and, much less often, whole cruises open to individual bookings. In addition, each ship carries 300+ cabin passengers at higher rates. Write and ask about possibilities to P & O Passenger Division, B.1 Educational Cruises, Beaufort House, St Botolph Street, London EC3.

Your living conditions when you get there

The humbler your accommodation, the cheaper your holiday. The chain of youth hostels here and abroad provides cheap clean dormitory accommodation, often in castles, mansions and other interesting buildings. (YHA, Trevelyan House, St Albans, Herts.) Camping, the genuine kind, can be even cheaper, if you have your own small tent. If you haven't, many hire shops rent out by the week all you need, including primuses, ground-sheets etc. As long as you're clean and tidy you can often camp in farmers' fields, but *ask permission first*. For further help, write to the Camping Club of Great Britain and Ireland, 11 Lower Grosvenor Place, London SW1, or buy *Camping Sites in Britain*. You can also get ultra light-weight equipment which you can carry on your back or your bike, which makes long walking or bicycle holidays anywhere you want a practical possibility: but this kind of thing comes expensive, so it's only worth considering if you're going in for it in a big way.

Boarding houses and farmhouses often give good value. Look in

Exchange and Mart or buy one of the annual books which have collections of addresses and descriptions.

How much pre-planned fun/ tuition you have

Self-evident, really. Discos, tennis, gliding lessons, all have to be paid for one way or another. The more that's laid on, the more you pay. Some kinds of pre-arranged holidays are going to be dearer than others – horse-riding is likely to cost more than painting classes, if only because you need one horse per rider: who cumulatively eat more and take up more room than one tutor. Some of these holidays, especially the more creative holidays, give first-class value.

You'll have to look around to discover a good range of possibilities. The English Tourist Board (4 Grosvenor Gardens, London SW1) produce a very useful book, *Holiday Activities in England*, 60p, giving details and addresses. Some of the more individual travel agents will help: or write to the British Tourist Authority, 64 St James's Street, London SW1. You'll find advertisements in newspapers, especially the *Observer*, the *Sunday Times*, *Guardian* and *The Times*. (Sometimes their travel services will help too.) You can often find information about holidays involving various arts, crafts, occupations etc. by reading the appropriate magazines. Local Adult Education Institutes have details of holiday courses run in colleges and halls: even if you're not a member you can go in and ask. You can find out about active holidays from the Sports Council, 70 Brompton Road, London SW3.

Whether you need/want a working holiday

Often young adults find it hard to afford more than the most elementary kind of holiday. If they're self-employed, unemployed, or students, the only solution is a working holiday. These can work marvellously, and provide change, stimulus and real entertainment *provided* that it's realized from the start that a working holiday is what it says: a *working* holiday.

Find out before you commit yourself what's involved. Ask about the hours, the pay, the conditions. Sometimes the margin between voluntary work and exploitation can be very narrow: shift work, or the distribution of part-time work, can reduce true leisure hours to virtually nil.

This may not matter if you enjoy the work or appreciate the side benefits. But the point remains that work is work, and you have to be able to tackle it. If you go grape-picking, for example, you may relish the wine, the company, the different way of life, but the picking itself is back-breaking, exhausting, hours-long, physical *work* under an un-English sun. Understand what you're letting yourself in for before you start.

There are various ways of coming across jobs like this, but the safest is through a reputable agency. If you're a student, the NUS (3 Endsleigh Street, London WC1) is a good place to start. For

Words of warning

Is accommodation included? If not, find out for certain where you're going to live and how much it's going to cost. Don't be put off by vague reassurances. You can find yourself paying out — especially in the hotel business, especially abroad — more than you're bringing in.

Are there any unspecified deductions? Sometimes holiday workers find themselves 'fined' for e.g. breakages, or charged for hire of essential tools.

When will you get paid? How certain is it that you will get paid? Be very wary of companies you've never heard of and private individuals who give you any reason whatever for sounding dubious (see opposite). If you're booking a job abroad through an agency here, raise this point with some urgency. Some workers have subsequently been left high and dry.

Is the job genuine? Apart from the non-jobs (see p. 312) some holiday openings are not what they seem. If you're a girl, your chances of disillusionment are probably that much higher. If your job's abroad, be particularly careful : the further you go, the greater the risks. Remember that in some countries women are legally chattels, not individuals — you might find yourself, to your surprise, 'belonging' to your employer. There have been too many cases of girls going abroad as barmaids, dancers, secretaries, who have found themselves manoeuvred into debt, and then blackmailed or forced into prostitution.

If you have *any* doubts, find out before you go. Consult the Foreign Office.

local jobs, the British Tourist Authority, 64 St James's Street, London SW1, can provide information about where and how to look. For vacation jobs overseas send for a copy of *Working Holidays Abroad* (£1 incl. post) from the Central Bureau for Educational Visits and Exchanges, 43 Dorset Street, London W1. Vacation Work, 9 Park End Street, Oxford, publishes directories of vacation jobs here and overseas: check with them for current prices.

If you're interested in voluntary work, where there's little or no pay, but often keep provided, there are several organizations you can approach. You can get conservation work of various kinds through Acorn Camps, The National Trust, 42 Queen Anne's Gate, London SW1; or through the British Trust for Conservation Volunteers' Work (apply to the Trust at the Zoological Gardens, Regent's Park, London NW1). You can inquire about community work of various kinds to the United Nations Association, 93 Albert Embankment, London SE1; the Quaker Youth Service, Friends Service Council, Friends House, Euston Road, London NW1; the International Voluntary Service, 91 High Street, Harlesden, London NW10. You can also find other socially useful vacation jobs (not usually including accommodation), par-

ticularly helping in children's playgrounds, advertised in local papers and *Time Out* (for London).

Finally, if you want an absolutely restful, effort-free solitary holiday for absolutely nothing (plus a little pocket money into the bargain) write to the Common Cold Research Unit, Harvard Hospital, Coombe Road, Salisbury, Wilts. You get free rail fare and free keep (in your own room in a self-contained flat) in return for being a cold virus guinea-pig. (Most people don't catch colds.) You have to be over eighteen, and you'd better enjoy a solitary life, because one of the essentials is keeping away from other people. It's ideal for anyone writing, studying, or just wanting to get away. Bicycles are provided!

3 GOING ABROAD

Passports

To holiday anywhere abroad you need a passport. You can get a British Visitor's Passport (valid for one year) by applying for and filling in a form available at any Post Office. This costs £4 and is acceptable in many *but not all* countries abroad. A ten-year passport costs £8 (for thirty pages) or £16 (for ninety-five) and has to be obtained through a passport office. There are several regional passport offices: for your application to be dealt with quickly you have to apply to the correct office.

London – Passport Office, Clive House, 70 Petty France, London SW1.

Liverpool – Passport Office, 5th Floor, India Buildings, Water Street, Liverpool.

Newport – Passport Office, Olympia House, Upper Dock Street, Newport, Mon.

Peterborough – Passport Office, Westwood, Peterborough.

Glasgow – Passport Office, 1st Floor, Empire House, 131 West Nile Street, Glasgow.

Belfast – Foreign and Commonwealth Office Passport Agency, 1st Floor, Marlborough House, 30 Victoria Street, Belfast.

You need your birth certificate and two identical copies of a recent photo of yourself, plus a signed witness to your identity from someone who has known you for over two years. If you weren't born in the UK you'll also need other documents. (See p. 2 of *Notes for Guidance* issued with the passport application form.) Getting a passport normally takes about three weeks, longer in the summer months. If you make mistakes filling in the form it will take even longer, so read the *Notes for Guidance* carefully. Don't be put off by all the words – many of the sections won't apply to you anyway.

Visas

In addition to your passport, to travel to certain countries beyond the Common Market you'll also need individual visas from the countries concerned. Check what's needed with the Passport Office. If you have a non-UK passport, even though you are resident here your visa requirements will be different. Be sure to check on this, and leave enough time to get the visas you need.

Vaccinations

Vaccination requirements vary from country to country and month to month. Many countries (e.g. USA) always require smallpox vaccination,* others (e.g. Spain) sometimes. For some countries you are not compelled to have certain vaccinations, but you should get them for your own protection (see also p. 110). You can get general information from the consulate of the country concerned, or from the Department of Health and Social Security. In the event of last-minute scares, you can try the Embassies or Tourist Offices concerned (you're likely to find the telephone lines jammed) or, sometimes better, the air lines or airports dealing with the countries in question.

There will normally be a small charge for the vaccination (see

---

* *A woman in the first three months of pregnancy should* not *be vaccinated.*

Participants abroad

Even if you're only going abroad for a couple of weeks, you'll get more out of the place/people if you know a bit about what/who you're visiting. Call at the appropriate tourist offices for any leaflets which might come in handy. Good guide-books are not expensive: even small pocket ones contain a lot of interesting and helpful information. The more you know beforehand about a country's customs and history, the more memorable your holiday will be.

Remember *you* are the foreigner. You will be both disliked and resented if you shout in English at the top of your voice, laugh loudly at local ways, and flout local customs.

Although we are fortunate in that English is an international language, and there's usually someone somewhere around who speaks it, you will get people's backs up if you appear to take this for granted. So, even though you may hate appearing touristy, take a phrase book with you if you don't know the language. Take the trouble to learn a few basic words: 'yes, no, please, thank you, good morning, good afternoon': basic numbers, some questioning words, 'where?, how much?, when?' and a few words of praise, 'how beautiful, how kind'.

Even the most minimal of vocabularies both indicates a willingness on your part to make an effort to communicate, and gives you confidence to venture to shop and eat off the tourist track in modest non-English-speaking establishments. The more you learn, of course, the better.

It's easier to get around without excessive and unwelcome interest if you dress reasonably closely to local custom. I don't mean adopting national dress, which would hardly be practicable unless you were living there, and sometimes unwelcome even then, but conforming to local ideas of seemliness. Where local dress is high-necked and sombre, if you settle for scoop fronts and jazzy colours you'll certainly get stared at; you may get sneered at too. If you want to learn more about the country you're visiting, protective colouring works better than personal display.

If you want to explore, you'll find that normally the tourist belt is pretty narrow. If you walk a mile inland, you'll be in a different world: take a local bus, travel a few miles down the road, and there'll be a total lack of signs proclaiming Bed and Breakfast or Tea as Mother Makes it. (Don't, by the way, judge a country by occasional manifestations in tourist sections of petty, greedy and grasping behaviour — you wouldn't want our manners judged by the thrusting techniques of some of the hawkers round Buckingham Palace. Once away from the tourist areas you may be pleasantly surprised by the un-pushiness of those you meet.)

It's true that if you're a girl you are in most countries far more circumscribed than if you were male. Unless you are out to be seduced, a decorous standard of dress and behaviour helps; so does a sceptical turn of mind. Remember that the kind of looks and manner which would raise no eyebrows here can appear deliberately provocative against different social ex-pectations: also that, in countries where unmarried girls have little or no freedom, visiting females are regarded not so much as fair game as regular sporting fixtures, where fouls are taken for granted as an essential part of the play. Which doesn't necessarily mean you have to run a mile at every friendly approach — international friendship is possible even inter-sexually — just that it's reasonable to take undying vows of love with a large pinch of salt.

p. 110), and you will have to pay to have a certificate stamped and authenticated at your local town hall. Avoid last-minute vaccin-ations. Not only may any later reaction upset you, but some, e.g. against cholera, require two or three injections at intervals before they're effective. In London you can get information plus free vac-cinations and certificates from the Hospital of Tropical Diseases, 2–4 St Pancras Way, London NW1. (Book in advance.)

Money

You can of course take abroad in cash all the foreign money you'll need, but this is hardly prudent. The risk of loss or theft is high. Instead, you can buy travellers' cheques in various denominations of £2 and upwards. You sign these as soon as you get them, and countersign them abroad only as and when you need them. You can take them out either in sterling or in the local currency – this could save you worry if exchange rates wobble. You normally get a better rate of exchange at banks, tourist offices and bureaux de change, so avoid running short on bank-closing days. (Bank times abroad are different from here; many shut Mondays, also on odd public holidays, saints' days etc.) The changing agency deducts a commission; generally a small percentage, but just occasionally a whacking big one. Check before you go the conditions in the country you'll be visiting.

You can also use a cheque card (if you have one) plus cheque book to cash ordinary cheques at any bank displaying the Eurocheque sign: you can use Barclaycard in the same way provided you have a Barclays Bank account.

Whether you have travellers' cheques or cheque book plus cheque card, look after them very carefully. Find out before you go what happens if they get lost or stolen. Different banks have different arrangements. Some forward money immediately, some keep you waiting, some won't refund until after you've returned. Any uncashed cheques will be refunded when you get back.

Don't forget that you can get lots of leaflets and information from the various national tourist offices. Phone lines are usually busy. Best to go and collect all you can yourself.

Health insurance. Make sure that, when you travel abroad, you are adequately covered against illness and accident.

If you are going to a Common Market (EEC) country you will be entitled to a certain amount of medical treatment *provided* you are a UK citizen and work for an employer here and *provided* that you take with you form E111 (and sometimes also your National Health card). You need to apply for this *in advance* by asking for and completing form CM1 (available at any Social Security office).

Even so, these reciprocal arrangements entitle you only to treatment available under local legislation. You may still have to pay part of any cost involved. Regulations vary from country to country, and keep changing. It's not easy to find out where you stand. Inquire at the embassy and tourist bureau of the country concerned.

Even if you are going to a Common Market country it may make sense to take out private health insurance. It's essential to do so* if you are not covered in this way (for example, if you're a non-UK citizen) or if you're travelling to non-EEC countries. If you're travelling by car or cycle, you can often arrange this through the AA, RAC or CTC: if not, inquire at any travel agent or insurance office. The security is well worth the small charge.

If you have never been in non-National Health Service countries, you may not realize just how punishing medical expenses can be even for minor accidents or brief illnesses. Anything more serious could beggar you for months or years.

People come in all varieties.

Some talk easily to anyone and everyone. Others hardly dare open their mouths. Odd ones actually enjoy writing letters, while for most of us the pleasure of receiving them is marred by the thought of replying. Some gossip happily on the phone for hours on end, while others dread even picking up the receiver.

Yet however we feel about it, we live in a world surrounded by others. We have to be able to communicate with them, whether it comes easily or not: sometimes because we want to, often because we have to.

If, like most of us, you feel you quite often fail to get across, take heart. Realize (1) that we all fail sometimes; (2) communication is something most people get better at anyway as they get older; and (3) there are ways of speeding up the process. To a certain extent, communication is a skill which can be acquired like any other, and which improves, like others, with with practice.

By which I don't mean that you're in for an instant course in sociability. We all have different personalities which must express themselves in different ways. But over the next few pages you may find help to inspire you to chat when you need to, answer your Christmas letters before Easter, make an efficient phone call even if you still don't actually enjoy it.

1 WE HAVE WAYS OF HELPING YOU TALK

If you suspect, or know, that you're not as good at talking as you'd like to be, *you're absolutely normal*. Many people, including plenty who don't show it, feel exactly the same; especially when they're just launching out on their own.

This is the time you meet situations you haven't had to tackle before, different kinds of people, whole new ranges of experiences. If all this makes you clam up, it's hardly surprising. Knowing that you share the problem with lots of others helps. So does realizing that you don't have to sit round waiting for the gift of tongues. You really can learn to listen, respond, get across your thoughts and feelings when you have to.

Four basic rules

No matter when, where, who you're talking to or what about,

you'll find any conversation becomes much easier if you follow four basic rules.
1 Listen.
2 Be interested.
3 Have something to say.
4 Say it.

1 *Listen.* Without listening, true conversation is impossible. All you get instead is a monologue – or two monologues. Knowing how to listen is the first step to knowing how to talk.

Which doesn't mean letting everyone else's words flow over you. It means concentrating and taking in what's said. Once you can do this, you'll be more than half-way to being a good talker.

2 *Be interested.* To listen well you need to be interested – and this can be a problem, since it's true that some people's conversation is so boring you need to pinch yourself to keep awake.

However, most people are at least potentially interesting. They can talk about their jobs, their families, their hopes. If you constantly find there's no one around worth talking to, then could be it's you yourself who are boring. In which case you could start by expanding your interests. See p. 205 for ideas.

3 *Have something to say.* If you listen and you're interested you can't help having something to add. A comment. An objection. A reminiscence. A joke. Even simply an exclamation. All around you

may not stop to listen with bated breath: you don't have to be world-shattering, you simply have to make sense.

4 *And say it.* Supposing that time and again you get so far but no further. You listen, you're interested, you have something to say, yet the words don't seem to get spoken – or, if they do, the conversation dies shortly afterwards?

Here are some suggestions you might find useful.

1 Take a few deep breaths. This may sound odd, but it has a steadying effect.

2 Remind yourself, once again, that you're not abnormal.

3 Wait for a gap in the conversation and make yourself say *something*: just a few words will

show you're among those present.

4 Don't strive to be brilliant. The mere thought will strangle the words on your lips.

5 Avoid flat statements. Add a comment or a question which will help the talk along. 'I've never flown – does it make you nervous?'

6 Never answer questions with a plain yes or no; say 'yes, because' or 'no, but'. 'No, I haven't been to Norway, but I'd love to go and see the fjords.'

Keeping these rules in mind will help you through all kinds of talk, whether it's small talk, serious talk, or talk-with-a-purpose.

Small talk

Small talk. Chatting to workmates, strangers at parties, once-a-year relatives. Talking about the weather, beer, TV; rheumatism, Renoir or rock and roll. Discussing subjects we're not passionately involved in with people we're not deeply attached to. A waste of time?

Well, it can be, of course. But it can also be amusing, and stimulating; at the very least, it's practice. You're unlikely to be able to tackle friction between you and your loved one if you can't even open your mouth to agree how-cold-it-is-for-the-time-of-the-year. Besides, the closest relationships have to start somewhere, most usually with idle chat. You may see a stranger across a crowded room; but if you won't bring your-self to communicate, he/she is going to stay just that.

Different people, different situ-ations, call for slightly different tactics.

Workmates

You may or may not end up finding bosom pals among your workmates, but whether you do or don't you've still got to rub along with them. The hardest time, of course, is when you're new. In tea-breaks or off-moments, you'll certainly be expected to start by listening rather than pushing yourself forward. Answer ques-tions in a friendly way. Add the odd comment if you can. Don't let yourself be overawed into total silence. Think of something to ask – where the vending-machines are, how much overtime there is. The important thing is to avoid becom-ing known as That One There who never opens his/her mouth.

Unless you're a tough character who enjoys jumping in at the deep end, avoid controversial topics un-til you know your way around.

And avoid gossip. Chat about other people is human nature. But malicious gossip is unpleasant and dangerous. Remember that this kind of spiteful talk causes real harm – and that you certainly won't escape if unpleasant in-formation (or pseudo-information) is being passed around.

What if you find that you simply can't click into the kind of con-versation that your workmates hold?

First, are you positive it's their fault and not yours? You can't ex-pect people you work with, your associates by chance and not by choice, to be soulmates, but you can expect them to be ordinarily friendly. Make every effort to adapt, especially if this is your first job.

But if you've really tried and yet know you're in a situation you can't handle (a prejudiced foreman, an older supervisor who can't bear new ideas) unless there are over-whelming reasons for staying put the best course may be to get out.

One last point. Don't, through boredom or a desire to impress, impart intimate information or discuss problems which should be kept for other times and other people. You could regret a mo-ment's rash confidence for a long time.

The opposite sex

Those who've been to a co-educational school, or squabbled for years with brothers and sisters, might find it hard to believe that others less lucky can come over all trembly at the mere prospect of talking to someone around their own age of the opposite sex. But it can happen, and it often does.

If you know you risk getting

tongue-tied, remember that girls/ boys aren't Martians but human beings very like yourself (see also p. 175). They get bored, amused, apprehensive, gay, bad-tempered, in much the same way and for much the same reasons as you. When you're merely meeting and chatting, any differences or awkwardnesses between you are far more likely to be a result of different experiences or different personalities than male *v.* femaleness.

Try to establish something you have in common. Ask where he/she works/lives; what he/she likes doing, what kind of films/music/ books he/she prefers. Listen to the the answers. It's easy not to when you're feeling nervous. Don't be afraid to reveal harmless information about yourself – after all, liking ice hockey and fish and chips is hardly a state secret – but save your deepest feelings for later, if ever: this is only small talk, right?

Don't lie to impress. You'll almost certainly be caught out. Don't agree with everything he/she says even when you don't in order to flatter. You'll probably sound incredible and you'll certainly sound boring. And if he/she is given to deep meaningful silences *don't* let yourself rush on to fill the gap with rash unmeditated confidences. It's probably just bashfulness on his/ her part, but some naughty people, more experienced than you, use silence as a deliberate technique.

Don't expect to find him/her automatically fascinating, interesting or even plain tolerable. If you've tried to talk, to listen, to communicate, and it just isn't working, don't worry. He/she might be a dead bore anyway. Or simply not on your wavelength. Or bothered with problems which have nothing to do with you. It certainly does *not* mean that you're a failure.

Again, the more practice you get the easier you'll find it, and the more likely you are to be able to distinguish the real person behind the chatter. Real friendships, with same-sex or opposite-sex, mostly grow slowly; and for most of us the growth starts – and flourishes – with talk. (If you've problems getting to meet people, see pp. 173–5.)

Older people

Older people come in all sizes and varieties just like the rest of us.

If you can establish points of interest between you – ancient Britain, QPR, cycling, chess – you're well away. But if not – and this can be tricky – the safest and most interesting solution is to try to draw them on to talk about what-I-saw-when. Don't put your foot in it. Asking someone who wasn't born till 1930 what it was like in the Depression won't win you friends. (It's safest to assume that someone is actually *younger* than he/she looks.) But provided that you keep putting the right questions, all you need do is sit back and listen. Which can be fascinating: listening to what older people have seen or experienced can be time very well spent.

Avoid general discussions. Some older people enjoy arguing or debating, but many don't want any arguments at all. (Which doesn't mean to say they don't want to give you their opinions: they may; at length.) But it does mean that they don't want their ideas challenged. Whether you want to dispute them is up to you, depending on your personality, perseverance, and the subject at issue. I'm only pointing out that someone who has spent sixty years acquiring his/her set of ideas is not likely to alter them drastically as a result of a half-hour's opposition.

And never patronize older people. They've all had experiences you've never faced and cope with problems you can't yet imagine.

Parties

Plenty of people look forward to parties with more terror than anticipation. No wonder some party-givers try to help by keeping the sound-level so high it's impossible to communicate in words at all. Sooner or later, though, you're bound to have to.

Don't panic. Start from the obvious assumption that you must have something in common with everyone there – either you all know the party-giver, work for the same firm, or belong to the same society – so it shouldn't be impossible to find a starting-point. How long have you known Bob? Where were you before you came here? Did you go to the club's last outing? And take it from there.

Don't unnerve yourself with the conviction that because it's a party you *have* to scintillate. Remind yourself that the other guests are all human – more or less – that some of them will be as nervous as you, and that most of them will be happy to respond to a friendly approach. All you have to do is be able to keep your end up, help others to have a good time, and relax and enjoy yourself. Nine times out of ten, you will.

Incidentally, in Victorian days, there was an unspoken rule that in social situations you never discussed politics, sex, money, or religion. At parties it's often best to keep these prohibitions still in mind. Although it seems drastic to avoid all the most interesting topics, remember that you risk upsetting people you don't know well in somebody else's premises at somebody else's invitation. I'm not suggesting that you should pretend to agree with something you don't; simply that it's not necessary to go round deliberately lighting fuses.

And for your own sake *don't*

make personal criticisms about other people in the room: the fat girl in the hideous red brocade is bound to be the sister of the boy you're talking to.

Serious talk

Small talk is in many ways a limbering up for the grand performance; for those times when we want to get across our thoughts and feelings about subjects which seem to us to matter very much – often precisely those topics which might be out of place at a party.

These are important occasions. Times when we're working out our true relationships to other people and what we genuinely believe and care about. So when they happen it's important not to dodge the issues raised, and instead to try to make the most of them.

How to say what you think

If you feel very strongly about certain topics, and yet find it hard to express your ideas, one basic reason might be that you simply don't know enough about them. The more you find out, the more manageable discussion becomes.

This may seem obvious, but there appear to be plenty of subjects – the Pill, advertising, Andy Warhol – about which people hold strong views but know very little.

Finding out and being sure of the facts which support your opinions will make it easier for you to express them. Try not to get over-excited. Listen particularly hard to those who oppose you. They may tell you something you never knew, make you think of something that hadn't occurred to you before. At the end of a long and often exhausting discussion you may simply have to agree to disagree, but you won't have wasted your time.

Debating on this level can become an absorbing and fascinating pursuit. If you want to learn more about handling arguments and discussion, including analysis, logic, and some of the tricks experienced debaters get up to, get hold of *Straight and Crooked Thinking* by Robert H. Thouless, Pan, 1974.

How to express what you feel

Many people – especially those

brought up against a conventional English background – are extraordinarily bad at expressing emotions.

It's not simply the conventional complaint that they can't say 'I love you', they can't say either 'I'm furious', 'I'm happy', 'I'm grateful'. This inability shows itself in different ways. Some people feel their insides knotting up so they can't say anything. Or they find themselves shouting indiscriminately about quite other matters. Or they start but give up, because they feel they simply *can't* express it themselves, or because they think they'll get laughed at, or because they're frightened of getting hurt.

Yet of all the kinds of conversation, being able to express what we *feel* is probably the most important. Unexpressed unhappiness can turn into violence or despair. Unexpressed tenderness can be misunderstood or never recognized.

The first step to being able to express emotion is to understand that it's important, to aim to try, and to keep trying in spite of setbacks. It can be difficult even for much older and more experienced people. But it does become more possible as you learn to handle both your emotions and your words to express them.

Don't worry over your choice of words or you won't get started.

It's enough to state very simply what you feel. 'I'm angry.' 'I'm thrilled.' 'You make me very happy.'

Make the effort. Don't kid yourself that those around you will guess anyway from the way you look. It may work if you have a particularly expressive face and they know your every gesture, but I wouldn't rely on it. You may feel you're conveying deep despair, but the message that comes across could be that you've got a nasty temper. You can't expect people to go round guessing every time you're emoting, and if you make a habit of it they'll soon stop trying anyway.

Talk-with-a-purpose

Seeing the doctor, going for job interviews, complaining to shops, occasions like these all demand talk-for-a-purpose. To a large extent you can predict what shape the conversation will take, you can work out in advance what you want to say, and even make a guess about some of the answers. So do some homework beforehand, and you're less likely to be taken by surprise.

Doctors

You don't see your doctor for fun. You go because you feel there's something wrong with you (either physically or mentally) and most often because you have specific symptoms you want to discuss.

Don't forget your doctor is human. He/she's probably both tired and overworked and will certainly appreciate it if you state what you have come for as simply and clearly as possible. It's a good idea to write out a list of points. It's surprising how easy it can be to miss out something which later seems important.

Don't go on to diagnose yourself and then demand the latest wonder cure. You have to get your doctor's advice, so *listen* to what he/she says.

And don't forget to say 'thank you'.

Job interviews

You'll have thought before you go into the room why you want the job, why you think you'll be good at it, what you want to know about it.

It's up to the interviewer to put you at ease, tell you where to sit, and ask you the right questions. Say good morning, follow his/her lead, and answer any questions as directly as possible with any precise information which you think is relevant. Avoid vague replies. 'I think I'll be good at the job because I've already had three months' experience,' *not* 'I feel it would sort of suit me.'

Don't run on about your personal problems. There are some personal questions which may affect your potential boss – are you still living at home, can you afford to keep yourself on the wage, have you dependants – but otherwise your personal life is not or should not be his/her concern. If you launch out, uninvited, into personal sagas you risk embarrassing rather than persuading.

An efficient interviewer should ask you whether you have any queries. This is the time to ask about any details not yet covered. If the interviewer doesn't give you this opening, then wait for a suitable opportunity: don't ignore your problems – the time to raise questions is *before* you start a job, not afterwards. (But do wait until towards the end of the interview. You won't do yourself any good by rushing in and starting right away with 'How much time do I have off? What size bonus do I get?')

Suppose your potential boss hasn't done his/her homework and simply leans over the desk and says: 'Right, go ahead.' Unfair, but don't give up. Say what you've already worked out seems to be important, and don't let yourself run on and on through sheer nerves. (Working out whether your interviewer is being lazy, incompetent, or simply bloody-minded might help you discover whether this is the right job for you.)

Applying for a job should be a

two-way thing. It's important to both sides, employer and employee, that each should be satisfied with the other. The purpose of the interview is to establish this.

Keep this in mind (assuming that your interviewer is doing the same) and you can't go far wrong (see also p. 301 and on).

Complaints to shops

First, make sure you want to return something because the screws have fallen out, or the seams have been cut so thin they've pulled apart, and *not* just because you don't like it or wish you hadn't bought it. Phoney complaints ruin the pitch for everyone else.

If you're sure you've a genuine cause for complaint, go along to the shop with, if possible, a dated receipt showing when you bought the article, or, if you've lost it, a cheque showing proof of purchase. (This is not important for a shop selling its own branded goods, but it usually is for large departmental stores.)

However cross you are, start by being polite. Remember that the assistant(s) you first meet are not to blame for the goods you've bought, and have in any case no power to put things right.

As you enter the shop or department say, 'Please could I see the manager/head of your department/buyer' – depending on the size of the store – 'to complain about the gloves/toaster I bought here last week'. Most reputable shops will then produce someone in authority, to whom you can explain in detail what has gone wrong. Don't get excited unless you see it's necessary. Most shops are concerned to put things right, and will do their best. (There is no need to go through all this with Marks and Spencer: it's enough to take the offending article to any assistant on the counter concerned, who will then call a supervisor.) Faulty goods should either be replaced or your money refunded. *Don't* accept a credit note unless you're quite happy to do so – you can't thereafter change your mind and ask for the money.

Supposing all your eloquence fails to produce results? It depends partly on how tough you are and how far you're prepared to take matters. If you haven't seen the top person yet, ask to see your opponent's boss. If you are already seeing the top person, you can threaten further measures. One possibility is to find out whether there is a trade association you could write to. (Your library could help you here. And you could find it helpful at this point to send for a pamphlet called 'How to Complain . . . and How to Avoid Having to'. Write to the Information Department, British Standards Institution, 2 Park Street, London W1.) Consult your

CAB or Office of Fair Trading. Often the intervention of an outsider produces results.

If after this you're still unsuccessful, you may decide to take legal action. This is now much simpler and cheaper, and, where small sums are involved, you can handle it yourself without a lawyer. Nine out of ten such cases, threatened with legal action, are settled before the case comes to court. For what to do, see p. 348.

Two negative notes

When to say no

People who enjoy talking are often so keen on making the conversation go with a swing that they find themselves saying yes when they really meant to say no. They can't bear to disagree. If you know you often find yourself in this situation, stop now and think it over.

And next time you find yourself going along with ideas you don't hold, or agreeing to arrangements you've no intention of carrying out, stop the words on your lips.

Learn to say *no* when it's necessary.

Only two letters, but it can be one of the most vital words in your whole vocabulary.

When to shut up

If you like talking, and you're good at it, please remember that there are times when it's even more important TO SHUT UP.

However witty, interesting and informative you may feel you are, people do not necessarily want the benefit of your chat morning noon and night.

Silence is golden
especially when
someone's ill
or reading
or working
or thinking
or watching a film
or a play
or listening to music
and when you're on the point of giving away a confidence.
So know when to keep your mouth buttoned *up.*

2 TAKE A LETTER

The playwright Sheridan hated letter-writing so much that he would throw three quarters of the ones he received into the fire, and leave the rest unopened on his table for a year at a time.

Without going quite so far, few of us actually look forward to writing letters. Which can be a pity. It's often the only practicable way to keep in touch with friends. It's usually the most straightforward way to get things done. And it's certainly the only way – unlike a telephone or person-to-person conversation – to prove exactly what your orders, complaints or opinions really were.

Thinking about the letters you have to write is usually much worse than tackling them. And since most of us, unlike Sheridan, have to get down to it in the end, here are a few suggestions to help.

First things first

Take your sheet of paper and put your own address in the top right-hand corner followed by the date. This is so obvious, but every day complaints to newspapers, orders to companies, letters to friends, never get answered because the address for the reply is missing.

Even if you're writing to someone you've written to often before, he/she may have a rotten memory or thrown away the torn-off coffee label with your address scribbled on it. And another good friendship expires.

Letters to a friend

These can be the easiest of all. Imagine him/her walking through the door, and simply start writing. Don't think you have to be witty or posh, or *anything*. Write down

how you talk. And simply tell him/her of all the things that would cross your mind if he/she were there.

When you've finished all you want to say, stop. Don't feel you have-to-get-down-to-the-bottom-of-the-page. Nothing could be better guaranteed to turn your letter into a chore instead of something you might actually enjoy doing.

It's easier for most people to keep in touch with friends by sending very short notes (even postcards) at fairly frequent intervals rather than one long letter every nine months. If you write often, the small, interesting, amusing things which are in your mind at that moment seem worth passing on. But if you're only writing after a prolonged interval, all these seem too insignificant to be worth mentioning: and then since, like most of us, you've had few dramatic experiences during this time – you haven't been given the Pulitzer, or solved a murder, or even been offered promotion – you're left with nothing you feel is worth saying.

Unless you know you're one of nature's epic-letter-writers, little and often is the safest way to keep your friendships from disintegrating.

Bread-and-butter letters

Yes, I know this kind of thing can

be boring. But make an effort to write a note to say thank you for an invitation, a party, a present. All you need to say is 'thank you', followed, ideally, by something which makes the recipient feel that it is you personally and not a zombie holding the pen. 'Thank you. I loved your curry/met a great girl/always wanted a box of kippers.'

There must be *something* you can say. If you're stuck, pause to reflect on two boys I once met who, at the ages of nineteen and seventeen, were sent for Christmas toy boats from a great-aunt who clearly hadn't realized how time had passed.

As they said, the thank-you letters were quite tricky that year.

Any other letters

I suppose you could loosely call most other letters (to order goods, complain, ask for information etc.) business letters; except that as soon as you use these fatal words people start to panic and think they have to write a mystic language.

This is rubbish.

Business letters can in fact be perfectly manageable. You have a purpose in view. All you have to do is to state it, as simply as possible. 'I sent you 375 tokens for your super-de-luxe pen-knife four weeks ago. It has not arrived. Please find out why not, and send

it to me. Thank you.' (Incidentally, 'thank you' at the end of a business letter can be useful. It shows you are prepared to be on friendly terms.)

The people you're writing to aren't interested in your problems or latest news, so don't include any personal details unless you think they're strictly relevant. An efficient business letter need often be no more than two or three lines long.

However brief, make sure you include all the relevant details.

If you're ordering something: size, colour, how many, the date you saw the advertisement, what form of money (postal order, cheque, giro) you're sending.

If you're making a complaint: when you bought the article, whether you have the receipt (don't send it, quote any number or date etc.), what's gone wrong, whether it's under guarantee. (Take a copy, and see p. 348.)

Applying for a job

This can be one of the most important kinds of letter you have to write. What matters is to take trouble from the very start; even if you're only sending for an application form, see your note is well composed and readable, not a scrawl on a tatty scrap of paper.

See that your writing's legible. *This is vital* (see below). If your writing's really atrocious, bribe a

Handicapped by hideous handwriting?

You may not want to learn to type, but loathe tackling letters because you know your handwriting lets you down. Maybe it's irregular, ill-formed, or even virtually illegible.

If so, it's possible to reform it, and enjoy doing so, without too much intense effort. Many people today are turning to an italic form of writing — simple, elegant and — important in today's rush — clear to read even when written at high speed. Basically, all you need to know is how to hold your pen at the right angle, shape your letters correctly and join them together in the most direct way or not at all.

Buy a pen with an italic nib (Platignum and Osmiroid both produce good inexpensive models) and a handbook. Ladybird have an excellent brief description with lots of diagrams (the *Ladybird Book of Handwriting*) and Penguin another (George Thompson, *Puffin Book of Handwriting*, 1976) which gives fuller illustrations of alternatives.

It doesn't take long to learn the principles. After that, every time you write a list or a letter you have another chance to practise.

friend to type it for you (unless, obviously, the application must be in your own handwriting) or get hold of a typewriter and type it yourself, no matter how slowly. An illegible letter won't get read.

When you're filling in a form, read it, and make sure you're actually answering the questions. If you haven't a form, and you're writing an unaccompanied application letter, you'll almost certainly have to write and rewrite it to include everything smoothly and without superfluous words.

Before you begin you'll have to be positive, of course, that you're a reasonably eligible employee (for help here, see p. 305). Once you start composing, points that you will probably want to include are:

– where you saw or heard about the job

- why you think you'll be able to do it well
- what experience you have
- how relevant your education is
- what your present job is
- why you want to leave
- when you could start
- how available you are for interviews
- what references you can offer.

Keep your letter as short as possible, without leaving out valid facts, Write a good, natural English, without either slang or clichés. If you can think of a couple of personal details that seem relevant, by all means include them – it'll cheer your reader up – but don't write a whole screed about your remarkable personality.

Check and double-check to make sure there are no spelling or grammar mistakes (see p. 256). Always be particularly careful not to misspell the name of either the managing director or his company.

Who to write your business letters to

Sometimes people put off writing business letters because they don't know exactly who to address them to. If in doubt, try to work out what sort of department might have to take action as a result of your letter (Sales Dept, Packaging Dept, Advertising Dept, Complaints Dept, Information Dept) and then address it to the Manager or Head of that Department. Or, if you're writing to a club or society, address it to the General Secretary. If you're applying for a job, you will generally know (either from an advertisement, or personal contact) who to write to – if

Try a new pen

However you choose to write, it's harder to write clearly with either a ball-point or a felt tip (unless it's really new). You may find that simply buying a good new pen can lead to noticeable improvements. Go to a local shop and try out different models. If you've never owned a proper pen before, you may be surprised what a difference this can make.

not, address your letter to the Personnel Manager (of a large firm) or the Managing Director (of a smaller one).

Once you've decided, put the title, department, address etc. at the top of your letter on the left-hand side, immediately under your own address and just before launching into the Dear Sir bit. There are two reasons for this: to help see it gets shuffled round inside the firm faster, and – more important – to make sure that your copy, when you take one, reminds you later who you've written to and where.

What about taking a copy?

It depends. If you're sending off money (especially by postal order or in stamps), or it's a particularly important letter (an application for a job, a complaint) then you should. If you're not typing, then using a sheet of carbon and writing with a biro will be effective enough. Or if you live near somewhere with a public duplicating machine (maybe a main-line station) you could take a copy with that.

How to start and end your letters

To your friends, of course, you write any old way you like. With bread-and-butter letters you probably ought to be more wary, playing safe with 'Yours', 'Yours sincerely', or – more daringly – 'Love'.

When you're tackling business letters, there is a straightforward conventional rule. If you don't know by *name* the person you're writing to, you put at the top 'Dear Sir' or 'Dear Madam', whichever seems to make more sense, and, at

---

Filling in forms

We all have to fill in forms at some time or another. Don't be put off by the often cheap paper and mucky-looking print. Most forms (not all) are easier to understand than they look at first sight. Read a section at a time. Make sure you understand it, fill in the relevant scrap of information, and only then move on to the next part. If there's anything you don't follow, ask the advice of someone who does. Either get in touch with whoever issued the form (the government department or whoever you're going to send it back to) or – safer in the case of commercial forms – your local CAB. *Don't fill in or sign anything you don't understand or agree to: this can be very important* (*see p. 340*).

Answering a formal invitation

The conventional way to answer a conventionally formal invitation is in the third pe rson.

If you get an invitation like this:

> *Mr and Mrs Louis Howgate*
> *request the pleasure of*
> ....
> *company at the marriage of their daughter*
> *Jessica Elizabeth*
> *to*
> *Mr Geoffrey Douglas White*
> *at 2.15*
> *on Saturday 4th December*
> *at St Edmund's Church*
> *Nethercote Street, Chipping Sugden*
> *and afterwards at*
> *5 Hill Street, Chipping Bower*

you don't, if you want to stay in the good books of Mr and Mrs Howgate, and therefore indirectly of their daughter Jessica Elizabeth, reply by scribbling 'Yes thanks' or 'Not (expletive deleted) likely' on a torn-off piece of paper.

Conventionally, you reply on a square of card (a correspondence card, which you can buy in packets at most stationers'), or, if you don't want to go to this trouble, on a good-quality sheet of notepaper, on which you write thus:

> *Miss Selena Bagshot*
> *thanks Mr and Mrs Howgate*
> *for their kind invitation*
> *to their daughter's wedding*
> *and is pleased/delighted/happy to accept.*
> (or: *but regrets that he/she is unable to accept*
> *owing to a previous engagement.*)

If you know Mr and Mrs Howgate and Co. well, you might like to turn the card over and elaborate on why you won't be turning up – because you'll be in Scunthorpe, or hospital, or whatever – but this is an optional extra.

You may feel this is a lot of outdated fuss, but there will probably be times when you'd rather know what is expected, even if you decide against doing it, than not know at all.

the end, 'Yours faithfully' or 'Yours truly'. If you *do* know who you're writing to, put 'Dear Mr Hoopwhistle' at the top and sign it 'Yours sincerely'.

(If I can't make a guess at whether I'm communicating with a Sir or a Madam, I simply put Dear Sales Manager or Dear Secretary or whatever.)

If it strikes you as somewhat hypocritical to declare yourself sincere (or indeed faithful) to someone whose existence is a total blank as far as you're concerned, you can simply, if rather coldly, put your name without any parting salutation. And it's generally best to steer clear of the final flourish which might occur to you: 'Your insulted but ever-hopeful customer'. It might look rather different to the eyes that scan it later than it did to you when you dashed it off.

3 LOOKING THINGS UP IN DICTIONARIES

I once saw a card in our local tobacconist's which said: 'WANTED a LADY 2 KIPUR RUM KLEN' which certainly shows that you don't *have* to be able to spell or write correct English. All the same, it can be important – especially, for example, when you're applying for a job; and in any case, knowing you can handle the language you're using helps, at the very least, to give you confidence.

So if you sometimes find yourself not using words because you don't know how to spell them, or hesitating over the right choice of verb, invest in a dictionary. The *Concise Oxford* is perhaps the classic choice, the *Penguin English Dictionary* a particularly good modern one. *The Bad Spellers' Guide* (Wolfe Publications) is a handy pocket reference book.

If you need more help over grammar than you can get in a dictionary, you might try *A Practical English Grammar* (A. J. Thomson and A. V. Martinez, OUP, 1960) and *Improve Your English* (J. E. Metcalfe, Elliott Rightway Books, 1969).

4 STAMPS AND SO ON

Within the UK there is at present a two-tier postage for letters.

Abroad. For *Europe* letters and cards go automatically air mail at surface charges. *Outside Europe* both surface and air charges vary according to weight, distance, and whether the country your letter's going to is Commonwealth or not. Ask at your post office.

Don't forget, if you're sending letters outside Europe, that sending them surface mail *must* mean they take more time. Apparently correspondents abroad frequently complain that we insist on sending urgent letters by surface mail.

Air letter forms. This is by far the simplest way of communicating with friends outside Europe. You buy them at your post office. They're long enough for the average letter, you don't have to take them back to the post office to be weighed, and you can send them anywhere in the world. But don't put anything inside, not even a signed photo of yourself; the letter will either go surface mail after all, or your correspondent will have to pay extra.

Sae When do you need to send stamps or a stamped addressed envelope?

Not to friends and relatives, unless you're conveying a not-too-subtle hint.

Not to manufacturers unless specifically asked for, when asking for information or enclosing a coupon: their postage to you is or should be part of their advertising costs.

Always to voluntary societies, non-commercial organizations or private individuals unknown to you. Don't forget that charities like Shelter number their letters in hundreds and thousands. You can work out for yourself the high cost of postage involved.

Reply coupons. If you're writing abroad there is of course no point in sending British stamps, unless you know your correspondent is a stamp collector. He/she won't be able to use them. What you send instead is an *international reply coupon*, which you get at the post office and which your correspondent will be able to exchange for the requisite stamps.

Insurance. Parcels and packets, for both here and abroad, can be insured. You pay an extra premium, increasing as the insured rate increases. The parcels go by ordinary post, but you are insured against their loss and to some extent against damage or breakage. Details from your post office.

If all you need is *proof of posting*, you can ask for a certificate of posting when you send off your parcel. (It costs 1p.)

5 BRR-BRR...BRR-BRR... BRR-BRR...

Some people would rather write five letters than make one phone call. Telephone boxes break down at their approach. They get crossed lines, wrong numbers, lines permanently engaged. Their telephone world is full of voices which tell them sharply to speak up, cut them off in mid-sentence, leave them hanging on for ever.

However, there's no denying that there are times when telephones are extremely useful. Trying to find a room. Ringing the doctor. Making an appointment for an interview. And even telephone-haters can contrive to cope.

Number please!

Before you make a phone call you need to know the number. The *exact* number. If you're not sure, and you want a local number, look it up in the telephone directory. You'll find all surnames arranged in alphabetical order.

Identical surnames are in alphabetical order of initials. First names, even when given in full, are disregarded; only the initial(s) counts. So Roe H. B. comes before Roe Harold D. Where both surnames and initials are the same, the order is determined by the street name of the address. Blakemore, J. L., Long Lane comes before Blakemore, J. L., Tudor Drive. Entries which are only initials A. I. Co., A BC etc.) head the beginning of each letter section.

The Post Office does its best, but all the same tracking down someone with one of the more common names takes time and patience. If you can't trace your particular person, don't forget that the first

name you know him/her by may not be his/her *first* first name – I spent ages wading through pages of Williams looking for someone I'd always known as Andrew to find out later that he was in the directory as Thomas A. And remember too that there are often several ways of spelling a surname – Phillips, Philips, Philipps, Phillipps.

If you can't find the number you want, or the number is not a local number, you need to ring *Directory Inquiries*. (This service is free, whether from a public kiosk or a private phone.) In London, for London numbers, dial 142; for numbers elsewhere in the UK and Eire, dial 192. Outside London, you'll find the local Directory Inquiry number at the front of your directory.

The person who answers your inquiries is not magic. He/she will need to know the name, the initials, and especially for common surnames, the address. If the reason you haven't been able to trace the number yourself is because it's a new one, or recently changed, it helps to say so right away.

What to dial

Most exchanges and telephones in Great Britain are now automatically connected and controlled, and most calls can be made (STD) simply by dialling an all-figure number.

So: in most cases, *if you have an all-figure number*, you simply go ahead and dial this. (On non-automatic exchanges, check with the operator.) However, if you are *inside* the area indicated by the first two numbers of an all-figure number, omit these two first digits.

I know this sounds complicated. What it means is that, for example, all London exchanges begin with the two numbers 01. If you are *outside* London, and want to ring any London number, you will need to ring first the London code, 01. But if you are already *inside* the London area, you do *not* dial 01; instead you start dialling the seven-digit number which remains.

If the number you want to ring includes a *named* exchange (Eastry 4729) this is probably because it's not yet connected to the STD system. But check first with the dialling code booklet or the operator. New exchanges are being connected all the time; also many

subscribers simply don't know the number code for their own local exchange, and continue to give its name even after connection to the automatic system.

If you find the named exchange does have a code number, write this down. Then write down the rest of the number. You can easily end up with nine or ten digits, every single one of which must be absolutely correct, so don't rely on your memory unless you know you're a mathematical genius.

Save money by keeping your calls brief and choosing the cheapest possible time to phone. Mornings before 1 pm are dearest of all. Cheapest times are 6 pm to 8 am weekdays, all day Saturday and Sunday.

Significant sounds

The *dialling tone* is the medium-pitched buzz you hear when you pick up almost any telephone, private or public. This means that the phone is working and you can now start dialling.

When instead you find *silence* the phone is probably only temporarily disconnected. Replace the receiver and try again in a few seconds. If, after trying repeatedly, you still get no response, the phone is out of order. Report it from another (working) phone.

Ringing tone. Brr-brr pause brr-brr pause brr-brr pause. The number you want is now ringing. If

---

Whenever you telephone:
- *make sure you know the number*
- *dial the numbers evenly and not too fast*
- *don't pause between numbers*
- *wait long enough for the connections to be made*
- *don't shout* and
- *don't whisper*.

---

there is no reply and the number is still ringing after thirty seconds or so, either there is no one there or no one who wants to answer. Ring off and try later.

(However: when you're ringing a very busy number, and you finally get a ringing tone after a series of engaged tones, you might do better to hang on and let it ring. Your call is now in the queue. Don't put the receiver down, or you may never get so far again.)

A high-pitched buzz means that the number is unobtainable.

Engaged signal. Brr pause brr pause brr pause. Someone else is connected to the number you want. Replace the receiver and try again in a minute. If the number you want is constantly engaged or there's no answer and you think there should be, there may be a fault on the line. Check with the operator.

Peep-peep-peep-peep. When you're ringing from a new (grey) call-box, this series of rapid pips means that someone has picked up the receiver at the number you're ringing and is ready to speak.

Two people talking (when you pick up the phone, or immediately after dialling a number) means you're on a crossed line. Either listen in fascination, or put back receiver and report to the operator. (You're charged otherwise.)

Personal calls

If you can make an STD call, it's usually cheaper to ring through and find out quickly whether or not the person you want to speak to is available. If you can't, or it may take some time to trace the individual you want, you can make a personal call by contacting the operator and asking to be connected directly with the person you name. This service costs extra, but you're only charged for the call from the moment the person starts talking, and not at all if he/she is unavailable.

Transferred charges

If you're moneyless, you can ring the operator and ask to make a transferred charge call. The operator contacts your number and asks if the subscriber will accept it (which costs extra on top of the normal rate) and, if so, tells you to go ahead.

ALL EMERGENCY CALLS
ARE FREE
PICK UP THE PHONE
AND DIAL 999

or as shown in the dial label.

See also p. 262.

Other phone services

You can also use your phone to:
  hear the weather forecast
  find out the time
  listen to the latest pop
  hear the stock market report
  write out today's recipe
  enjoy a bedtime story
  learn the test-match score
  and acquire much other useful information.
  Consult your dialling code booklet.

Telegrams

You can send a telegram from any phone (or from a post office on a special form). Dial the appropriate code (which you find opposite Telegrams in the front of your directory) and dictate your message. If you're ringing from a private phone the charge goes on the bill, if from a coin box you'll be told how much money to put in.

Greetings telegrams, on a special form, cost extra and can be dictated in advance for delivery on a particular day.

When to ring and what to say

Whenever you telephone, remember that whoever you're trying to ring is, almost certainly, not sitting there waiting for your call, but busy with his/her own affairs. He/she may be delighted to hear from you, but at the precise moment the phone rings you are interrupting. Aim to make your call at an un-awkward time.

If the one you're calling sounds fussed when you get through, ask if the time's convenient, and if not say you'll ring back later. (This is particularly important with people you don't know well.) If you forget to ask, and they tell you they're busy, don't go off in a huff, and don't assume (unless it keeps happening) that you're unwelcome.

Some people like chatting on phones. Some don't

If you do, make sure the other person does too. If you don't, let this be generally known to anyone who's likely to ring you up, then when you announce after two minutes' chat 'I'm sorry, I've got to go,' your abrupt departure won't be taken personally.

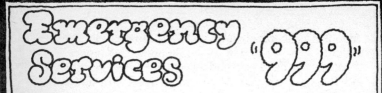

999 is the phone number to dial for emergency services almost through the whole of the UK. If there is any local difference, you'll find it marked clearly on the dial of the telephone you're using. You need no money: 999 calls are free.

When you dial 999 you come through to a central switch-board. The operator will ask you what service you need and will put you through. When Fire, Police or Ambulance answer, give the number you're ringing from, details of what help's needed and where it's needed. Try to keep calm and speak clearly. Time will be wasted if your message is only half understood or you ring off before you've given all the necessary information (this happens).

Emergency services are for emergencies only
This means using them only when you need help then and there, can't wait to get it through a slower more routine way, or you can't deal with a situation yourself.

In practice, what this means, for example, is that you dial 999 for the police when you see lights going on in a house you know is unoccupied, not when you've lost your dog. You dial the Fire Service when you want them to put out a fire, not rescue a cat from a tree. You ring for an Ambulance when there's been a road accident, not when someone's broken an arm but is capable of making it to the casualty department unaided.

At the same time, the police ask you to dial 999 whenever you spot something suspicious (even if your call turns out to be unnecessary) rather than ignore it; the fire service want you to call them before a small fire turns into a large one (see also p. 51). What emergency services don't want is trivial or frivolous calls which may take help away from those who need it.

When you need help and advice, but less urgently, there are other people you can call on. Fill in your own useful phone numbers here.

Your local police: phone no ....
Your doctor: phone no ....
Your nearest hospital: phone no. ....
Others: ....
....
....

When you're trying a private number, but no one you know personally – in answer to an advertisement, say – don't phone either too early (before 9 am) or too late (after 10 pm).

If you're ringing a shop or a firm, a good time seems to be about 10.15; after the staff are in and settled down and before the rush of work accelerates. Bad times are lunch-hours and the last half-hour of the day.

Doctors' surgeries often have fixed times for callers. Find out and remember the times your doctor prefers, and stick to them unless there's a real emergency.

When you ring up a non-private person – a station, an office, a store – remember that you come first to a main switchboard. It's no good plunging straight in on your problem, you need to be put through to the person who's going to deal with it.

If you know the extension number, ask for it.

If you don't, ask for the likely department.

If you can't work this out beforehand, explain to the switchboard telephonist as briefly and clearly as possible: 'I'd like to speak please to whoever deals with towing away abandoned cars.'

If you ask to speak to a specific person, you may be put through initially to his/her secretary. Unless it's a private and personal matter, be prepared to explain what you want to speak to the boss about.

When you're through to the right extension on a non-personal call, start with 'good morning' or whatever, say who you are or on whose behalf you're speaking, and then state what you're ringing about as simply as possible. Wait for the response, and make sure you're listening. If you think you're likely to get flustered, write down in advance a check list of points. Note the answers – writing them down, if necessary. When you're sure you've finished, say 'Thank you. Good-bye.' And ring off.

If your phone call involved any important issue – booking a hotel room, agreeing to pay the expenses of a repair – send a letter (with a copy) confirming your conversation (see p. 254).

Taking a phone call.
When your phone rings,
don't just say hello,
give your number.
Keep pencil and paper
by the phone.
Always write down
straight away anything
important (phone nos.,
addresses, dates, names,
times).

Need your own phone?

You may not be in a position to choose whether or not to have a telephone of your own: either your flat, or room, or hostel, has a phone available or it hasn't, and whether it has or hasn't probably won't affect you vitally either way.

But if for some reason you feel it could be important to have your own phone – because your work or your health demands it, or you think your social life will suffer if you haven't – don't forget to note these points.

1 Telephone rental (at present £39 per year) is payable quarterly in advance.

2 Calls are cheaper than from a coin-box, but since you don't pay for them at the time, only every three months with the quarterly bill, it's fatally easy to ignore how they mount up. The more calls you make, the longer you speak, the higher your bill. It's quite possible, even without long-distance calls, to be faced with a bill (including rental) of £15–20. Can you cope with this kind of demand? Putting a box near the phone to pay into day by day works with some people, but not with others. Would it with you? (You can get a meter from the PO to show you – and others – how much you're spending; but it costs £5 to install and £6 yearly to run.)

3 If a phone is in your name you are responsible for all calls made from it, whether or not you authorised them. Irresponsible acquaintances can make this a nightmare.

4 You may become the recipient of annoying or obscene calls. This is unlikely, but can happen. The course to take is to put the phone down immediately it becomes

clear it's not a genuine call, and if it's repeated report it both to the Post Office and to the police. (If necessary, the Post Office will arrange to have all calls intercepted.)

5 You may be rung up at inconvenient times. A friend had to leave his handsome room because his landlord got fed up with phone calls at 2 and 3 am. One solution is to leave the phone off (the Post Office don't like this) or to apply for a special plug-in phone.

If the expense and possible hazards of being responsible for your own phone make you stop and think, and yet you feel you must have one, the best idea may be to concentrate on finding a room or flat in a building which has a community coin-box telephone as part of its amenities. (Which would probably mean that this would become your first priority in home-hunting; see p. 15).

Risks ~ Elementary and Advanced

'Call no man happy until he is dead.' Most of us become increasingly aware the older we get how chancy life can be. Accidents happen, misfortunes strike, not just ourselves but our relatives and friends and our friends' friends. No one can escape all life's hazards; and if we tried to eliminate all danger beforehand we'd end up quite incapable of dealing with the slightest divergence from routine.

A certain amount of risk-taking is essential and inevitable: since our personalities vary, attitudes and the risks taken vary too. Some want the stimulus of frequent hazards: they may deliberately take chances with their lives, their work, their friendships. Others are cautious, unwilling to take an unmeasured step. Somewhere in the middle are those who cope with risks that turn up, but rarely expose themselves to others.

Only you know which category you fall into. If you suspect you're a compulsive high-risk-taker, you could end up a danger to yourself and others. It might be worth talking this over with someone experienced and sympathetic. If you have no local counselling service, write to the Youth Advisory Centre, 31 Nottingham Place, London W1. Or at least channel your risk-taking into areas which endanger fewer other people – moto-cross rather than aggressive driving and so on.* (But no risk-taking can involve yourself alone. Your actions may affect friends, relatives, involve total strangers.) If you know you're restrained and calculating, your attitude could be right for you, or perhaps unnecessarily limiting your horizons. If you're neither one nor the other you can find yourself foxed by not being able to make your mind up when to take a risk and when not.

Clearly, risks and risk-taking go on right through life. But there are areas in which young adults are particularly vulnerable, and where a miscalculated risk can have *permanent* consequences. It can be a harsh lesson to discover that some mistakes or accidents can change a person's course for life.

Here then are some of the areas in which you are most likely to meet risks with potentially serious consequences. Not surprisingly, most of them are incurred in generally otherwise pleasurable pursuits. So if what follows seems sometimes disproportionately pessimistic, remember that in the normal way (a) you're never likely to underestimate the agreeable aspects and (b) this is the side that gets most emphasis in advertisements and popular fiction. What follows is a look at a rather larger picture than is often shown.

1 ROADS ROULETTE

By far and away the biggest and most immediate risk for young people today of death or serious injury is on the road. Accident figures are regularly and monotonously quoted in the press and on TV, but I wouldn't mind betting that if you were asked out of the blue how many people on average were killed and seriously injured each year on British roads you would be many hundreds, perhaps thousands, out. Have a quick guess: and then look at these figures.

In 1975, 6,350 were killed and 77,000 were seriously injured. This means an average of *over 17 a day dead, 210 a day seriously injured*: and a disproportionately high number of these victims are in their late teens and twenties.

The casualty rate for younger car drivers (under twenty-five years old) is *over two and a half times that for older drivers.*

* *There are still too few opportunities for competitive and daring sports; see p. 206 for some suggestions; how about questioning your local council or MP?*

The highest rate for drivers and passengers of cars is in the *twenty–twenty-one group*.

The casualty rates for young motor cyclists and scooter-riders are also disproportionately high for under twenty-fives: highest of all between the ages of seventeen and nineteen.

What these dry figures mean is that statistically you run some of the highest risks of accident and injury before you reach the age of twenty-five. What's more, that *you're over twelve times as likely to end up maimed or in hospital for life as neatly and tidily dead.*

We can't unhappily prevent other people slamming into us. But we can take elementary precautions against being ourselves accidents waiting to happen.

1 *If you own a motor vehicle, make sure it's properly maintained.* This means regular servicing, not waiting until things go wrong. An added incentive is to remember that regular servicing works out cheaper than being taken to court, being ordered to put right deficiencies you'd been hoping to ignore, and having to pay a fine on top as well. If you intend to cope with this side yourself, bear in mind that it must be done correctly and thoroughly. Inefficient DIY decorating just means wallpaper falls down: inefficient ad-

justments to steering and brakes can kill. Get the manual for your model. Start by tackling only non-moving bits or parts not under stress. Go on to others only with adequate instruction from an expert. Most evening institutes run excellent classes in car and motorbike maintenance.

2 *Pay attention always to day-to-day details* (tyres, radiator, battery etc.; see p. 220). Listen to the way your vehicle behaves, and don't ignore warning signs. *Driving a car or motorbike with bare tyres or no brakes is not only illegal but lethal.*

3 *Don't drive at all* if you:

– have drunk more than the very minimal permitted amount of alcohol*

– are feeling the effects of any kind of drug or medicine. (Some medicines cause drowsiness or distort vision and hearing. Others react with even small amounts of alcohol. If you're prescribed any medicine or drug, ask about possible reactions.)

– are hungry, tired, or in a temper.

4 *Take elementary precautions.* In a car, use safety belts and adjust them properly. (Yes, I know there's the odd accident which always gets a lot of publicity where someone escaped because he/she was not wearing a belt: but this freak accident is many times out-

* *And you can never be sure what this is – see p. 284. Safest of all of course is never to drink at all before you drive.*

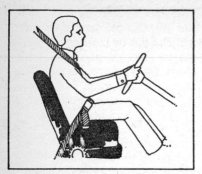

weighed by those who escape because they were. Surgeons who spend their working hours repairing victims, and experts who spend their time studying accidents, are in no doubt that wearing safety belts saves lives and looks.)

On a motorbike, make sure that your helmet fits you, and is strapped on correctly and tightly. Chincups can be dangerous unless the strap tension is properly adjusted.

Carry a first-aid kit and a fire extinguisher. Some smaller, cheaper extinguishers are unreliable or even unsafe. All extinguishers should be changed every six months. Buy yours from a reput-

able shop and take their advice, even if it means paying more.

5 *Don't expect others to drive as well as you.* No one does. Not even you. Be on the look out for potentially dangerous vehicles and situations (heavy lorries nearing steep hills, cars festooned with puppets, a caravan approaching you at the head of a traffic build-up).

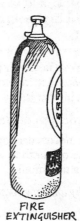

FIRE
EXTINGUISHER

6 *Increase your driving skill.* Passing the driving-test is only an indication of very elementary competence. Many accidents happen in the first few months after qualifying. Apart from gaining increasing experience as you drive, you can also go on to advanced driving courses: these vary in demands and cost, but you sometimes save money on reduced insurance later. It costs much less to have a practice session on a skid-pan. Write to the AA, Fanum House,

---

If you're a passenger

don't be driven (or ride pillion) if the driver is incapacitated (as above in 3); or is disqualified; or is accident-prone – evidence shows that a relatively small number of drivers cause and keep causing a large proportion of accidents. Don't go out without enough money on you for alternative transport, or a stout pair of shoes and a warm coat for brisk walking. In a car, remember that the front passenger seat is the most vulnerable, and use a safety-belt. On a bike, remember that it is now a legal obligation for a pillion-passenger also to wear a helmet.

Basingstoke, Hants, for particulars of advanced driving courses and skid-pans in your area.

Cut out common driving errors

Everyone makes driving errors at some time or another. Aim to cut yours to a minimum.

Here's why and how some accidents happen.

Why

Obviously, very many accidents are caused simply because driver(s) involved are drunk (see p. 285), ill, or otherwise incapacitated: because they're incompetent or inexperienced: because they get rattled or lose their cool. Stay sober, sane and serene, and you increase your chances of remaining in one piece. (And if you're being pressured by other drivers, make a deliberate effort not to respond to provocation.)

But still others are caused by:

– failure to respond to weather conditions
– miscalculations through night-driving
– inability to adjust speeds to roads.

Failure to respond to weather conditions. Pouring rain reduces visibility and drastically reduces

First Aid Kit

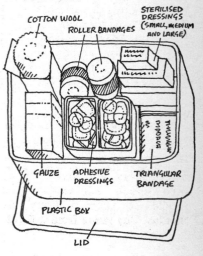

the grip of tyres on the road. A mere sprinkling of rain on a hot dry road can make it as greasy as a skid-pan. Heavy hoar frost and snow are usually visible enough to slow cars down, but black ice isn't. Fog is a killer. It damages the sense of speed and distance. Use fog-lights or dipped headlights. Notice what conditions are like and adjust to them in plenty of time.

Miscalculations through night-driving. Allow time for your eyes to adjust after leaving a brightly lit building. Slow down when moving from a built-up area to unlit roads. Light up early. Use dipped headlights on badly lit suburban roads. Drive within the limits of your headlights. If you're dazzled by carelessly undipped oncoming lights, slow down and focus on the *near side kerb or shoulder* to prevent yourself being drawn towards the road centre.

Inability to adjust speeds to roads. In Britain you can move from a narrow winding country lane to an A-road to a motorway within minutes. All require different speeds and different attitudes of mind. Don't drive along a country road assuming there'll be nothing round the next corner. There may be. Don't speed along an A-road as though it were a motorway. It isn't. And remember that motorway driving is something special again. Particular danger points

are entering and leaving motorways: *consciously* adjust your speed accordingly. Make yourself look further ahead in order to anticipate possible crises. (100–150 metres isn't too far.) Avoid bunching like the plague – if you can (see below). *Watch out in fog.* Take care in darkness and especially at twilight: you leave lighted areas for unlit too quickly for the eyes to adjust.

How

Basic driving faults

Many accidents happen because drivers make one (sometimes more) of a number of avoidable mistakes. Here is a list of often hazardous situations.

Stopping or starting without due warning.

Driving too close to the vehicle in front. You should always have enough space in front of you to be able to do an emergency stop without driving into what's in front. Theoretically, you need at least 1 m per 1·5 kph of your speed; more (up to twice as much) in bad road conditions.

Turning left without signalling. (And remember left-turning lorries will swing out first.)

Turning right without due care. Check with your mirror, give plenty of advance warning, draw out, slow down, change gear in time; resist the temptation to clip the corner.

Incorrect overtaking. Never overtake from immediately behind the vehicle in front. Pull out leaving space between the two of you (giving yourself a longer view, and a chance to get back again if you need to), check the road's clear ahead, and accelerate when still well back to give yourself the necessary speed. Overtaking is one of the most dangerous hazards. Three-lane roads are death-traps.

Failing to observe basic rules and regulations. Failure to observe the Highway Code can cause you and others trouble and pain. (If you've lost the copy you had for your driving test, get the latest version from any HMSO or W. H. Smith's.) Among dangerous manoeuvres you constantly see are:

– careless, stupid or illegal parking

– foolish reversing, especially e.g. from a minor road into a major instead of the other way round

– U-turns in congested main roads

– overtaking over double white lines, at blind corners, near hill crests.

Often risks are taken quite unknowingly. This is particularly true where road markings are ignored or misinterpreted. (For example, when the ordinary broken white line in the middle of the road lengthens to become a dashed instead of a dotted line, this indicates a hazard ahead.) When you see markings or signs you don't understand, find out what they mean – from the police, AA or RAC.

Some accidents are truly accidents, and totally unpredictable. Others are the result of a brief lapse of care or skill at the wrong time and the wrong place. Others happen when errors of two different people combine to produce a major reaction.

Better maintenance, better driving, better care, can and do reduce accidents. So take it to heart. As they say, the life you save may be your own – or your girlfriend's or boyfriend's, sister's, brother's.

You can find very useful information on driving techniques, car maintenance, accidents, first-aid for travellers etc. in the *Reader's Digest AA New Book of the Road*.

Accident

When an accident happens, what you yourself can or should do depends obviously on how serious it is, whether you're involved or not, and whether or not you or anyone else is injured. Here are steps which can or should be taken – not necessarily in this order – by you or others. Which ones in practice are possible or essential depends on the type and seriousness of the accident.

Things to do

1 Turn off the ignition.

Zebra crossings

You do not have priority on a zebra crossing until the moment that you step *off* the pavement and *on* to the crossing. It's quite clear, from the number of irate citizens you see fuming by belisha beacons, that many don't realize this basic fact.

Don't step out in front of speeding traffic. Give vehicles time to brake. Don't unnecessarily infuriate a driver by forcing a sudden stop when just behind the road is clear.

Be wary in wet weather. The damp surface of the road obscures the warning stripes, especially at dawn or twilight. Remember too that most accidents happen when pedestrians step from the shelter of one stopped vehicle straight into the path of another.

2 *Aim to prevent one accident turning into another*. Warn other traffic, especially if it's happened near a bend or corner. If any car involved is carrying a red warning triangle (compulsory in many countries abroad, but not yet here) place it 50 metres (150 metres on a motorway) behind the accident. If any car has hazard lights (flashing indicators) switch them on. Or open the car boot.

3 *Get help where necessary*. Use the nearest available telephone for a 999 call; if there is no phone, wave down a passing motorist and ask him/her to contact the emergency services. If anyone is injured, ring the ambulance service first: then the fire service, if there's a danger of fire (if there's smoke or escaping petrol visible): then the police (but see note opposite). Make sure that details of the accident and where it's happened have been clearly understood (see 999, p. 262).

4 *If necessary, apply first-aid techniques* (see p. 124). Don't attempt to do more than you know how to. Never move accident victims unless they're in danger of being run over, or if there's a risk of fire. Sometimes more harm is caused by 'help' after an accident than by the accident itself. Often all that can or should be done is to cover the victims with coats or blankets to help reduce the effects of shock until skilled assistance arrives.

5 *If you're involved*, and not too badly shocked or injured to do so, write down these particulars as soon as possible:

– registration numbers of vehicles involved

– names and addresses of drivers

(and, if the drivers don't own the vehicles, of their owners)

– names and addresses of insurance companies (and number of certificate of insurance if shown)

– details of any refusal to give the above information

– details of injuries

– description of damage to vehicles

– names and addresses of witnesses

– individual numbers of any members of the police force on scene

– details of facts leading up to accident: date, time, weather conditions, any wheel marks on the road, speeds of vehicles concerned, width and surface of road, road signs, traffic lights, lighting, anything else which seems relevant. Add a rough sketch if this seems helpful.

6 *If you're a witness*, but not involved, leave your name and address with a policeman or someone who is involved. Even if you feel you saw very little, just the bit you did see might fill in gaps to make a clearer picture. Witnesses are particularly vital in cases of private prosecutions (see below) or insurance disputes. Help if you can: don't just leave it to someone else. You might be in the position of needing a witness yourself one day.

Note. If you are the driver of a car involved in an accident which causes damage or injury to any other person, or other vehicle, or any horse, cattle, ass, mule, dog, pig, goat, sheep,* you *must* stop, give your own and the vehicle owner's name and address, and the vehicle's registration mark, to anyone with reasonable grounds for asking for them, or, if there is no one present, report the accident to the police within twenty-four hours. You must also produce your certificate of insurance either at the time of the accident or to the police within five days.

The police are not *obliged* to take any legal action when they receive the report of an accident. They may decide to prosecute for dangerous or careless driving, but they are under no *compulsion* to do so, and often take drivers to court only in cases of personal injury or major damage.

Legal help

If you are directly involved in any but the most trivial accident, you should see a solicitor. The more serious the accident, the more necessary this is. Visit your Neighbourhood Law Centre (if you have one) or contact a solicitor through your CAB (see p. 341).

If you are, or feel you are, the injured party, you may wish to

* *Should you be keen to recall this list, remember 'How Can a Motorist Drive Past Grazing Sheep'.*

Beware Bicycles!

If you have been or are a cyclist you'll know just how vulnerable you feel. If you're a driver, you'll know how thoughtlessly some cyclists can behave. If you're both, you'll know how to appreciate the other person's point of view, but if you're only one or the other it can be hard to realize how easily your own behaviour can cause an accident.

Cyclists are often not very noticeable especially in wet or grey weather. You increase your chances of being spotted by wearing light or bright coloured jackets or capes. At night it is *essential* to have working lights at both back and front. When you ride a bicycle without lights, or with weak batteries, you're taking a very real risk. This is even truer if you're dark-skinned. A black person on an unlit bicycle in a dark side-street is virtually invisible.

Certain manoeuvres are particularly dangerous on a bike, especially turning right and overtaking. Warn other traffic of your intentions, and make use of the (too few) bicycle-only lanes and the new bus-only lanes. Watch out for cars and in particular vans and lorries which have just stopped. Far too many drivers fail to see cyclists and open doors straight in their front wheels.

If you're a driver, remember that cyclists are quite as entitled to use the roads (except motorways) as you are. Don't drive so close to them you almost clip their handle-bars. Leave plenty of space between you. The bigger the vehicle you're driving, and the faster you're travelling, the more gap between you you should leave : cyclists are affected by your slipstream.

Be alert, particularly near junctions and roundabouts, for cyclists changing direction. Use your horn to give warning only with great discretion — you can blow someone off a bike as easily as pushing them. Give warning of your approach in plenty of time.

When you stop, make sure before opening your door that that you *always* check your mirror and open your door slowly and with care. This is particularly important if you have no wing mirror (get one fitted) because a cyclist overtaking your parked car will be in a blind spot to you as he/she passes your offside back wheel. A moment's carelessness here can kill. Child cyclists are particularly vulnerable.

take out a private prosecution, especially in a case where the police do not decide to prosecute. You must give notice of your intention to do this *within fourteen days after the accident*. Later is too late.

Beware of anyone grabbing you after an accident and urging you to sign a form authorizing them to prosecute on your behalf. Such people are not legally qualified, and want only to snatch a quick percentage of any damages awarded. *Sign nothing*.

2 HITCH HAZARDS

It seems a shame to have to put in a caution on hitch-hiking, when giving lifts is socially useful and often a pleasure to driver and hitch-hiker alike.

However, there can be no doubt whatever this comes under the heading of a risk, mainly but not entirely on the hitch-hiker's side. The police warn strongly against it, particularly for girls, particularly for a girl on her own. The risk of assault and attack is real, not imaginary. The police have reason to suspect that there are many cases which don't get reported: not surprisingly, the girls concerned would rather try to forget what's happened than be forced to relive it first at a police station and then perhaps in court.

Male or female, you also run risks of personal injury in the case of accidents. If this happens, and the driver's insurance is defective or nonexistent, you may get no kind of compensation.

If you must hitch-hike, go in pairs (though this is no real safeguard) and avoid like the plague cars which display no road-fund licence. (They're probably uninsured, and the driver may be disqualified as well.)

If you're the driver, you're certainly more in charge of the situation: but you too run risks, of assault and robbery and sometimes blackmail. It is also worth remembering that if you have an accident in which your passenger is injured, he/she can sue for damages.

3 SEXCAPADES

It may seem absurd to turn from road accidents and the risks of hitch-hiking to sex, but it does no harm to remember that sexual encounters can have their casualties too. Futures can be changed and sometimes damaged: two

unwanted consequences – of unplanned pregnancies and contracting some form of VD – are never far away.

Never forget that:

– *any one act of intercourse or near intercourse may result in pregnancy*

– *the majority of girls suffering from the early stages of gonorrhoea show no symptoms whatever*

For details of these and other equally important facts please turn to pp. 118 and 187.

4 IT'S A GAMBLE

You've almost certainly gambled at some time or other – bought a raffle ticket, or filled in a pools coupon, or put a bet on a horse or dog. Having the occasional flutter does no great harm: BUT

– over a period you might spend more (even far more) than you realize

– you stand a 1 in 50 chance of becoming a compulsive gambler.

The British are a nation of gamblers. Betting is one of the country's growth industries. Horse racing alone attracts bets of over £1,000 million a year. Bingo clubs, betting shops, casinos, all draw millions of people every week. So if you bet, you're betting in good company. And if you lose, you're losing in good company too.

Clearly, gambling is by no means

particularly a young person's passion. However, since the earlier you start the longer the period of time in front of you in which you just might get hooked, it's worth considering gambling as at least a potential risk.

If you bet with any regularity, you might start by keeping a check on how much you spend. Ask yourself whether you get £x-worth of pleasure and excitement, or whether you might not get a more satisfactory return if you laid it out in other ways. (And don't tell yourself you're bound to win some time. You're not.)

Choose your chances

Not all kinds of gambling are the same. When you buy a Premium Bond you lose only the potential income your money could be earning. When you buy a raffle ticket you're as likely to be doing it to help the charity as because you want to win. If you go in for bingo you're joining in 'a neigh-bourly game played for modest prizes'. If you fill in pools coupons every week, there's no chance of being cheated or manipulated – which is a possibility in e.g. private games of cards: deliberately contrived 'beginner's luck' isn't just an imaginary tale. It happens.

Keen gamblers will tell you that calculating the odds sharpens the mind and increases your chances of winning. The first part of the statement may be true, but it's doubtful if the second follows. An essential point to bear in mind is that, while bankrupt gamblers are two a penny – you may know one yourself, or someone who's heading that way – bankrupt bookies, casino owners and pools promoters aren't.

Incidentally, the number of people who fall for the 'Find the Lady' trick never ceases to astonish me. I have watched men jostle each other to throw down large bets in Oxford Street, the flea-market in Paris, in back-street Roman cafés. I have never, ever, seen anyone taking money away. (If I did I'd be pretty certain the winner was an accomplice.)

Unlucky for some

For most people gambling is no more than a way of buying a brief excitement, a short invest-ment in hopes and dreams. For some it becomes compulsive: a way of life. *Gambling can become an addiction.*

Addictive gamblers need to bet as alcoholics need to drink. They'll spend everything they possess, and more. They will lie, cheat and steal. Sex, family, friends, work, all become unimportant. Only the next bet matters.

Psychiatrists don't understand fully *why* a proportion of those who gamble become addicted, while most others don't. There seems to be no possibility of physical addiction, as there is with alcohol or drugs. People in all walks of life, all types of background, education and intelligence, are equally vulnerable. Some experts think that a big win early on sets the gambler a challenge to go on and aim to top even this. Others think that, on the contrary, the compulsive gambler is obsessively determined to lose.

Addictive gamblers are, like most addicts of any kind, among the last to recognize their own addiction. These are possible warning signs:

Has anyone mentioned that you spend too much time/money on gambling?

Have several people told you this? More than once?

Do you find yourself spending a lot of time when you appear to be doing something else actually thinking about bets you've made or that you're about to make?

Do you always or very often get a physical reaction when you lay a bet or await results? Rapid heartbeats, sweating, dizziness?

Have you ever used for gambling money which you know (or others have told you) should have been used for basic necessities: e.g. rent, food?

Have you ever 'borrowed' or been tempted to 'borrow' for betting money which was not yours but in your reach (e.g. from a till, friend's wallet, petty cash)?

Do you rarely or never quit while you're winning?

If you answer 'yes' to any one of these questions you could be heading for trouble: if you've answered 'yes' to more than one the danger is very real. If only to reassure yourself that you're not in fact an addict or potential addict, get in touch with Gamblers Anonymous, National Service Office, 17–23 Blantyre Street, Cheyne Walk, London SW10 (01–352 3060). This is the headquarters of a loosely knit organization of gamblers and ex-gamblers set up to help others suffering from the same addiction, and to give support to their families.

As with most forms of addiction, self-cure is extremely difficult. Gamblers Anonymous draws on personal experiences to give sympathetic help and long-term encouragement.

5 WHEN DRINKING GETS DICEY

Alcohol in moderation helps shy people relax and oils the grating wheels of social intercourse. Beer is thirst-quenching after heavy work, wine aids digestion, and can even be a source of iron. For many young people pubs are among the few places they can meet and entertain friends on common ground.

Many people drink and go on drinking for years without even so much as getting drunk once; some go on occasional binges; others have drinking sessions which end in abuse or violence. Most sadly of all, some drinkers develop into alcoholics.

Many doctors are more concerned about the problems presented by alcohol than by drugs, because numerically far more people are affected. Convictions for drunkenness among young people have risen and are still rising: for three main reasons. (1) Many (though certainly not most) have a disproportionately high amount of spare spending-money. (2) In proportion to incomes and other goods, spirits – the most addictive of alcoholic drinks – are cheaper now than they have been here for many years. (3) General problems over unemployment, homelessness, personal relationships, help to create conditions of stress which leave victims vulnerable to alcohol's less pleasing consequences.

What's your poison?

What you drink and the effect it has on you depends on a number of factors, perhaps the main one being its *alcoholic strength*. This is measured by its alcoholic content, expressed as a percentage. The alcoholic content of a beer can be even lower than $4\frac{1}{2}$ per cent: the alcoholic content of wine is usually from 11–17 per cent: that of spirits from 40–55 per cent. The higher the alcoholic content, the stronger the drink.

However, knowing this and appreciating what this means isn't all that simple because (a) Alcoholic contents are rarely marked on the bottle. (b) Unless you're serving the drink yourself, you're not likely to notice the information even if it is there. (c) Knowing the alcoholic content is only a beginning anyway.

So here are some general clues to give you basic information about what you're drinking and how not to get drunk on it.

Beers and stouts. Most have a comparatively low alcoholic content. While drinking only one or two glasses is fairly innocuous,

those who knock back one after another will be downing the equivalent of several whiskies.

Homemade beers, increasingly popular, are generally *very much stronger* than commercial beers.

Strong beers (winter ales, barley

wines etc.) are stronger again, and intended to be drunk in smaller quantities. Alcoholically speaking, you should think of them as wines rather than beers.

Ciders. They vary considerably in alcoholic strength, but tend to be stronger than ordinary beers while weaker than wines.

Local, often non-fizzy, draught ciders in the West Country can be much stronger than large-brewery brands. Local people are always happy to tell you tales of holiday-makers found in ditches after too much scrumpy.

Wines. They can be made from practically anything, but most commercial wines are made from grapes. Sweet wines tend to be more alcoholic than dry ones, red is supposed to produce the worst hangovers, young wines are more treacherous and can make you sicker quicker than old ones.

Home-brewed wines vary in alcoholic content, but again they can often have a higher alcoholic content than commercial wines.

Fortified wines. Sherries, ports, vermouths are wines which have a proportion of brandy added. They're stronger, drunk in smaller glasses, absorbed into the blood stream faster.

Spirits. Produced by distilling and drawing off the alcohol from previously fermented liquors. Brandy is distilled from wine, whisky from malted liquors, rum from fermented sugar-cane extract, vodka from fermented potato juice. Spirits therefore have *a very much higher content* than the undistilled liquors they are made from. In most cases in this country they are then diluted by adding a little water, soda, tonic and so on: the result is a short drink of comparatively high alcoholic content. When spirits are diluted by adding another alcoholic drink (e.g. gin and vermouth) the result is a drink slightly less alcoholic than one the same size of pure spirit, but obviously stronger than spirit + water-based fluid. Undiluted spirits are not only very strong but rapidly absorbed into the blood stream.

Warning. Distilling spirits is not only illegal but dangerous. There's only a narrow margin between producing ethyl alcohol (drinkable) and methyl alcohol (deadly). The odd case which crops up, generally abroad, of illegal distillations killing or blinding scores of people demonstrates the very real dangers involved.

How not to get sloshed

You can see from all this that spirits are stronger than wines, wines stronger than ordinary beers, and so on. What you can't tell, necessarily, is what effect any given drink at any given time will have on you. This depends partly on your physical state, partly on the way you feel, partly on how used you are to alcohol anyway.

Never forget, if you are or are about to be in a situation which demands skill, judgement, precision, common sense, that alcohol, in even very moderate amounts, blunts the sharpness of every faculty. If you need to keep your wits about you, or you want to keep in one piece, especially on the roads (see p. 284), *don't ignore this basic physiological fact.*

Be particularly on your guard too if you're new to drinking. Take things very slowly. Even one drink can have quite an effect on someone who's never tasted alcohol before. Don't let yourself be pushed or jeered into drinking more than you want. And though it may sound nasty, don't forget that you may meet people who actively want to drink you under the table. Be prepared to take defensive measures, whether by the time-honoured method of poisoning the pot-plants, or by merely saying no and meaning it.

Since there are times when it's not only disagreeable but foolish, dangerous or illegal to be under the influence, here are a few practical facts which often get overlooked.

1 *You're feeling the results of the drink you've already drunk, not the one you're drinking.* It takes time for any alcohol to be absorbed into the bloodstream and to affect the body. So whatever you feel now you'll feel more acutely soon.

2 *Learn early how much you can safely drink.* (Not safely drink to drive, or safely drink before some delicate piece of personal negotiation, but safely drink in undemanding circumstances without feeling more than mildly cheerful and before showing any more advanced symptoms such as speech-slurring, unsteadiness, etc. See p. 282.) You may find this in normal circumstances is perhaps a litre of beer, a half bottle of wine, one double whisky, or whatever. Then, if you find yourself in a booze-up, unobtrusively count your drinks as you take them. It's easy otherwise while you're talking to down them much faster than you realize.

3 *You can't necessarily tell how strong a drink is by the way it tastes.* The less experienced you are, the truer this is. Beware particularly of mixed drinks where the taste of the additive effectively conceals the base. A triple gin or vodka swamped with orange tastes to the unwary not much different from a single. Go especially easy with punches, which may be anything from glorified fruit

Half/whole seas over

Not everyone is affected by drink the same way, and not everyone gets drunk the same way. Some people can drink heavily and become virtually incapable, yet show almost no signs except to those who know them well. Others turn giggly after only a couple of drinks, but are basically little affected and rapidly sober up. Some are strong-stomached but get violent headaches, others vomit while their heads stay relatively clear.

Here is a sliding scale of the various stages someone can pass through as he/she gets progressively drunker: but drunkenness doesn't always follow this pattern or proceed neatly from one stage to the next.

Cheerfulness
Inhibitions loosened
Judgement affected
Personality intensified
Pugnacious or tearful stage
Slurred speech
Unsteady walk
Double (treble) vision
Memory loss
Blackout

The old Latin tag, *in vino veritas* (in wine truth), seems to be true: someone who's drunk reveals his or her personality heightened and carried to excess. Someone who's pessimistic becomes depressive, someone who's pugnacious becomes violent, someone who's cheerful becomes unbearably ebullient. If you don't feel like doing a psychological strip, watch out.

squashes to potent spirit/wine concoctions (and sometimes at some parties even contain industrial alcohol. Watch out, and if you have any doubts, stick to something safe). Uncommon drinks often deceive: if a drink is new proceed with caution.

4 *Don't switch from grain to grape.* That is, don't switch from beer to wine, from wine to whisky etc. Some people find the combination doesn't affect them, others find it makes them ill. If you must experiment, do it some time some place where it doesn't matter. Meanwhile, don't put brandy on top of beer, don't chase up wine with whisky.

5 *Avoid drinking on an empty or near-empty stomach.* If you're well fed beforehand, or you're drinking with a meal, or there are plenty of padding snacks around you're far less likely to get drunk or sick.

6 *Beware if you're tired or tense.* In either case alcohol can react on your head or stomach with unusual vigour.

7 *Don't mix alcohol and drugs.* Which means any kind of drugs, medically prescribed or otherwise. Even aspirin or anti-histamines, followed up too soon by a glass of beer or wine, can cause dizziness or sickness. If you're following a course of drugs of any kind, ask your doctor if they are likely to react adversely with alcohol (and check with pp. 291–300).

8 *Some people are allergic to particular alcoholic drinks* regardless of alcoholic content. Some can't take whisky, others vodka, others gin: one small diluted glass is enough to make them sick. If you discover this is true of you, steer clear of whatever makes you ill.

Alcoholic consequences

Even a little alcohol affects your judgement a little bit. This may not matter in many circumstances: it merely makes your friends seem a little wittier, life a little more bearable, the future a little more hopeful. It can matter very much if you're required to use that judgement in critical conditions.

There are certain times when alcohol, and the impairment it causes, can be catastrophic.

When you're driving

A very large percentage of road accidents are caused or affected by alcohol. You don't need to be drunk to be a danger to yourself and others. Even a relatively small amount of alcohol can cause you to miscalculate speed and distance. Naturally, the more you've

The law on alcohol and driving

It is an offence to drive or attempt to drive while unfit through drink (or drugs) : a person is considered unfit if his/her driving ability is impaired. In these circumstances no blood test is required.

It is also an offence for a person to drive or attempt to drive a vehicle if the proportion of alcohol in his/her blood exceeds 80 mg. per 100 ml. This is an offence whether or not driving ability appears to have been impaired. (Though, since random spot tests are not at present legal, the vehicle is likely to have been stopped because of careless or dangerous driving, followed by an arrest for drunken driving. However, there are occasions when a driver stopped for driving offences not necessarily affected by driving ability — e.g. exceeding the speed limit — may also be asked to take a breath test.)

It is also an offence to be under the influence of alcohol while *in charge* of a vehicle. The police may prosecute in these circumstances as long as the car keys are on the driver or in the car, even if not actually in the ignition, and will leave it to the courts to decide on the driver's intention to drive or otherwise.

The crucial figure, 80 mg. per 100 ml., describes the proportion of alcohol in the bloodstream. It is not easy to translate it in terms of drinks per person. A large person and a small one drinking identical amounts will show different levels in their different bloodstreams. The more you've drunk, the more recently you've drunk, the emptier your stomach, the lighter you weigh, the higher your blood/alcohol level. Very roughly, for someone averaging 11 stone, an 80/100 level may amount to $1\frac{1}{2}$ pints of beer or three single whiskies.

Since it takes time for the body to eliminate alcohol, someone who has drunk heavily the night before may still be over the legal level when driving to work next day.

Breath tests. If the police suspect the presence of alcohol in a driver's body, or if they suspect him/her of committing a traffic offence while driving the vehicle, or if there has been a road accident, they may require him/her to take a breath test.

Refusal to take a test without a reasonable excuse is an arrestable offence.

If this test is positive, a blood test will be required. Refusal to provide a blood specimen, again without reasonable excuse, is an offence which can carry the same penalties as being found guilty of a drink/driving offence. A driver however may substitute a urine sample. The limit here is 107 mg. per 100 ml. (The higher figure doesn't mean that the driver can safely drink more as long as he insists on a urine instead of a blood test: it's merely a different method of analysing the amount of alcohol in the body.)

Penalty. The penalty for any of the above drink/driving offences is *compulsory* endorsement and disqualification for twelve months (unless there are special mitigating grounds against the sentence being carried out). In addition, further penalties may be imposed, from a fine of £100 and/or four months' imprisonment for a first offence to an unlimited fine and two years' imprisonment for later convictions.

had, the more accident prone you get and yet, frighteningly, the more skilled you can convince yourself you are.

The British Medical Association's report on 'the relation of alcohol to road accidents' states that 'a concentration of 50 mg. of alcohol in 100 ml. of blood while driving a motor vehicle is the highest that can be accepted as entirely consistent with the safety of other road users'. This is, roughly speaking, the equivalent of 6 dl (1 pint) of beer or two small scotches.* Above this level driving ability begins to decline, and continues to decline with ever greater rapidity. The BMA goes on to say that it is 'impressed by the rapidity with which deterioration occurs at

* *See panel.*

blood levels in excess of 100 mg./ 100 ml. (approximately 1·5 litres of beer or five whiskies). *This is true even in the case of hardened drinkers and experienced drivers.'*

If you drive, don't drink, remains the ideal: but there may be occasions when this can, as a slogan, create a kind of backlash, when people who've had a couple feel they might as well be hung for a sheep as a lamb and so keep right on drinking. Don't let this happen to you. A glass or two of wine with your dinner, a glass of beer with your ploughman's lunch, is unlikely to do any harm *as long as you stop at that.*

And if you know you've drunk more than you meant to, don't take a risk, take a taxi.

In the first year after the introduction of breath and blood tests, 1,152 fewer people were killed and 11,177 fewer seriously injured. This demonstrates vividly just how destructive the combination of drink and driving can be.

When sex comes into it

Too often a night spent painting the town is followed by a long, long hangover. Be wary if someone seems bent on pouring you drink after drink – especially if it's someone who's a stranger to you. Your suspicions are very likely to be well founded. Many cases of rape, attempted rape and assault follow on top of excess alcohol. Even where there's nothing as sinister as this involved, relationships can be created and maintained which are unwanted and unfortunate. Although women tend to be the victims here, this is by no means always so. Males can finish as flies even after setting out to be spiders: this is particularly true, obviously, where homosexual contacts are involved.

Alcohol may sometimes be therapeutic when two people's attempts to form a relationship founder on their mutual inhibitions. But on the whole it's dangerous to mix alcohol with sex unless there's a genuine, long-standing, non-alcoholic relationship between you.

When you feel depressed

Traditionally, people drink their sorrows away, but this can often be the worst thing for them. Alcohol is a depressant, not a stimulant. Like other narcotics it can, in small quantities, dull the edges of pain and despair: but in bucketsful it makes the already wretched feel worse still. Better to seek help for what troubles you. For starting suggestions, see p. 129.

When you're in explosive situations

If you know you've a low flashpoint, often find yourself involved in arguments or quarrels, watch out if you drink. Look in any popular Sunday paper for evidence of quarrels with tragic endings which might never have flared up without a liberal splash of alcohol. (See also p. 342.)

When work's involved

Drink and work don't mix. This is true whether it's a labourer staggering on to a building site or an executive falling asleep over a board-room table. Too much at the wrong time can put a severe dent into your future prospects.

Warning. Alcohol also plays a part in many spontaneous and often violent crimes. Breaking and entering, car thefts, robbery with violence, are among the anti-social acts committed, often on the spur of the moment, by those who have had too much to drink and who, when sober, are frequently appalled by what they've done. 'I only did it because I'd had one over the eight' is not an adequate line of defence.

Hangovers

If you suspect or know you've had too much, drink a glass or two of water before you collapse. In the morning – if you survive that long – steer well clear of the hair-of-the-dog-that-bit-you 'cure'. Drink still more fluid (non-alcoholic). Remember that the effects won't wear fully off, for driving or other purposes, for several hours.

Alcoholic aspects

As with most other forms of addiction, no one at present really knows why some become addicted to alcohol while others, in apparently similar situations, don't. Some specialists think there may be some chemical imbalance in the blood; others that there's some psychological predisposition; or that only the unbalanced and immature are vulnerable.

Young alcoholics are still rare. Of the estimated 500,000 alcoholics in Britain, by far the greatest number have left their teens and twenties far behind. However, teenage drunkenness and teenage alcoholism (not the same thing) are rising: and since this is so it's wise to realize that alcoholism is a threat, even if for most only a remote one.

An alcoholic is someone to whom drink has become the main purpose in life. You are not an alcoholic if you have occasionally been drunk. You are not an alcoholic if you drink fairly regularly, but without increasing your intake or without wanting to increase it. Among potential danger signs are these: falling into the habit of drinking spirits regularly rather than beer or wine; increasing, and progressively increasing your alcohol intake; thinking nothing of drinking six strong drinks every twenty-four hours; beginning to lie about the number and amount of drinks taken; concealing alcohol, or carrying it around, for fear of running short.

If you feel you have any cause for worrying about your or your friends' drinking habits, you will find it helpful to get in touch either with the National Council on Alcoholism (45 Gt Peter Street, London SW1) or with Alcoholics Anonymous (11 Redcliffe Gardens, London SW10).

A particularly informative pamphlet, available for 15p post free from the NCA, is *How to Know an Alcoholic*, which explains clearly and undramatically what effects alcohol can have, the progressive stages of alcoholism, and the various methods of recognition and treatment.

6 'STINKING SMOKE'

Even in the short term, smoking is damaging. It can make you short-winded, and give you a persistent cough. It makes your breath, hair and clothes smell. (You may not be aware of it, but non-smokers certainly are. A masseuse in a Turkish bath told me that she could always tell a smoker from the 'stink of nicotine'–her words–that oozed from every pore.)

It can harm others. A certain proportion of women every year have miscarriages, stillbirths and premature babies simply because they're smokers. Moreover, there's evidence that even when babies are born apparently normal, smoking has already damaged the embryo: by the time they're seven, children born to smoking mothers are shorter, read less well, and are less well adjusted than the children of non-smoking mothers. Smoking in confined spaces not only makes the atmosphere unpleasant for non-smokers but actively triggers off in some unwilling victims bronchitic and asthmatic attacks.

It's an increasingly expensive habit. Because it costs so much it too often turns an adequate income into an inadequate one. It isn't always luxuries like foreign holidays that go up in smoke, but everyday necessities like food. If you smoke you probably, like most smokers, underestimate what you spend. Try this extremely obvious experiment (but I bet you haven't done it before – or if you started that you rapidly stopped!).

Write down here every evening the cost of any packet of cigarettes you've bought that day – it doesn't matter whether it was for you, a friend, or because you were going to a party. Keep this up for at least a fortnight. (A week isn't enough. You'd let yourself cheat. No stock-piling of fags beforehand permitted.)

1st week:	2nd week:
Monday . . .	Monday . . .
Tuesday . . .	Tuesday . . .

Wednesday . . .	Wednesday . . .
Thursday . . .	Thursday . . .
Friday . . .	Friday . . .
Saturday . . .	Saturday . . .
Sunday . . .	Sunday . . .

GRAND TOTAL COST . . .

Rather more than you'd reckoned on?

In the long term, cigarettes are dangerous. Thirteen times more smokers than non-smokers die of lung cancer. Cigarettes also cause chronic bronchitis, increase the risk of coronaries, and contribute to the onset of other unpleasant illnesses. Doctors, who have reason to know better than others just how nasty these diseases can be, smoke very much less than the rest of the population.

Since smoking is less rapidly suicidal than drug addiction, less socially dangerous than alcohol, it tends to be overlooked as a serious risk. Yet diseases closely related to cigarette smoking kill far more people every year than either alcohol or drugs: and if cigarette smoking does not diminish, by the 1980s it's been estimated that 50,000 people a year could die from lung cancer alone.

So why do people start smoking? Because their families do. Because their friends do. Because it gives them something to do with their hands. Because they have the illusion it makes them look adult. Because they feel it helps when something goes wrong. Because they feel it perks them up. Because they feel it calms them down. Because, especially in adolescence, they have no clear picture of what they may be letting themselves in for.

Yet this doesn't affect certain facts. That cigarette smoking starts by being unpleasant, can end by crippling or killing, and in the meanwhile week by week absorbs cash which might be spent on producing happier results.

The longer you smoke, the more heavily you smoke, the more potentially dangerous the habit becomes. If you smoke filter-tips, you reduce some of the hazards, but you don't remove them (and you still smell as unpleasant and spend almost as much). Pipe-smokers and cigar-smokers escape some of the risks, but again not all.

If you decide to stop smoking, you can – often much more rapidly and less painfully than you might

think. A sympathetic, informative and helpful leaflet, called *How to Stop Smoking*, helps you decide your personal reasons for smoking and the most effective plan for you to follow. Ask at the health department of your local authority, or write to the Health Education Council, Middlesex House, Ealing Road, Wembley, Middlesex.

From the moment you actually stop smoking you start to mend the damage already done. With every month that goes by, the risk of your suffering from the smoking you've already done diminishes and keeps diminishing.

All this, and you save money too!

7 ON GUARD

In spite of much publicity to the contrary, this remains by and large a peaceable country: and certainly far more so than it was in the last century. (Edwin Chadwick in the 1830s estimated that 11,000 Britons died yearly from acts of violence.) I think it's worth pointing this out if only because those who go round expecting attacks sometimes end by provoking them. Violence is still an exception; violent attacks by strangers even more so. (In most murders, murderer and victim are known or related to each other.)

Evasion is the most practical form of defence. If you want to stay out of physical trouble (most do) don't go looking for it. Steer clear, especially if you're on your own, of streets and pubs with bad reputations (though often enough their reputation's much worse than the reality). Stay away from unlit streets, especially just after closing time. If the atmosphere in a pub or party's turning sour, and you're not likely to be able to sweeten it, you don't have to wait around for it to explode. If you're a girl, don't get yourself manoeuvred into impossible situations – don't get drunk in pubs with people you've just met, don't accept lifts from them or go off walking with them on your own; don't hitch-hike (see p. 275); whenever you're on your own late at night, keep to well-lit streets and walk on the right-hand side of the road (then you can't be dogged along it by a crawling car).

If you know you have a quick temper, remember that many acts of violence are never premeditated, and that many disputes end with consequences out of all proportion to any initial provocation. Beware too of the effects of group psychology. Any group of people can experience and arouse in each other far stronger reactions than any one of them would feel without the others there. If you're often in a group, be on the alert for this phenomenon, which can lead people to behave with aggression normally quite out of character.

Avoiding potentially dangerous situations, plus a confident manner and a normal walking pace, will help to keep you clear of most attacks. For additional protection, with the bonus of a boost to the confidence, learning judo can be a help. You will not become a black belt in ten easy lessons. Judo is a sport which demands time, practice, and self-control, but even a few months' real application can make a difference. Women in particular are often naturally gifted: they're supple, and generally lack the male response to counter violence by violence. Reputable judo clubs are all affiliated to the British Judo Association, 70 Brompton Road, London SW3; write to them for local addresses.

Meanwhile, police advice, especially to a girl, is to knee or kick your attacker in the groin if possible, and to make as much noise as you can. (Probably a counsel of perfection, in these circumstances, is also to try to notice any physical characteristics or distinguishing marks – scars, warts, eye colour etc. Two or three solid facts are worth any number of vague impressions.) If the worst happens and you're outnumbered and knocked to the ground, roll into a ball to protect your stomach, face and fingers as much as you can. As a professional stuntman pointed out, the most delicate bits are all in front.

You are, I hope, extremely unlikely to need this unpleasant advice. While you can't learn self-preservation simply from reading about it, a very useful handbook is *The Book of Survival*, by Anthony Greenbank (Wolfe Publications, 1967).

8 HOW DANGEROUS DRUGS?

Many young people resent the emphasis on drug addiction as a teens-and-twenties problem. They point out that there are many times more alcoholics and barbiturate-dependents than, for example, heroin addicts, and that most of these are middle-aged. Which is true: statistically, the number of young people dependent on drugs is very low. You're far more likely to catch V D or end up as a road-accident victim.

But there is another side to the picture. Drug dependence develops much faster than alcohol or nicotine addiction. Every case is a potential source of sorrow and waste. A certain proportion of pot-smokers *do* go on to hard drugs. And the average life-expectancy of a heroin addict is two years. People take drug dependence as seriously as they do because, unreasonably perhaps, the death or personality disintegration of someone of twenty seems more tragic than a similar state of affairs in an alcoholic businessman of fifty.

Whether you yourself have ever come or will come up against drug-taking in any way depends on where you live, your kind of school, your choice of job, your background and upbringing. In many parts of the country it's quite possible that drug-taking, in any form, will never approach you more closely than reports in the papers. In other parts, though, you will meet people, or at least know people who know people, who experiment with drugs in some form or another. It can happen that it's when you're on your own for the first time, aware of your independence, with no one around, maybe, to notice or ask questions, that the possibility of taking drugs becomes less of an abstract consideration and more of a concrete opportunity.

Naturally, people don't decide for or against drug-taking solely as the result of a conscious, rational choice (see below). But since most people are not governed exclusively by emotion – luckily for the rest of us – it's important at least to know some of the facts involved: to find out what drugs are, what dependence is, and what the differences are between different kinds of drugs.

It's not possible here to go into descriptions of individual drugs in great detail. For more help and information, try *Out of your Mind?*, by Peter Newmark (Penguin Education, 1968, 50p); or *Pot or Not – a Plain Guide to Drug Dependence*, 17p post free from Family Doctor House, 47–51 Chalton Street, London NW1 1HT. The Association for the Prevention of Addiction, Long Acre, London WC2, will send on request a list of further books and pamphlets. For more detailed technical information and background, consult reports from HM Stationery Office – Government bookshops – of committees on drug dependence both here and abroad.

A note of warning: generally speaking, the most accurate information comes from those most directly involved. This is not true where drug dependence is concerned. *Never believe, without confirmation from further objective sources, what a drug-taker tells you about his/her drug.* He/she may not know him/herself. Or he/she may, quite simply, be lying.

What are drugs?

A drug is a substance which, whether swallowed, injected or inhaled, changes in some way the chemical balance of the body.

When a drug is used with medical approval (penicillin, antihistamine) it is with the intention to change the balance in the patient's favour. None the less, no drug is without its side-effects: in certain circumstances, or certain dosages, or to a minority of people, any drug can be actively dangerous. No drug is harmless, not even aspirin. (There's evidence that some – mostly older – people can and do become damagingly dependent on aspirin.)

Nicotine is a drug. So are tranquillizers. So is alcohol.

But of course the drugs which most people are concerned about are those rarely taken for medical reasons: drugs which can be unpredictable, tolerance-increasing, and dependence-producing.

What these terms mean

Unpredictable. Even a doctor, prescribing a regulation amount of a pharmaceutically accepted drug, can't be absolutely certain of the results. Drugs which are taken for non-medical reasons are infinitely less predictable. Uncertainty about the quality or strength of the drug doesn't help. (Many illegally obtained drugs are heavily adulterated. Often the additives – anything from sugar to Vim – can be as harmful as the drugs themselves.) In many cases, particularly with hallucinogens, possible reactions are almost unguessable. No two people will react the same on the same occasion. No one person necessarily reacts the same on different occasions.

Tolerance-increasing. Many drugs develop tolerance in the takers. That is, the more the taker takes the more he/she needs to go on taking to get the same effect. (Rather like sugar. If you've got a sweet tooth, you know how half a teaspoon soon doesn't taste at all; you need one, then two, then three, to get the same sweetening effect you'd once have got with a half.)

Dependence-producing. In its simplest terms, a dependence-producing drug is one which the taker becomes increasingly unable to do without. The time taken can vary from weeks to months, depending on the kind of drug, the dosage, and the taker him/herself.

No one knows for certain what causes dependence. Some specialists think it's largely a chemical reaction in the body; others, that it's a psychological predisposition. All they do know is that specific drugs are *in themselves* more dangerous than others; and that some people are more likely to become dependent than others.

They distinguish between two kinds of dependence: physical and psychological.

Physical dependence means that the taker comes to need the drug in order to feel normal. Without the drug he/she is physically ill: sick, shaking, suffering from hallucinations etc.

Psychological dependence means that the taker, deprived of the drug, does not necessarily show any signs of *physical* illness but

Drugs and crime

are often closely connected: *First,* many drugs stimulate anti-social reactions in takers (they may become aggressive, or convinced the world is plotting against them, or totally irresponsible, or ultra-jealous) which may result in violence. *Second,* unless takers are registered addicts they will be dependent for their supplies upon illegally obtained supplies, and thus risk getting caught up in a criminal network. *Third,* many drug-takers take to crime themselves (prostitution, stealing, smuggling) either to pay for black market drugs, or because the drug-taking damages or destroys their capacity for work.

suffers from, for example, acute anxiety because deprived.

It's often not easy to distinguish between the two states. The practical results can be the same. Once someone is dependent on a drug, it becomes the essential – often the only – element in the taker's life. Obtaining it becomes more important than any personal relationship, food, shelter, work or personal interests. As a doctor said, 'A drug addict loves his or her drug as a mother loves her baby.'

Different drugs, different risks

Warning. Don't forget that the Misuse of Drugs Act 1971 provides heavy penalties for possessing or dealing in most of the following list. (See p. 296.)

Cannabis (marijuana, tea, grass, hash, dope, pot)

Many forms, many varieties. Mainly smoked. A highly concentrated liquid form, producing still largely unknown but potentially dangerous results, has recently been introduced. The kinds of cannabis at present generally found in the UK are on the whole unlikely to produce dependence. (Some doctors disagree.)

Cannabis can produce feelings of pleasure, giggliness, mild intoxication. It may release the impulse to creativity by removing nervous tensions, but since it can also affect the will-power and the ability to work necessary to produce results it often produces illusions of creation rather than creation itself. (Which sounds rather grandiose, but it's rather like what happens when you dream. During the night you're convinced you're witty, brilliant and logical, but in the morning you wake up to very different feelings.)

In the short term, cannabis-taking may cause lack of concentration and apathy, and exaggerate a natural unwillingness to meet problems and deal with them. Evidence seems to be building up that, over a period, frequent and prolonged smoking leads to physical deterioration of certain brain cells, causing such effects as loss of memory and inability to make decisions. Not enough is known about possible long-term effects, but it has been suggested that cannabis-taking may cause chronic psychosis.

Cannabis is clearly not risk-free.

However, it is a fact that some people can smoke cannabis for a long period without apparently damaging themselves or others: also that some people can smoke cannabis for one or two years, give it up, and never touch another drug again.

It is equally a fact that a proportion of cannabis-takers go on to other drugs: drugs which are infinitely more unpredictable, dependence-producing and damaging.

You can't tell – no one can – into which category you might fall.

There are two fallacies, closely connected, which need clearing up.

The first is that cannabis is a kind of weaker form of other stronger drugs. This is simply not true. *Cannabis is chemically different from other drugs (which are also different from each other). Except in some of its potential effects – light-headedness, dislocation of time and place – it has nothing whatever in common with other drugs. Beer is closely related to gin because they contain the same essential ingredi-*

Drugs and sex

usually have very little to do with each other. Some drugs may increase the capacity for sexual fantasy while diminishing actual performance. Many drugs are an alternative to sex rather than an approach to it. It's true that drug-taking may lead to prostitution, but it's for the cash, not the carnality.

Drugs and the law

The Misuse of Drugs Act 1971 attempts to distinguish between the dangers of different types of drugs, and between possessing (therefore presumably using) drugs and supplying them to others.

Drugs are divided into three categories, with different penalties in each category both for possessing and supplying.

Class A includes cannabinol, cannabinol derivatives, coca leaf, cocaine, diamorphine (heroin), lysergamide, lysergide (LSD), methadone (physeptone), mescaline, morphine, opium pethidine, poppy-straw, psilocin, 2.5.Dimethoxy and 4-Dimethylphenethylamine (STP). It also includes injectable amphetamines such as ampoules of methylamphetamine (Methedrine).

Class B includes cannabis (marijuana, grass), cannabis resin (hashish, kief) and amphetamine.

Class C includes methaqualone (Mandrax).

The maximum penalty for *possession* * of a Class A drug is seven years and/or an unlimited fine: of a Class B drug, five years and/or a fine: of a Class C drug, two years and/or a fine. The maximum penalty for *supplying*,* dealing in, exporting, (importing) of a Class A drug is fourteen years and/or a fine: a Class B drug, fourteen years and/or a fine: a Class C drug, five years and/or a fine.

Some experts are critical of these categories and the implications the divisions and the relative penalties convey. For example, there is a big distinction between cannabis and amphetamines (compare the descriptions on pp. 294, 297), yet lumping them together suggests they are alike. The potential penalty for supplying cannabis is as high as for supplying

* 'Possession' is possession without being authorized – unless for example you are a registered dependent. 'Supplying' does not necessarily mean dealing: handing over a drug, free, to a friend also constitutes supplying.

heroin, which again appears to suggest a false correlation. Mandrax seems to be relatively innocent, while in fact its effects, when combined with alcohol, can be highly dangerous. Barbiturates, possibly the most frequently abused drugs (not counting tobacco and alcohol) don't appear on the list at all.

The police, in pursuit of inquiries into drug misuse, are entitled to stop and search anyone they have reasonable grounds for supposing is carrying drugs (see also p. 343). If they have reasonable grounds for believing drugs are being used or about to be used on private premises, they have considerable rights of entry, search and seizure, both with and without warrants. (These are complex: for analysis, see the NCCL factsheets on Search of Premises and Seizure of Property.) The possibilities here for police abuse of civil rights have -aroused more comment In recent months. The law here may be changed or legal rights more closely defined. For up-to-date information, contact the National Council for Civil Liberties (see p. 341), 186 King's Cross Road, London WC1.

ent, alcohol: but cannabis is not, in a parallel way, related to other drugs.

The second is that those who can take cannabis without apparent harm will also be able to take other drugs with similar immunity. This is not so.

It's important to stress this point, because after smoking cannabis some people look for, or are persuaded to take, other drugs in the conviction that nothing can go really wrong. This confidence is highly mistaken, and is likely to be proved so.

Stimulants

Amphetamines (Dexedrine, Drinamyl, Methedrine, Preludin, Benzedrine – speeds, dexies, bennies) and cocaine (coke, snow) are stimulants, the kind some people take to keep going through all-night parties. These drugs excite the nervous system, creating feelings of confidence and ability. They can cause exhaustion, sickness, hallucinations. Takers don't become physically, but may become psychologically, dependent. Tolerance increases rapidly.

Hallucinogens

LSD, Mescaline (acid). Only a pin-head amount is needed. Their effects are almost totally unpredictable: they can cause states of ecstasy or total nightmare. (These are the drugs that cause people to step out of top-floor windows, attack others, try to walk on water.)

They are very unlikely to cause physical dependence. There are three main dangers.

Physical: takers can harm themselves and others.

Mental: all these drugs can highlight any tendency to schizophrenia and lead to *permanent* personality changes which might otherwise never have taken place.

Long-term: reactions can last up to two years after taking a dose, causing takers to have 'psychotic episodes' without warning.

Opiates, narcotics

Heroin, morphine, opium, Methadone, physeptone (junk, dope, H, horse, phy) are all narcotics. They produce drowsiness, detachment, relief from anxiety.

Tolerance and physical dependence develop more rapidly than with any other drug. Dependence may start developing in as little as a fortnight. Chinese heroin, is impure and additionally dangerous. Narcotics affect embryos: the baby of a heroin addict is likely to be born an addict. Injecting narcotics can produce side-effects: infection, jaundice, gangrene leading to amputation.

Sedatives

Barbiturates (Nembutal, Seconal, Amytal, Luminal, Tuinal – barbs, reds, blues, sleepers) and non-barbiturate tranquillizers (Mandrax – Mandies) are the most frequently taken drugs in Britain. Barbiturates are not controlled under the Misuse of Drugs Act, so are more easily available. Although used mainly by the middle-aged, their use (particularly powdered and injected) is growing among young people. Barbiturates sedate and dim the faculties; large doses make takers violent. Tranquillizers taken with alcohol cause quick intoxication. One tablet taken with alcohol can produce symptoms of extreme drunkenness; several can kill.

They can cause both physical and psychological dependence, though this takes longer than with opiates. It's easy to take an unintentional overdose. Barbiturate-injecting produces unpleasant side-effects (particularly gangrenous ulcers) even more certainly than heroin-injecting.

What starts people off on drugs?

This brief analysis of some of the effects, both direct and indirect, of drug-taking, shows that not one can be guaranteed wholly harmless, and that most can have unpleasant or violent consequences, not only for takers but for those around them.

This being so, it may seem strange that anyone should expose themselves (and their friends) to these risks. Yet people do. They may start in a spirit of experiment, or because others urge them to try, or because they don't want to be odd one out. They may know few or no facts about the drugs they're offered; or they may not believe them. Sometimes they fail to appreciate – or are deliberately misinformed – *about the vital distinction between cannabis and other drugs*. Most often they are people with crises they feel they haven't the courage or capacity to meet: taking drugs becomes a substitute for facing life.

Cases for treatment

Although drug dependence most often starts as a result of taking illegally-obtained drugs, and is therefore clearly evidence of this illegal activity, it is the intention and desire of the law and the medical profession to treat the dependent as a patient and not as a criminal.

Any recognized dependent may have drugs legally prescribed. Opiates and narcotics may only be prescribed through a number of specialist clinics and units attached to hospitals. Barbiturates and amphetamines may be prescribed by GPs. It's possible to approach a clinic direct, or to be referred by a GP. In some areas social workers and priests may also advise and refer.

It is possible to work one's way free from dependence, and the clinics aim to help those of their patients who wish to do so. Often difficulties come later, when former takers come face to face with the problems they took drugs to avoid. There are some residential rehabilitation centres, but not enough. Help is also given by social workers and day counselling centres.

Attitudes and situations vary in different parts of the country. Release (01–289 1123; 01–603 8654 evenings, week-ends) have someone on tap to answer the phone twenty-four hours a day, keep up with developments throughout the country, and will do their best to give advice on all aspects of drug dependence. Their offices are at 1 Elgin Avenue, London W9.

Drug overdose

In any case where you find someone suffering from an apparent drug overdose, you need skilled help fast. Ring 999 for an ambulance, and until it arrives treat as for *poisoning* or *unconscious person* (see pp. 126 to 128), by putting in recovery position.

P.S. Someone suffering from one or more of the side-effects of drug-taking – e.g. a septic arm – can approach a doctor in the confidence that medical ethics will prevent his/her contacting the police. What further steps the doctor may take depends of course on the individual: he/she may question the taker or may choose not to probe: but the possibility of questioning should not deter someone suffering from potentially dangerous side-effects from seeking medical help. If you, or someone you know, is affected this way, don't ignore it. Again, contact Release and get advice.

Plea from police officers in an area with an above-average quota of drug dependents: 'Won't you please say *don't*. Don't experiment, don't have a go, don't try it for size, nothing. The young ones we see in here, it's enough to make you cry . . . One young girl, couldn't have been seventeen, so covered with punctures all down the side of her body, she looked as though she'd been badly burnt . . . And a young man, picking a scab off his arm because there was nowhere left to push a needle in. He was shaking so hard he couldn't do it, even the doctor we sent for had trouble . . .'

Some find work, some achieve careers, others have dead-end jobs thrust upon them.

Some find themselves in a job because they saw it advertised. Or it seemed the only one available. Or they're following some family tradition. Or their careers teacher

suggested it. People can find themselves launched on some particular type of work without quite knowing how it came about. Sometimes this arbitrary decision works out quite happily. Other times it takes months or even years to realize that they would be happier or better off in a completely different line of country.

Yet discovering the kind of work you can and want to do isn't easy. Sometimes careers advisory literature can be deceptive. Even the mere sight of a display of careers books can mislead by giving the impression that there are endless jobs and careers available – that all you have to do is pick the one you want. In fact your possibilities, as you probably already realize, are limited by various factors. Your age. Your education. Your particular talents. Your temperament. Your financial state. The number of jobs available. And, indirectly, on other people's wishes and prejudices.

None the less, it's also true that even taking all this into consideration, there are often more potential jobs available than you realize. The difficulty is finding out about them and making the right decision.

If you're already working at a job you enjoy, or training towards a career, then most of this section is not for you. But if you've no firm ideas, or you're working but don't enjoy what you're doing, then perhaps you'll find some helpful preliminary suggestions here.

1 YOUR KIND OF WORK?

No job is 100 per cent perfect. None is likely to offer you every-thing you want. Some of you will be lucky enough to have more options than others. Few of us escape having at some point to make a conscious choice – to decide on this kind of work rather than that, this job now rather than that job tomorrow. Here are some considerations which may help you when you're trying to decide what specific *type* of work would suit you.

Do you realize what it entails? If you're considering being employed as an assistant in a baker's shop it's not too hard to work out what you'll be doing – standing behind a counter, handing out bread, giving the right change, cleaning shelves and floors. But with other jobs the description is so vague it might mean anything ('special assistant') or so different from your past experience ('trainee sales rep.') that you may not have any real idea of what you'll actually be *doing*. Find out what the pattern of your day will be. Try to visualize what this means in terms of effort, stress, interest.

Where's the 'job satisfaction' in it for you? Most people would far rather enjoy their work than not. After all, they spend a good deal of their lives on it. Unfortunately, job satisfaction doesn't necessarily go hand in hand either with good pay or good prospects. Again, you may have to make a conscious choice – to decide whether to cut and plant and trim in the parks or join the nearest factory conveyor belt at twice the wage. Some of the most interesting jobs are less well paid or have little security: in others, ridiculously, you can eventually gain promotion and increased pay only by leaving the work you enjoy, and do well, for other jobs on what is loosely called the administrative side.

Don't be too influenced by what others say, unless they know you very well indeed. It's natural for them to judge from their tastes and experiences, and when amateur advisers tell you that a particular job wouldn't suit you, very often what they mean is that it wouldn't suit them. Only you really know your own temperament and capacities. Don't be misled either by false notions of status. Better by far to enjoy being an efficient decorator than become an unwilling bank clerk. (For some negative help here, see p. 306.)

Can you cope with the boring bits? All jobs have dull bits; some more than others. Different temperaments can put up with different kinds of monotony. Some people hate close figure work, but wouldn't mind loading sacks on lorries: for others the opposite would be true. Advertisements (and employers) skip over the more tedious details. Anticipating them, and working out beforehand whether you can handle them for

the sake of the rest of the job, can save everyone time and irritation.

What if it's all boring bits? Let's not gloss over the fact that many jobs not mentioned in careers guides, but done by tens of thousands, are extremely monotonous from clocking-in to clocking-out. Some tolerate this by temperament; or because of the companionship; or for the high wages (though these don't necessarily follow – plenty of exhausting and demanding factory work is badly paid); or because there seems to be nothing else available. Industry and management are only beginning to tackle this problem: sometimes by using gliding-time in factories to give workers longer periods of leisure, or by moving workers from job to job to give variety, or by totally reorganizing the basic job system. If you are contemplating, or find yourself in, this kind of totally monotonous work, then you might find it helpful to think out why you're doing it and how much you object to it. If you decide that you don't mind it all that much, or that your reasons for doing it are adequate, good: if not, there might be ways of finding a job you'd enjoy more, either by moving away, taking less money, or gaining further qualifications.

How much training, or chances of getting further education, will you get while working? In some jobs you'll know all you need to know after the first half-day. In others, you learn gradually over months and years. In some, you'll learn entirely on the job: in others, you'll attend training sessions or get the chance to attend classes through day-release in Colleges of Further Education or Technical Colleges. To have the opportunity of attaining skills and qualifications is not only satisfying in itself, it gives you the confidence that you're becoming a more useful and desirable employee. It makes sense to go out for as much training or teaching as you can get.

Is this a purely short-term job, or does it have long-term prospects?

Sometimes the answer's obvious. If you're a labourer on a temporary building-site, your job finishes when the building does, and you'll be only slightly more qualified or experienced at the end of it than you were when it started. On the other hand, if you're an apprentice in the printing-trade, you're starting on a well-marked path that leads in the end to full craft status. But there are other jobs where it's not so easy to work out whether you're going to progress in capacity or salary or responsibility. Once a typist you may stay a typist for evermore – or you may go on to be a personal secretary or an executive or head of the company; it depends partly on you but very much more on the requirements and outlook of your particular employers. If this particular side of the job interests you – and it should – try to find out what the company's policy is and what has happened in the past to other people with your kind of job.

Do you get money now or later? This is partly a corollary to the last two questions. The less the training, the dimmer the long-term prospects, the higher proportionately your pay-packet is likely to be. (Though not always – money, job satisfaction and responsibility are sometimes not closely integrated: see above.) And vice versa; the longer your training, and the longer it's going to be before you're actually producing useful work, the less profitable you are to your employers and the less money you'll earn. On the other hand, if you start by pulling in high money for unskilled or semi-skilled jobs, you must remember that you're unlikely to earn more as you get older. Indeed, as you look ahead, you can see that not only will you have increasingly less security (for younger people will be able to do your job as well or even better) but you're likely to find yourself earning proportionately less too: while ill-paid trainee jobs generally (though not always) promise steadily higher salaries in later years plus increased security.

What this means to you only you can work out. It's not easy to scrimp on a beginner's pittance while your friends are lashing out on clothes and cars: but being interested in your job, and appreciating what your training may mean in the future, can help you through the inevitable thin years. But there again, a short-term, highly paid though unskilled job could be well worth it, and not just in terms of the clobber or cassettes you could buy, but because you could use the money to see the world, to spend on further training, to set yourself up in business, or simply to give away.

What are the national *long-term prospects for this kind of job?* I know this sounds a bit highfalutin – after all, you aren't a prophet, are you – but it's only practical to try to look ahead and guess what's likely to happen in your particular field. Ask those who know. Be on the alert for references in papers. Many of us don't want to stay in the same kind of job all our lives, and most of us will end up changing course at least once; but we would all prefer to make up our own minds when we want a change rather than have it decided for us. There's surprisingly little attention paid to this particular aspect of job-choosing. Far more people train as actors than will ever find jobs, more go through art school than will ever be able to paint or design professionally. Yet in other areas there are many more jobs than there are people capable of taking them. This is particularly true in various skilled occupations: there aren't enough therapists, watch-repairers, electrical servicers, and so on. Naturally, not everyone wants or is capable of, for example, tuning pianos; but if you have more than one possibility it makes sense to choose a job in an undercrowded rather than overcrowded field. The job market is changing all the time: keep this particular side in mind when you have the opportunity of asking advice.

What about side-effects?

Does the particular work you're considering tie you to a particular area, or could you do it in another part of the country, or even abroad? Nursing qualifications equip you for a job in many parts of the world; decorating bone china commits you to a particular industry and so to particular areas. This could matter if you want to travel, or if you prefer not to be too much committed to one particular trade or district.

Could you leave your work for a period, and then return to it later? This is a point which could matter very much, especially if you're female. There are jobs which are relatively easy to pick up again after a lapse of childbearing years, like teaching, and jobs which aren't, like industrial management.

How far are you interested in benefits attached to various types of work? Sometimes banks offer employees preferential interest rates for mortgages; shops give theirs discounts on goods; travel agencies offer facilities for cheap travel; some firms finance language courses, and so on. There is little point in choosing a job simply for its side-benefits while disliking the job itself; it would be daft, for example, to choose teaching because of the number of weeks in the year when you can escape from it; but if

you're hesitating between two different fields it's reasonable to pick the one which seems to offer most all round.

When it comes down to specific jobs, *are there other, smaller, perks* which might affect you? Sports facilities, social clubs, pleasant surroundings, help with transport, and so on?

It's worth spending time and thought working out your attitudes to these questions, because the answers you give can influence important decisions. If you're fortunate enough to speak to a good Careers Adviser (see below) he or she is likely to cover much of the same ground, but if you're not lucky enough to be able to contact some fully qualified person, or there's too little time available, some of this important background thinking may get left out. None of these questions has right or wrong answers; only right, or less right, answers for you personally.

2 CAREERS CONSULTANTS

Now comes the tricky bit – matching up what you'd like to do, could do, feel qualified to do, with what other people expect you to do.

This is where you need help, preferably individual help; and help is available.

If you're still at school or college there should be either a Careers

Negative notions

If you're still at the stage where you've no idea what you're going to do; or you thought you knew but you're not too happy about it; or you've got a job and you don't like it; then here's an idea which you might find helpful. Take a piece of paper and make three columns thus:

and in the appropriate columns fill in these statements.

	In my job I would		
	positively like	not mind	positively dislike
Working as part of a team	☐	☐	☐
Working on my own	☐	☐	☐
Sitting down for long periods	☐	☐	☐
Standing for long periods	☐	☐	☐
Doing demanding physical work	☐	☐	☐
Doing demanding mental work	☐	☐	☐
Working alone and unsupervised	☐	☐	☐
Working out of doors	☐	☐	☐
Working indoors	☐	☐	☐
Getting dirty	☐	☐	☐
Working in a noisy atmosphere	☐	☐	☐
Working in a polluted atmosphere	☐	☐	☐
Doing shift work	☐	☐	☐
Doing night work	☐	☐	☐
Meeting new people	☐	☐	☐
Using the phone	☐	☐	☐
Using my hands	☐	☐	☐
Tackling figure-work	☐	☐	☐
Doing repetitive work	☐	☐	☐
Learning new things	☐	☐	☐
Talking	☐	☐	☐
Shutting up	☐	☐	☐

Working regular hours	☐	☐	☐
Working irregular hours	☐	☐	☐
Working unusually long hours	☐	☐	☐
Staying in one place	☐	☐	☐

Fitting these into the right holes should start you thinking of other points of your own to include. Think of jobs you've wanted to do, or mentally turned down, and work out what particular aspect attracted or repelled you.

When you've finished, look at your list. Often what you *don't* like can be revealing. We're often more negative than positive – we've learnt the hard way what we don't like, even if we're not too sure about what we do. And although all jobs are bound to include a proportion of elements we don't take to, at least understanding your likings and dislikings will help you avoid a job which turns out, in practice, to include a high proportion of just those aspects you least enjoy.

Positive thinking

What do you like doing? What can you do?

Start another list, probably much shorter this time, with, on the left, what you feel you can do, and, on the right, the evidence for claiming this accomplishment.

This might include, in list A, items as various as 'ironing' or 'playing the violin' or 'driving' and, on the right, notes such as 'six years' practical experience', 'LRAM Grade VII' or 'full driving licence for two years – no endorsements'. Put down all the things you can think of, within reason; sometimes seemingly unimportant accomplishments can point the way to future jobs.

Ambitious – or realistic?

Try to combine idealism and objectivity: not easy.

Some aim impossibly high; often girls in particular aim too low. Avoid this. You're doing yourself out of a worthwhile job. Never catch yourself thinking, well, who needs a job like that anyway? I'll be married in no time. Who knows? You might not marry. You might leave your husband. He might leave you. You could be left a widow before you're thirty. In any case, you'll still be a young woman, by today's standards, when your children are grown and gone. (And even before then, are you sure you're going to be satisfied to earn your keep by concentrating purely on domestic chores?) More jobs are open to you than you think.

Advisory Service or at least a Careers Officer to consult. Take advantage of this. Like everything else, services and specialists vary from place to place and individual to individual, but much of it is shrewd, experienced and intuitive. Even where time and money are short and advisers are rushed, you can at least discover basic facts like essential qualifications, training period, starting salary, and so on.

You'll get more out of your interviews if you've put in some initial research. Most school, and many college and public, libraries have a good selection of careers booklets and leaflets of all kinds: see especially those put out by the Central Youth Employment Executive and by the publishers CRAC. (Check the publication date – usually on the back cover – to make sure the information's still correct.) HMSO put out some

---

Equal pay should become a fact. *A Guide to the Equal Pay Act 1970*, from employment offices, gives detailed general advice. There's also a brief leaflet called *Equal Pay for Women and what you should know about it*.

For other problems over discrimination in employment, see pp. 348–50.

excellent booklets in a series called *Choice of Careers*, which you can order through a bookseller or newsagent, find at a local Employment Office, or buy at any HMSO bookshop (address in your telephone directory). There are many helpful books available, some in paperback: your local library will probably have several in stock. Ruth Miller's *Careers for Girls* (Penguin, 1970) is particularly clear and informative: so also are *Careers for Girls* by Gavin Brown, and its companion *The Careers Handbook for Boys* (Pan Books). *Which Career?* by Catherine Avent (Robert Hale, 1970) is somewhat more specialized. *Starting Work*,

by Catherine Avent and Eleanor L. Fried (Parrish, 1972) is an excellent general book on work and careers choice. Among several series aimed at describing what a job really feels like is one called *Educational Explorers*. Often specific trades or industries have booklets describing openings and requirements. Get in touch with the appropriate professional body

or trades union and find out what's available.

If you're under eighteen and still in full-time education, your local Careers Officer is ready to spend time on you and to give you much useful information. He or she will probably know more than you and your friends about local vacancies and opportunities, and can also tell you about openings in other parts of the country which might not occur to you.

If you're over eighteen, you can either consult your Careers Officer or go straight to your local Employment Officer; which you choose depends partly on you and partly on what time and facilities are available. The newest high street 'Job Centres' are welcoming and well staffed. Whether you can discuss your problems in the depth you would like depends on local circumstances. In some big cities you will find attached to them – free of charge – Occupational Guidance Centres.

Some magazines and newspapers, among them the *Sunday Times* and the *Daily Telegraph*, offer advice on careers and on specific individual career problems. There are also various commercial organizations which, for varying fees, offer vocational guidance. These usually put you through a series of (interesting) tests, followed by interview(s) with psychologists and advisers, who will sum up your results, qualifications, and disposition and suggest possible careers to consider: one of the most reputable is Educational and Career Analysts, Career House, 90 Gloucester Place, London W1. The National Advisory Centre on Careers for Women, 251 Brompton Road, London SW3, gives interest tests to teenagers and advice to women of all ages.

There also exist many less orthodox job opportunities which are often not so easy to hear about. Not just starting your own business, making your own crafts and so on. There are also openings for people working in various social and caring fields: not purely voluntarily and unpaid – rich young spinsters are less available these days – but where you can at least keep alive while helping others. A useful source of suggestions is Uncareers, 298 Pershore Road, Birmingham 5. Advertisements in, for example, *Time Out*, suggest others. A further possibility is to contact Community Service Volunteers, 237 Pentonville Road London N1. Here you have to give full-time service for four months to one year: you get expenses plus board and lodging.

3 WHAT QUALIFICA-TIONS?

Naturally, working out what you would most like to do is not much help if you turn out to be short of the necessary qualifications. (Sometimes, unfortunately, these paper qualifications have little to do with your ability to do the actual job; there is growing discussion about this particular aspect at the moment, and it could possibly be worth talking about this with someone with the experience to advise you.) Sometimes it's possible to choose instead a closely related job for which you *are* qualified: laboratory assistant instead of research scientist, for example.

Otherwise, there are various ways in which you can study in order to obtain necessary degrees or diplomas. Evening classes, Colleges of Further Education, Polytechnics, Colleges of Technology, the Open University – all are possibilities. The Open University in particular is interested in people without any formal qualifications. For full information, send for the *Guide to Applicants* to the Admissions Officer, OU, Walton Hall, Milton Keynes, MK7 6AA.

For all advice and details of various possibilities, consult your local Further Education Information Service.

If you want a complete picture of how to qualify for any imaginable job, look at *British Qualifications*, published by Rogan Page, 16 Gray's Inn Road, London WC1.

Your library will get you a copy.

4 STUDENTS' SWINDLES

You will also become aware of various commercial organizations, not connected in any way to the the national education system, and not backed by government money, which offer different courses and training schemes in return for (often substantial) fees. Many of these, especially, for example, correspondence courses, are well and legitimately run and offer a sound training with meaningful diplomas opening the way to future jobs.

Others are not.

Two types of organization which are particularly suspect are studios which offer to train models and businesses which promote some kind of course connected with computers. A few are genuine, selective in whom they take, giving a worthwhile training, and offering a real chance of a job at the end of it. Others cynically accept whoever comes, offer a meaningless 'course', and turn out their students at the end with a worthless piece of paper.

Don't shell out any money, or sign on for any course, without knowing what you're letting yourself in for. Ask for advice from your Careers Officer or from someone in the relevant field of work. Find out about the organization's reputation, their pro-gramme, and whether their diploma has any value at all.

With the number of unskilled jobs available decreasing all the time, it's important to make the most of any opportunities for training you can get – after all, a skilled person can always do an unskilled job, but the other way round doesn't work. It's equally important to make sure any training you do get is a valid one.

5 WHERE TO START LOOKING

So you've decided what you want to do, you've got what it takes, and you're all poised to find the right job.

There are various ways to go about it.

The most obvious, and often the most satisfactory, is to consult *an official agency*. Your local Careers Office (if you're still under eighteen) or Employment Exchange or new-styled Job Centre (if you're over) will have details of many local vacancies. Some people are still unaware that many Employment Exchanges also maintain a Professional and Executive Register. This exists to provide a meeting-place for employers and would-be employees for jobs demanding a certain standard of education, training and experience. Although so far used mainly by older people, increasingly employers are coming to look to it to fill vacancies for certain specialized or trainee jobs. If your particular Employment Exchange has no such register, they'll put you in touch with one that does.

Depending on the kind of job you're looking for, you may also find one of the many *commercial agencies* helpful. However, some are far less conscientious than others. Often the interviewers, unqualified and set to work after a half hour's 'training', know little more about jobs and possibilities than you do yourself, and are more concerned with fixing you up somewhere than fitting square pegs into square holes. Don't let yourself be pushed into taking a job you feel isn't right for you. Try to find out beforehand from those who have already used such agencies what kind of treatment they experienced.

Advertisements in papers are another excellent source. Naturally, most ads for desirable jobs will receive more than one applicant: it's not so much who answers first as who seems the most suitable which matters. So think what you've going to say before picking up the phone; plan your letter carefully. (For help, see pp. 251 and 261.) Even if you fail to get the job, the experience of applying will help you next time.

Certain ads should be looked at with some suspicion: if there's no indication what the job actually is, or of specific requirements, or of the kind of money offered. Particularly during the summer months, there are many non-jobs advertised which exist only to take money off the unfortunate applicants. If you do ring up in answer to a vaguely worded advertisement brimming over with promises but skimping on information, be very much on your guard. If the person the other end of the phone won't tell you any details of what the job is, it's not worth going along. If you are lured, refuse to pay out any money for 'samples', 'magazines', 'training brochures'. No reputable business works like this. Don't agree to buy stock unless there's a firm money-back-if-unsold guarantee (and even then, scrutinize the guarantee very carefully, small print and all). Be very wary of attempts to induce you to sell goods on commission without guaranteed pay. This may be all right if all you want is pin-money, but unlikely to come anywhere near to providing you with a living wage.

Don't forget that many jobs in specific trades or industries are advertised not in national newspapers but only in the *trade press*. So, especially if the kind of job you're looking for is off-beat, find out what the relevant magazine is called and read it regularly. (Ask your newsagent, or your librarian if he's baffled.) Advertising, grocering, dancing, farming, and so on – all have their own magazines. You can sometimes read here of opportunities for juniors or trainees which would never otherwise come to your notice.

Cards in windows, hand-scribbled notes in shops, Vacancies Available signs outside factories and stores can all do the trick. Like all kinds of advertising, cards and so on do no more than communicate: it's up to you to discover whether the job in question is up your street or not.

One not so obvious but frequently successful way of finding a job is to *go out and ask for one*. This doesn't occur to many young people, and those who do think of it are often too unsure of themselves to go ahead, but it can and does work. You have to be sure before you start that you're a reasonable candidate: wanting to be a hairdressing apprentice if you can't bear standing or a secretary if you can't type is a waste of everyone's time. But if you've worked out how and why you're qualified for a particular kind of job, then there's no harm whatever in asking if there's a vacancy available. A prospective employer can only say no.

Whether you call directly, telephone or write, depends on what you're aiming for. If it's a job in a local shop or firm, you can generally just call in. If it's a large store or business, and one which has its own personnel department (find out by ringing or asking) you can either phone or write a letter to ask for an appointment. If it's an office or studio full of hardworking people, and with no one who has a full-time responsibility for hiring employees, you will only alienate by telephoning out of the blue. Either ring and explain to the switchboard the kind of job you're looking for and ask the name of the most suitable person to write to, or write directly to the managing director.

If you want to tackle your jobhunting this way, don't merely write one letter or make one phone-call and leave it at that. Have half a dozen projects on the go at once, and don't stop. As one falls through, write to another. Otherwise it's easy to get depressed when you get turned down – and you probably will be. Most of the people you get in touch with won't actually have a vacancy there and then: but if you have a viable proposition the odds are that sooner or later something will turn up.

6 FIGHTING FAILURE

Suppose the net result of all your efforts seems to be failure? You can't get the job you want; or you can't get a job at all.

If this happens to you, and keeps happening over a period of weeks and months, then it might help to stop and take stock – preferably with the aid of someone like a Careers Officer.

(a) Are you aiming at something impossible at your present age or with your present qualifications? Be honest with yourself. It's natural to be ambitious, but sometimes ambitions lead us to overestimating ideas and talents.

(b) Is there a local shortage of vacancies in your particular line of work? If so, would there be better opportunities elsewhere? You can sometimes get financial help to move to skilled employment in another part of the country. Again, you need advice: and don't forget that it's tricky to move around without money in your pocket (see p. 11). It could be worth taking any kind of temporary job to build up your funds.

(c) Is there a national shortage of openings? You could be a first-rate actor, for example, and still unable to get work. If you are in this kind of situation, then you either have to accept it as part of

Off to work you go

Perhaps the most surprising thing about starting work is just how tiring it can be. A new job, even one which you know is well within your capabilities, often leaves you feeling whacked by the end of the day. This is caused not only by the work itself, but by the pressure of other people, adjusting to new conditions, travelling, even comparatively trivial details like finding your place of work too hot or too cold.

Normally you'll find yourself adjusting within a week or two. Meanwhile, cut down on leisure activities, and do sensible things like eating well and getting enough sleep. Avoid friction by following instructions and turning up when you're meant to. Once you're working, breaking even minor rules (especially over e.g. safety and timekeeping) may mean the sack. Don't start by trying to reorganize everyone and everything. Even if you feel you could, keep quiet until you've found your feet. (And for some ideas about getting on with your workmates, see p. 242.)

the job, or opt for another one. Give yourself a time limit (six months, two years), and stick to it. This will help to make sure you keep actively looking; and to decide whether you're looking for the right job anyway.

(d) Do you put off potential employers – by turning up late, or drunk, or unsuitably dressed (see p. 145), or arguing, or giving the impression that you're the one doing the interviewing? It's easy to foul up a couple of interviews for no mistake of yours, but if you've been turned down time after time, and you're sure you're qualified, it might just be something about the way you act.

(e) Have you begun to convey a defeatist impression? Although it's easy to do this, the result's generally fatal. Few people want to hire a loser, and if you go round with a hang-dog look, or even saying things like 'I know I'll never get this job', you predispose people against you from the start. They may be sorry for you but they're unlikely to hire you.

(f) Do you feel you're the victim of prejudice? I phrase this carefully, because the fact that you feel yourself the victim doesn't prove that you are; only that you may be. Only if you feel that none of the above reasons seem to apply to you should you begin to come to this conclusion. If you believe racial discrimination is

involved, see p. 348; if sexual discrimination, p. 350.

7 OUT OF WORK

Because you're more likely to find a job (and, hopefully, a job you'll enjoy) if you think and act positively, practically everything you've read so far looks on the bright side. But in today's rapidly changing economic climate it's unfortunately true that you can be ready and eager to work, feel that none of the remarks above applies to you, and yet find no job available at all.

What happens next depends on you, your circumstances, and where you live.

Be ready to take advice. If any possibility comes up, don't reject it out of hand because it wasn't what you wanted.

You may get the chance of being trained under a new scheme through the Training Services Agency. Your Careers Officer or Job Centre will tell you about possibilities, or write direct to the agency at 168 Regent Street, London W1R 6DE. Skillcentres are also now training people of all ages from school-leavers upwards in manual and craft skills. You get paid while training: not lavishly, but you can also claim travel and lodging allowances.

Or you could look for a living-in job (see also p. 19). You can almost always find catering and

---

You and your union

No union can effectively represent those who belong to it unless they turn up at meetings and make their views known. If/when you join, be prepared to play an active part. *Going to Work* (from the TUC, Congress House, Russell Street, London WC1) helps tell you how.

---

domestic jobs; obviously, particularly at holiday times, but also right through the year.

In many parts of the country it's possible, depending on your skills, to work on your own or with other young people. Window-cleaning, small decorating or carpentering jobs, oven-cleaning, housework. Pay – provided you can do what you say you can – compares favourably with semi-skilled work in regular employment. You may have complications over insurance stamps, even tax, but your CAB will help you here. (If your work is going to take you into other people's homes, you'll need really good references that can be checked up on. Perhaps a teacher's reference to start with: later, from satisfied clients.)

Don't reject chances of work because they pay little more than you could get through social security or unemployment benefit.* Those who have worked – in whatever capacity – are much more likely to get improved jobs than those who have never worked at all. Almost always, you'll find you learn something. And, though doing nothing and getting paid for it may in theory sound great, the reality is generally very different.

8 CHOPPING AND CHANGING

If, after a reasonable length of time – could be weeks or months, depending on your job – you feel all is not well (the work's too tedious, or exhausting, or you've learned nothing), don't sit there brooding about it. Talk it over with someone; preferably your boss or supervisor. If you can't do this, or it leaves you still unsatis-

---

* *You aren't entitled to unemployment pay until you've paid a minimum amount of National Insurance contributions. (This amount varies according to age, dates of work etc.) If you've no job, and can't get unemployment pay, you're entitled to apply for supplementary benefit. (The amount varies depending on where you're living and how old you are.) Ask at your Social Security office.*

fied, or you're convinced you've made a mistake, don't stalk out on impulse.

Sit back and think. Most important: are you in the wrong line of work, or is it that you've picked the wrong place to do it in? Are you expecting too much too soon? In many jobs it takes time before you even begin to earn your keep, and some businesses work at a certain speed – *you* may be capable of moving faster, but the place won't reorganize itself around you. Even if you're really fed up, are you sure it's the right time to cut your losses, or might you gain at least some experience and further training if you stayed on? This is particularly important if you've left another job, or worse still jobs, within an unusually short space of time. Although this matters more in some kinds of work than others, employers generally are unwilling to take on employees with records of early or frequent leaving.

There are also of course more positive reasons for leaving. To gain more experience or responsibility or independence, or to get promotion you can't hope for in your present set-up. Sometimes initial promises never materialize. For example, often girls who go into an office job as typists with the lure of more interesting work ahead find it never materializes. (I warn you, good typists are in such short supply that no boss will willingly promote you. The better you are, the truer this is.)

If you've thought it all through, and you're convinced leaving is the right step to take, then don't hang around indefinitely because of cold feet. On the other hand, in most cases it's unwise to hand in your notice before you've got another job in the bag. It may be less easy to change than you think, and it can be particularly depressing to find yourself in limbo for what feels like forever.

Work that you enjoy doing, that you feel is purposeful and useful, can be a deeply satisfying and important part of your life, even though it's tiring and at times exhausting. Work that you dislike, which you find monotonous or pointless, is destructive, even when it's undemanding and even if it's well paid. We're very far yet in this country from working out a moral philosophy, or indeed an economic basis, which takes into consideration many of the questions increasingly asked about the relative values and problems posed by dirty, arduous, responsible, time-consuming, difficult, boring, complex, demanding kinds of work. These aspects affect you whether you notice it or not, and your attitude affects not only the work you choose and do, but how you feel about the work other people carry out around you.

Good luck with whatever you choose. And remember, you probably won't be stuck in it for life: today, most people in this country are going to make several changes in direction before they finally retire.

Pence Sense

Being able to manage your money doesn't mean being obsessed by it. On the contrary. Knowing you can keep yourself (and also be in a position to help others) is liberating. Being constantly worried about money and debts, or not worrying and bumming off acquaintances, isn't. What's more, it gets less so as time goes on – and as the people willing to put up with you diminish.

If you can keep yourself reasonably well you're one less person for society to worry about: and if thereafter you have money or time to spare you can always use it to help those who, for reasons often far beyond their control, simply can't.

1 FIRST NET YOUR INCOME

How you can afford to spend and live depends primarily on how much money you have coming in. This should be obvious enough, but it isn't: partly because, to start with, £x per week sounds so much you don't bother examining the actual sum, partly because in your first flush of independent enthusiasm you concentrate more on what you're going to do than on how you're going to afford it.

So before you start thinking any further make sure you know how much money per week (or month) you can reasonably count on.

If you work, that means knowing what your pay packet is. If you're promised extras (tips, bonuses, commissions), are these just promises from your employers, or have you any objective indication that these will actually materialize?

Next: what deductions will you have? *Income tax* is no longer going to be something other people pay: unless you earn less than the taxable minimum, *you'll* be paying too. In most jobs tax is deducted at source (PAYE). If not, you'll have to be responsible for your own returns, by setting money aside each week. Have you reckoned with *National Insurance* deductions? Or any other automatic levies – for union funds, weekly office coffee contributions, or supplying your own tools and equipment?

When you've finished these basic sums you may find that your income is less than you'd expected. If it now seems to you too low for you to live off, look at p. 323 to make sure that it's not your expectations or your (inessential) expenses which are too high. If you're only a little short, you might be able to do some extra or freelance work as well (but don't underestimate the effort and energy this involves). Sometimes it's possible to transfer to a different job paying a higher wage; or to study for additional qualifications which will ultimately mean more money (see p. 310). But if you're an apprentice or trainee, then you may well have to accept a lean period encouraged by the anticipation of better times to come. (If the prospect alone is not enough, perhaps a sympathetic relative or bank manager might make you a small loan? But beware of debts; see p. 331.)

You'll probably be paid either weekly or monthly. In either case, your money has to stretch out until next pay day – not so bad if it's only a few days ahead, trickier if you have to wait for over four long weeks.

The less used you are to handling money, the harder you'll find it. Start by dividing it into fixed amounts, weekly or daily depending on your personality and way of living, and stick to these sums. Don't draw cash ahead of time unless you're experienced, you know what you're doing, or it's an emergency. Get into a money muddle early on, and you'll find it hard to pull your way out of it.

If you're a student, you're likely to be dependent on a grant supplemented by, possibly, vacation earnings. Grants are fixed, and there's little flexibility: however, you may find extra sums for certain courses and in certain circumstances – for buying special equipment, for example, or for helping to pay for essential travel. Sometimes you may receive extra payments during vacations, especially if you're entirely self-supporting. If you're in difficulties, or you think you could be entitled to certain extras, inquire at your local education authority.

In addition, there's a whole range of extra grants or scholarships, from £10 to hundreds of pounds, which often go unclaimed because they're not sufficiently widely known. These include industrial sponsorship schemes, various charities, regional endowments. Consult *Grants for Higher Education* by Judith Booth for ACE (Barrie & Jenkins, 1973, £1.75).

During term-time you'd be wisest not to consider any kind of extra work unless you're fortunate enough to find a part-time job which ties in with your main work (e.g. coaching foreign students if you're reading languages). The amount of money you could earn is unlikely to compensate for the time and energy taken from your work and from your whole life as a student.

(You can hope to recoup somewhat by working during the vacation: though here again you have to weigh up earnings, hours, the demands of your own studies, and also maybe the desire to do unpaid but socially valuable volunteer work. See also p. 233 for suggestions.)

You're unlikely to have to pay *income tax*, except possibly while doing vacation jobs; but even then you'll probably remain beneath the earnings limit and so won't be liable. (Apply to your employer's local Inspector of Taxes for a form (P.38 S) authorizing you to work without having PAYE deductions made.) If you have any tax problems, your local Inspector of Taxes will be ready to advise you, or ask the NUS for 'Students and income tax' (17p incl. post) from NUS, Cromwell House, Fulwood Place, London WC1.

You're not obliged to pay *National Insurance* while you're a student, *except* when you're employed, in which case your employer will make the appropriate deductions (but see p. 322).

Most grants are paid *termly*, though a few are paid *yearly*. With so much lovely lolly arriving all at once, there's a natural temptation to live for the moment. Financially, you must reject this. It's hard to budget for long stretches at a time, but failing means bleak days and sleepless nights before the next lump arrives. You'll need to be even more scrupulous than your fellow workers on weekly or monthly pay packets to split your money up into regular amounts, and to use only what you're entitled to in any given time. Unless you're really skilled at handling money you'll almost certainly need, at least to start with, to draw up an actual budget and *to stick to it* (see p. 323).

Organize your outgoings

Working out how much money you have coming in is just about the simplest part of money management. After that the going gets tricky. The reason is that, as with other areas of life, choices have to be made: by you.

The lower your income, the more inescapable expenses you have, the fewer, obviously, your chances to choose. If you're a student on the minimum grant, living in hall, paying predetermined tutorial and college fees, you won't have much leeway. But even on this scale there are still decisions to be made: and the more you have, the fewer cut-and-dried costs, the more complex your money-handling's going to be.

National Insurance

The National Insurance scheme covers you in case of pregnancy, unemployment, illness and (much later) retirement. What benefits *you* are entitled to depend to a large extent on how many contributions you (or occasionally your spouse) have made in a certain period. Too many missed weeks could affect your right to benefit.

When you *work for an employer* it is his/her responsibility to make the appropriate insurance deductions: both of you contribute towards the cost.

If you're *self-employed* you're legally obliged to keep your contributions up. There may be complications: inquire at your Social Security office.

If you're a *student* you may or may not contribute: if you don't you run certain risks. Up to the age of eighteen, as long as you're in full-time education you get free credits for national insurance. After that you don't. Paying or not is left up to you. However, if you decide *not* to pay, you leave a gap in your contribution record which has certain consequences later: for example, you (if you're female) or your wife (if you're male) might lose out on future maternity benefit.

If you have options over whether or how much to pay, don't decide without knowing what's involved. Get advice at your local Social Security office.

Once a year you will get a statement showing how much your contributions have been during that year. Take the trouble to look at it, especially if you've worked for more than one employer. If your insurance contributions seem lower than you'd expected, it's worth checking up with Social Security that no mistake has been made.

Unless you've come into a fortune or you're set on an unusually ascetic life, you're very unlikely to be able to afford all you want to have or do. You'll have to choose between different wishes. Do you want a car and a tiny bedsitter, or a bike and a flat with space to move? Do you want to wear up-to-date clothes at home, or to travel in jeans? Do you want books, or drink? Have your hair set, or go to the theatre?

Of course, you won't want or be able to plan your life and its costs minute by minute and penny by penny, but as long as you bear in mind that you'll have to be selective at some point you'll avoid finding yourself in a situation where overspent poverty leaves you with no choices at all.

2 BEAT THE BUDGET

Budgeting, as someone remarked, is a way of worrying about money before you spend it as well as afterwards. However, if you're new to juggling financial responsibilities it's not easy to do without some kind of forward planning.

How you do this depends partly on experience and partly on temperament. If you're already managing successfully on your own, ending up most weeks solvent and with enough in hand for the odd whip-round, then most of what follows will seem pretty obvious. If you're just settling into your first bedsitter, hostel or college room, skip the next section and go straight to p. 324. But if you're already living on your own, trying, but lamentably failing, to make ends meet (someone keeps moving them) this is what you need to do.

How does your money go?

For at least a week or a month – depending on when you get paid – keep a complete list of *all* your spending for that period. Carry a notebook and pencil around with you, so you can jot down as soon as possible every single item.

At the end of this time, take a critical look at your sums, and work out where and how you spent most. If necessary, split the various items under different headings (rent; heating; cigarettes; food etc.) to help clear your mind.

You may see straightaway that comparatively minor economies will make all the difference between just managing and just not managing. Walking one fare stage. Going one week longer between haircuts. Doing without sweets. Or cigarettes (see p. 288). But you may need more than pruning: what's called for is a *total* rethink. What form this takes is entirely up to you. Could you find somewhere cheaper to live? Or do without a car? Or stop eating out? Or make your own clothes? If you're really hard up it's necessary to concentrate on essentials; *your* essentials, which are not necessarily the same as anyone else's. Once you have these fixed you can start to see how much, if any, scope you have for playing around with the rest.

Your perfect plan

In general, the poorer you are, the more important it usually is to arrive at a workable spending plan and stick to it.

Again, everybody's ideal budget differs. If you're starting from scratch, the one you work out may later turn out unrealistic, but at least you'll have thought through what you want to see happening. If you've tried before but failed, as all too clearly demonstrated by your Spending Analysis Programme (see above), then at least you'll appreciate some of the practical details involved.

Start with the *essentials*. Rent. Fares. Perhaps fees. Or petrol. Or anything else which you know you *have* to pay each week. Look at what's left. Now divide this as sensibly as you can between the different kinds of spending you're going to have to do. If you're completely without experience, call if possible on a friend or relative in similar circumstances to give you a hand. If you're already out and spending, review your previous

spending pattern to check that you're not indulging in wishful thinking – if you've previously been spending 75p per week on heating don't plan a budget which allocates only 30p to gas and electricity unless you also determine to switch off, go out, or wear your winter woollies.

Don't forget to put aside some money for *heavier expenses* that come up at much less than weekly intervals – fares home, or car licence, or whatever. And aim to

leave some over for what accountants call contingency spending – shoe repairs, unavoidable taxis, birthday presents.

You'll probably have to adjust as you go along, but not to worry. The main idea is to have a framework within which to move. Once you know that you have, say, a theoretical £4 a week for food and £2 for clothes, you can see that you can afford an £8 belt only by using a whole month's clothes allocation, or by resolving to live off fish scraps and market remnants so you can pinch money from your food allowance.

If you suspect (or know) that making a plan is one thing, and sticking to it quite another, take steps to prevent rash spending. Arrange for the bank (if you have one; see p. 328) to limit your cash-drawing to so much a week. Or lock your money in an unforceable money-box and give the key to a friend. Or keep away from shops which offer the most temptation. Or take with you only so much money a day. And *don't ever* use a cheque book, credit card, or run up accounts.

It's very tempting to overspend to start with. To succumb is only human, but it's vital to get back on an even keel as quickly as possible. Being harassed over money is one of the more avoidable hazards of an independent life.

There's no need to go on penny counting for ever. Once you have a budget which works, and you've kept fairly closely to it for a matter of weeks, you'll find you've acquired a feeling for what you can and can't afford. You can safely relax unless you find that once you do your money starts to melt again. (In which case go back to it pretty smartly.)

3 WHERE TO KEEP YOUR MONEY

If you get paid in cash weekly, and spend the lot before next pay-day, you may not see any point in opening any kind of banking account. But the moment your finances begin to get a little more complex, or you start to save even a few bob a week, you'd be wise to think of letting someone else look after it.

The National Savings Bank

This (until recently the Post Office Savings Bank) suits many people. You can put money in and take it out when you like (though there's a limit on large sums per day and per week). There are branches all over the country, open right through the day and six days a week. You can't write cheques on it, which is inconvenient but prevents impulse-buying: an advantage for any compulsive spender. Running your account costs you nothing. Indeed, if you leave money in for

Shopping around

You can make your money work harder by shrewd buying. For help with food, see Chapter III ; for clothes and cosmetics, Chapter V; for household goods, Chapter II. Unbranded goods can be as satisfactory as branded, but look at them carefully. (And for a *warning on electrical goods*, see p. 50.)

Goods sold in *markets* may be good value, even when flawed, but examine them closely. Perishable foods, especially fruit and vegetables, generally cost more on a Saturday (and higher still on a Sunday) ; but some stalls, and even some shops, sell off cheaply what's left just before Saturday closing-time. Supermarkets can be cheaper for own-brands, but often dearer for other pre-packed goods. If you buy several items, know what they're going to cost before you get to the cash desk. Mistakes have been known to be made. Always count your change.

Larger sizes are usually cheaper proportionately than small (not always). Buying e.g. detergent in bulk can save money if you've somewhere to keep it and you really will use it : not otherwise. Some shops, notably Tesco's, are now starting to sell one-person portions of food.

If you want to buy *larger pieces of equipment,* a good way to start is by going to your library and seeing if there are any comparative reports in the magazine *Which*. (You'll find a complete index at the end of each December copy.) If you're spending money on e.g. a sewing-machine or electric drill, you want to know you've picked the right one for your purpose. You may also find useful leaflets in your C A B.

When you're buying *new*, discount shops are somewhat cheaper, but they may not offer the same after-sales service. This could matter. Ask before you buy. Some in any case offer no lower prices than a good main-street department store. Check.

If there's a *guarantee*, study it to see what it amounts to. Some mean very little. Is labour included? Or parts only? Or only a portion of any subsequent repair? Are there any restrictions on who repairs it? Do you have to pay for transport? And so on. You're hardly likely to be making many large purchases, but just because of this it's important to make sure you get a good deal when you do.

In many cases you can buy goods *secondhand* which for your purposes will be as good as new. For bargains, see your local paper, evening paper or *Exchange and Mart*: or put in a wanted ad yourself. When you do buy secondhand, though, look carefully at what you're getting and make sure it's what you want. You won't have any comeback if it isn't. (You may have more security if you buy from a secondhand *trader*, as the Supply of Goods Act applies here.)

Fair Deal, an excellent booklet put out by the Office of Fair Trading, tells you all about your rights as a shopper, how to get the best from your shopping, and how the law can help, with much other advice. Look for a copy from your CAB, or send a large sae to Office of Fair Trading, Chancery House, 53 Chancery Lane, London WC2.

any length of time, you get interest on it – not a high rate, but better than nothing. When you have £50 in your current account you can open a special investment account, which pays a considerably higher interest rate.

Keep your National Savings book somewhere safe. It's very easy for a thief to use it at a branch where you're not known.

Giro

A new banking system run through the Post Office which is in some ways cheaper than the service operated by the clearing banks. You can deposit money at any Post Office, but you can withdraw only at one or two specific branches. You can pay bills by filling in Giro slips to those companies who hold Giro accounts. You can also arrange for Giro to pay regular bills (rent etc.) automatically. There's no fee for this, nor for any postage involved (though there's a modest charge for stationery), which means that this method works out cheaper than buying postal orders and posting them. You can also write

Giro cheques to pay people who have no Giro account: they cash them through their bank or any Post Office. At present, some places which will accept ordinary cheques are still wary about Giro cheques, but the number of acceptors is growing all the time.

Banks

Anyone over eighteen can open an account at a bank. There is no need to have a fortune or, normally, a guarantor. Once you have an account you can deposit money at any branch or even any branch of another bank. You can only withdraw money at the branch which holds your account, or at another branch by previous arrangement (unless you have a cheque card, see below). You can arrange for your bank to make regular payments. You can pay bills by cheque. You can use cheques (backed usually by some proof of identity – a driver's licence or something similar, or sometimes a cheque card) in most larger shops, and for paying bills by post. Charges vary, depending on the bank, your branch, how much you keep in your account. You can pay from nothing to around 10p per cheque. As a bank customer, you have the opportunity of getting a personal loan, also of having advice from your bank manager over any financial matters. However, you get no interest on your current account (except with the Co-op), and banking hours are inconvenient for many people; they close early most week-days, shut on Saturday, and often have long queues during lunch-hours. (Again, the Co-op is more flexible.)

Cheque cards. A cheque card is a card issued by the bank at which you hold an account and which you can show on demand when you want to pay by cheque. This guarantees payment to the payee of any cheque up to £30. Many banks are somewhat less than eager to issue a cheque card: some large stores, and places where you are personally known, don't ask for one. If you want a cheque card, read the small print on the application form. If you lose your cheque card plus cheque book, you may find yourself liable for all cheques made out until you notify the bank (though provided you notify them as soon as you can the bank may exercise discretion ove this liability). If you do have a cheque card, you can avoid most of the dangers involved if you *always carry your cheque book and cheque card apart*, and *always* know where they are.

Bank statement. The bank will send a statement of your account whenever you ask for one. It's a good idea to have one monthly. It gives you a complete list of all

Filling in a cheque

There are two kinds of cheques, crossed and uncrossed (open). Crossed are much safer. They can only be paid into a bank account, and therefore once written are useless except to the authorized person or company. An uncrossed cheque can always be turned into a crossed cheque by drawing two lines across it, but for most purposes you need only crossed cheques.

When you make out a cheque, start by filling in the counterfoil (the piece of paper attached to the cheque) or the form at the front of your cheque book. This is a valuable reminder to you of what you've paid out and when. On the cheque itself, fill in the date, with year; who you're paying it to (after 'Pay'); the sum paid, the pounds amount in words followed by the pence in numerals; repeat the amount in numbers in the box; sign it with your name in whatever form you have arranged to have as your regular signature. (Full name, or initials plus surname, it doesn't matter, but you have to stick to it.) Draw lines in any blank spaces. Start writing right up against the left-hand margin. Put the numbers close to the £ sign.

I know you can write cheques on cows and eggs but most people prefer one duly if dully completed as above.

payments made and how much you have or haven't left. Banks don't usually make mistakes, but you should still check your statement through. You can also, if you ask, have sent back the cheques you have made out and which have been paid through your bank: these cashed cheques thus act as receipts for payments. Keep them at least for several months in case there are queries or you get the same bill twice.

4 SIMPLE SAVING

'A penny saved is a penny earned.'

Although trite, it's true. As it's also true that, if you want to buy anything larger than an LP, you'll have either to save or borrow. Which you choose depends more on your personality than your finances. Some manage to save on a minute wage, while others earning far more can't.

The simplest way to save is to put a regular amount aside each day or week or month. You can ask the bank to deduct a fixed sum out of your pay cheque or put a weekly sum into the Post Office (keep your book somewhere safe). Pick whichever method suits you. The principle's the same.

As soon as you save even a modest amount, *you can put it to work to earn more*. If you put your money into the National Savings Bank (current or investment account), or into a deposit account in your bank, it will earn you interest as long as it's there. Provided you intend to save *regularly* for not less than five years, the government's new index-linked SAYE scheme makes sound sense. You put aside from £4–£20 per month, and at the end of five years you get back what you've paid in *plus* an amount to compensate for inflation: the money will be tax-free. Paying your money into a Building Society will not only pay you a fair rate of interest but may also help you later if you're looking for a house mortgage. Putting your spare money into Premium Bonds offers you a fairly risk-free gamble: you

get no interest, and the value of your money is likely to drop through inflation, but you stand an opportunity of winning and, unlike all other forms of betting, you won't lose your stake.

All these forms of saving are virtually risk-free. Building Societies and banks are unlikely to go broke. You won't lose your capital, and it will continue to earn a fair rate of interest until you decide to remove it.

If you want your money to work still harder for you, and earn you more, then *you'll find yourself running higher risks*. Moderate returns plus security go together; the promise of high returns is inevitably accompanied by the possibility of insecurity. Remember this when you see advertisements offering unusually high returns on investment, or any bizarre moneymaking schemes promising amazing profits. Look at what's offered very carefully indeed. Your risk could pay off – but you could equally well end up losing not only the interest on your money but the capital sum itself.

A further, entirely individual, way of saving is by *using your money to invest in your own interests*. If you have particular skills or knowledge, this can pay off handsomely. It could mean buying a wheel and a kiln: or collecting seventeenth-century religious tracts: or picking up old chairs to reupholster. This is putting your money to work directly for you rather than indirectly through other people. It is of course possible to get caught – you may find you haven't the time to work your wheel or no one wants your tract collection – but it can otherwise be a satisfying and liberating way of saving.

5 LOW-DOWN ON LOANS

They say that there's only one quicker way to lose friends than by borrowing from them, and that's by lending to them.

I think this is a bit cynical. Being ready to lend or borrow freely should be a sign of real friendship: *provided* that neither lending nor borrowing is all on one side; that the sums are modest; and that payment is always made when expected and always without being asked. Otherwise, yes, money can wreck friendships as readily as marriages.

If you catch yourself regularly borrowing small sums, make a real effort to check yourself. Borrowing like this can easily become a habit – you'll know it has when you spot people vanishing at your approach. When you do borrow, even if it's only 5p, make sure you return it as rapidly as possible. It's astonishing how little things like this can niggle for months or even years. Get a reputation as a bad borrower and you may never lose it.

If you're tempted to borrow a large sum from a friend, stop and think hard. Why are you borrowing? Is it really essential? How long do you want the loan for? Are you sure you can pay it back – or are you honestly just hoping? (And, if you're a prospective lender, ask yourself the same questions in reverse.)

Generally speaking, if you want to borrow more than the odd pound to tide you over the weekend, there are alternative ways of borrowing which are more satisfactory, even though financially more expensive, than borrowing from friends.

But before rushing to take on loans, fix your mind on these points.

A loan is not a present. It is a commitment to pay back out of your income a certain sum or sums at future date(s). If you have so far failed to put by what you wanted, how do you know you'll be able to deduct this sort of money in the future? Where's it going to come from?

Borrowing money means relying on future income coming in. This can cause a lot of worry. If you've been buying on HP, for example, getting sacked or being made redundant could mean losing not only your job but whatever you're buying as well. In any case, hav-

ing loans cuts down your freedom of action. You're less likely to fight points of principle, take another job with better prospects but a lower salary, and so on.

Borrowing money must cost more than saving. (Though this increased cost can be set against rising costs for the saver.) How much more depends on how you raise the money. Different ways vary considerably. In some cases you can end up paying back a lot extra. It's very difficult to work out the true cost of credit, which depends not only on the sum borrowed but how long it's borrowed for, but you can at least work out the difference between the nominal sum borrowed (or the cash price) and the total amount you'll end up repaying (or paying). You may be surprised.

Borrowing generally involves legal and binding commitments. Before you commit yourself, make sure this is the right answer. Sometimes, for example, you could buy something second-hand for little more than the deposit on the same kind of article new. (And you could even end up making a profit.)

6 CREDIT SQUEEZES

Getting into debt is easy. Staying in debt is even easier. People of all ages find their lives tangled and damaged by over-borrowing. The younger you are, the less experienced, the more sense it makes to do your utmost to steer clear of borrowing in any way at all.

But in this inflationary world there are many with a professional incentive to persuade you otherwise; it's important at least to know about the various kinds of credit which you may find offered to you.

In general, people under eighteen can't legally raise money in any of the following ways unless the agreement is made through another person or they're backed by a guarantor. Once over eighteen, they can take out loans on their own account. Whether you yourself can or cannot get credit depends on what and how you're borrowing, your financial status, job etc. Sometimes a guarantor may still be asked for.

Never act as a guarantor yourself for another person's debts unless you can afford to pay them off if necessary. You may have to: you will be legally responsible for them.

Monthly account

A monthly account is an arrangement with a store or supplier which allows you to buy goods on credit and pay for them only when billed at the end of each month. This is not normally looked on as a form of borrowing, but in fact it is – and at the moment there's no charge. Though you can only borrow for so short a term, the two or three weeks' respite can be helpful. However, it can be depressingly simple to buy on account far more than you intended, so if you have an easily tempted disposition you should beware. Anyone can open an account provided they can give a reference (a bank manager or employer) to testify to their financial status and stability.

Budget account

Many stores offer a budget account. With this you pay a fixed amount each month and may buy goods worth several times more than this: you can continue to do this each month up to a predetermined fixed amount. You pay interest on the amount outstanding each month: this is often called a service fee and the actual interest is often unspecified. It's again easy to make impulse purchases you can't really afford.

Overdraft

If you have a bank account and an understanding bank manager, and want a modest sum of money for a brief period, an overdraft can be the simplest and often the cheapest way of raising it. (You *must* ask your bank manager first before running into the red, or you'll end up with bouncing cheques and abusive letters.)

Personal loan

As above: if you have a bank plus friendly manager, and want to borrow more money for a longer period, ask for a personal loan. This is more expensive than an overdraft, but generally cheaper than any other form of credit, including credit sales and hire purchase. So this is a sensible place to start. If you have an account with Giro, you can raise a loan through an associated finance house.

You can also arrange loans directly with finance houses. These too are cheaper than other forms of credit, but are usually for sums over £100.

Check trading

Check trading is widely used in certain districts and areas. It works like this. The check trader, through a local agent, gives a check to the would-be buyer for a given sum of money (£20 or £50, or whatever). He/she can then use this check to buy goods up to its face value at any shop which accepts them. Then the purchaser pays back to the check trader's agent a fixed sum each week until paying off the face value *plus* an added percentage. It's a useful way of raising credit for those without bank accounts, or who only want to borrow small sums for small items not normally purchasable through hire purchase. On the other hand, the *real* cost of this credit is high, and there's a big risk that those who start buying this way end up stuck with it. They never have enough money to pay off outstanding checks *and* to put money aside so they won't need to buy this way in future. (This of course can also apply to all methods of buying on credit, but check trading as a system, possibly because of the personal element involved through weekly agents' visits, does seem to be that much more addictive.) Everything bought this way costs more than if paid for on the nail: the more that's bought, the higher the expense.

Hire purchase

Theoretically, when you buy goods through hire purchase you are not actually borrowing, since you are *hiring* goods which do not become yours until you make the final payment. However, in practice – apart from the legal implications, which are important – the effect is the same.

The hire purchaser puts down in cash a certain proportion of the

---

DON'T SIGN ANYTHING FINANCIAL UNLESS YOU'VE READ IT THROUGH FROM BEGINNING TO END. SMALL PRINT AND ALL. DON'T SIGN ANYTHING INCLUDING SUCH WORDS AS 'CONDITIONS AS UNDERSTOOD' OR 'ACCORDING TO COMPANY'S CONDITIONS' UNLESS YOU KNOW WHAT THOSE CONDITIONS ARE. NEVER SIGN A BLANK FORM. IF IN DOUBT, GET ADVICE FIRST. LATER IS TOO LATE. YOUR SIGNATURE COMMITS YOU ABSOLUTELY. (Ask at your Citizens' Advice Bureau. And see p. 340.)

total price as a deposit, and continues to pay fixed sums, weekly or monthly, until the purchase price (plus the 'service charge', i.e. interest) is met. The real cost of buying in this way varies from retailer to retailer and from one finance house to another, but is almost always higher than, for example, a personal bank loan. However, it's a simple and relatively straightforward way of buying goods when you need them, and during the hiring period the retailer and/or finance company are responsible for seeing that the goods are the quality you expected.

But, because initially you are hiring, and not buying, these goods, if you default on the payments the hiring company may repossess them. (Once you have paid one third of the total price the company will need a Court Order first, but it can still be done.) You can't sell *at any time* until all payments have been made. If you do want to sell before the end of your repayment period, the only way is to ask the hirer if you can renegotiate your agreement: you can't just pay off what's left in a lump sum. This kind of renegotiation can be expensive.

If you decide you made a mistake, you can end the agreement when you want at any time, but you must return the goods in good condition, pay any arrears and, in addition, with some exceptions,

the difference between this and half the total purchase price.

So you want to make sure, *before* you sign a hire purchase agreement, that you really need what you're buying, that you know you can keep up the instalments, and that you won't want to get rid of it before you've finished paying. Apart from anything else, there's nothing drearier than paying week after week for something when you can't even remember why you wanted it in the first place.

You can change your mind immediately after signing a hire purchase agreement *provided it was not signed in the dealer's shop or showroom, or in the premises of the finance house,* and provided the letter cancelling this is posted within three days of receiving your copy of the agreement.

Beware of a promissory note masquerading as a hire purchase form. Recently some dealers, among them certain car dealers, have been issuing these to would-be customers with the assurance that they were 'just the same'. They aren't, and if you sign one you are depriving yourself of certain rights. A promissory note will be much shorter than a hire-purchase form, generally consisting of only a few lines stating that in return for a loan of £x you will repay £y by instalments over a certain period. *Don't sign one of these* – or certainly not without first asking your CAB.

Credit sales

A credit sale looks very like hire purchase, but in some important respects it's very different. You're not hiring the goods: they become yours from the moment you sign the agreement. In practice, the two most important differences between a credit sale and hire purchase are that the company you're dealing with is *not* responsible (except to a limited extent, sometimes further restricted by the terms of the contract) for the quality and suitability of the goods supplied, and that there is no right of cancellation unless the agreement is for more than £30. So if the agreement is under this, look even more closely at what you're buying, and at the agreement itself. The moment you put your name on a form you *could* find yourself committed to paying out £29.50 for a load of old (or new) junk.

Pawnbroking

This can be a handy way of raising small sums of money for short periods if you're absolutely stuck. You pledge some sellable article (jewellery, watch, radio) as a security against a loan. When you pay back that loan, plus interest (a maximum of 20% per year – but there are also extra charges, valuation fees etc.) you

have your security returned. If you fail to repay, the goods can be sold. The real cost of borrowing money like this can be high, but it's useful in an emergency.

Credit cards

There are various credit cards issued by various banks or finance houses offering slightly different terms, but essentially similar. You can apply for one of these cards whether you're a bank customer or not. With it, you can buy goods on credit anywhere which accepts this form of credit. You sign a form every time you make a purchase, and each month a totalled account is sent to you. Each month a minimum amount must be paid; interest is charged on the amount outstanding. As with other forms of account trading, it's very easy to overspend.

If you do get a credit card, make sure you always know where it is, and check daily to see it's still there. There can be nasty shocks in store if loss or theft is not discovered for several days. If you leave your wallet or bag around it's uncomfortably easy for a thief to slip out your credit card and leave everything else untouched; by the time you've noticed it's gone you could be liable for payments of hundreds of pounds.

If you contemplate having a credit card, *look very closely at the small print on the back of any information or application.* This can (and generally does) include the condition that *you accept the responsibility of paying any sums signed for through this cheque card until notice is accepted* in writing *by the issuing bank or company.* This means that if your cheque card is lost or stolen at 5.30 pm you will have to pay all bills run up by the thief until you turn up after a sleepless night at 9.30 or 10 am the following morning. (American Express has an upper limit of obligation of $50 or equivalent in local currency.)

Money-lenders

Money-lenders will lend to people who can't raise loans elsewhere – who are therefore, usually, bad security risks. *Their charges are extremely high.* The annual interest rate may be 40 or 50 per cent or even higher. (These are the sort of people you see advertising 'All personal loans – no security – any amount from £10–£1,000' and so on.) *Never visit a money-lender.*

7 LOOKING AHEAD

You can't tell now what kind of money you may need in future. You could need a capital sum for further education, travel, helping relatives, setting up house. You'll probably want life insurance: the earlier you start it, the cheaper it is. So don't rush to spend everything you've got the moment you get it. When you really start earning you may well find yourself better off, and with more free money, than at any other time of your life. No one wants to live entirely in the future, but the chances are that it will one day materialize. Don't ignore it entirely. Save when you can, and the money you put by will be there when you can't.

If you want to study financial matters in much greater detail, the *Save and Prosper Book of Money*, edited by Margaret Allen (Collins, 1972) is factual, interesting, well laid out and easy to read. *Money Which* (ask at your library) also has much detailed and critical information.

It's the Law

A legal system is an attempt to create a framework within which everyone is equally free to live, move and have their being. It derives from ideas of right and justice, but it is not identical with morality: by and large our legal system rarely goes so far as to interfere with private morals. It's possible to behave appallingly, cause a great deal of misery, and break no laws, while someone else may be arrested and imprisoned for conduct which is illegal but less damaging.

In theory, the law exists to give the same protection to all – to prevent a set-up where some, simply because they're bigger, stronger, richer, cleverer, can shove others around. In practice, it doesn't always work out that way. Laws become outdated, reflect a society which has ceased to exist. Administration of the law is often extremely expensive, so that it can seem out of the reach of ordinary people who want to have put right ordinary wrongs. It has to be set in action and enforced by fallible human beings.

Nevertheless, it's worth pointing out that even as it stands the law, with all its faults, is generally impartial, the administration un-bribable, the majority of officers uncorrupt, and that there are many actively involved in trying to improve those areas – its expense and failure to adapt to new demands – where change is most needed.

1 FIND OUT FIRST

Whatever your feelings about the law in general, or about any specific individual law, if you are discovered breaking one you are liable to certain penalties. This is so even if you offended un-wittingly. Ignorance of the law is no defence (though it may be pleaded in mitigation). Often, obviously, you know without having it spelt out when you're breaking the law – when you're hitting your neighbour over the head, breaking his windows, stealing his car (but not, generally speaking, his wife: though adultery at other times in this country has been, and in some other countries still is, a legal crime).

But in other matters you may find you have broken the law quite without realizing it (selling an article not legally yours because you're still paying for it on HP). Or you may find yourself in debt or difficulties because some perfectly legal action on your part involved you in a way you didn't anticipate (e.g. by agreeing to supervise an L-driver who subsequently has an accident).

If you take actions which have legal force, the law will see to it that you abide by these, whether or not this is what you intended. If you sign a document, you are answerable for whatever is in that document (see p. 340). If you get married, or become a partner in a company, you automatically assume certain responsibilities and accept certain restrictions.

This is also true when you're abroad. In other countries there are other laws. Many will be the same as ours. Others will be different. If you contravene them, you are likely to find yourself paying for the contravention –

whether or not you accept the thinking behind them. There are many opportunities for finding yourself in trouble, from comparatively trivial offences – kissing in the street, wearing hair or clothes of a forbidden style – to more serious – handling alcohol or drugs. You may even find yourself committed under foreign laws to consequences which, if foreseen, you would have found wholly objectionable: for example, if a girl marries abroad a citizen of certain countries, she will find her children are never legally hers but her husband's and, if he dies, her husband's brothers'.

The further you travel away from countries which have legal systems based on or allied to our own, the easier it is to find yourself breaking unknown laws. In many cases concessions will be made to genuine tourists making mistakes in genuine ignorance: but not always.

The majority of unintended offences in western European countries are with police registration, driving, and drinking. Know what local laws are and, if you want to keep out of local police-stations, comply with them. Drug offences, or alleged drug offences, can have very serious consequences. So can smuggling, even of a minor nature; so can financial or currency contraventions.

Legally speaking, when in Rome

Look before you sign

If you've read through *Help!* you'll already have seen warnings, particularly in the pieces on housing and on money, against signing documents without due consideration. But because this is such an important point, and one which affects many people who might never otherwise come into contact with any legal matters, it's worth driving the point home.

If you are asked to put your signature to *anything*, whether it's a routine form, a contract, a document *of any kind*, NEVER SIGN unless you have read it through from beginning to end, understand every word, and agree with everything there. If there are references to any other pieces of paper which you haven't seen ('conditions as understood' 'conditions as referred to in Blue Paper VI para 2') don't sign unless you know what these refer to. Don't let yourself be rushed into signing. If you want time, ask if you can take whatever it is away to read it through. If you have any doubts *at all*, get advice. Start by going to your local Citizens' Advice Bureau. (Comment from a solicitor at a CAB who handles similar cases: 'If only people would always come and see us *before* they sign. Afterwards we do everything we can, but all too often our hands are tied. Once that signature is on the paper we have the devil of a job to prove it doesn't mean what it says it means.')

So ask first. Remember, no reputable company or organization will want to rush you into signing something against your will.

P.S. When something large is delivered to you, you're normally asked to sign a receipt. Somewhere on the front, possibly not on the page with details of your particular item, it will say 'Received in good condition'. If you're not going to open your package then and there (usually the carrier won't want to wait) be sure to include the word 'unexamined' before you sign. You may not otherwise have any comeback if the item turns out to be in fact damaged.

do as Rome does is a practical order rather than friendly advice.

Get personal advice

Giving brief legal advice is asking for trouble. Attempting to simplify complex matters inevitably risks misleading: moreover, in some important respects the law in England and Wales (for example over homosexuality) is not the same as in Scotland or Northern Ireland.

Nevertheless, although it's impossible to give detailed information about all the legal situations you might at some time be faced with, you'll find help over some of the most frequent hazards in the appropriate individual sections. For some advice about the law concerning housing, see p. 17; over sex, p. 188; over alcohol, p. 284; over drugs, p. 296; over driving, p. 284; over accidents, p. 273; over hire purchase, credit sales etc., p. 334.

In all important cases there's no substitute for personal advice. Sometimes there may be a specific organization prepared to give legal help with your specific problem – after a driving accident, for example, you may be able, if you're a member, to call for legal help from the AA or RAC. Otherwise, to start with, consult your local CAB, or any Neighbourhood Law Centre, or Release

(01–289 1123) or – especially for advice on any particularly controversial matter – the National Council for Civil Liberties (01–278 4575, 186 King's Cross Road, London WC1).

Financial help

One of the principal obstacles to the fair administration of justice has been its vast and increasing expense. This is a major problem, especially for those who are neither rich nor poor.

However, recently considerable efforts have been made to make legal advice more accessible. In some areas new Neighbourhood Law Centres will give free or almost free legal help. The CAB will give you initial advice without charge, and assist you with claims, forms, phone calls etc. Many branches have a rota system, with solicitors available to advise free of charge.

If you are accused of a criminal

offence, you may be entitled to Legal Aid. This depends on how much you earn and how much capital you have: even if you're subsequently found innocent you may well have to contribute.

The green form scheme provides for part-payment of legal advice and help. Again, contributions vary according to income.

New legislation at present in the pipeline may further improve the financial viability of legal services: check with your C A B.

2 LEGAL PROCEDURES

You can best avoid the attentions of the police by leading a godly, righteous and sober life. If you should deviate from this happy state of affairs, or possibly act in such a way that the police think you have, here's what can or should happen.

What follows does not intend to suggest that the police are out to trap you and do you out of your rights. It's important to remember

Not into temptation

Many young adults come before magistrates' courts not for any long-meditated misdemeanours but through momentary impulses, egged on by friends, or drink, or temper. If you find yourself being lured or driven in this way, do your best to resist. If it's bad enough coming up before the courts for something you felt compelled to do, it's utterly depressing when it's for some offence that now seems pointless or that you can no longer understand. Group pressures plus drink/drugs account for a lot of violence and crime. Other people's stories lead to shoplifting, pilfering, petty fraud. Quite apart from the moral aspect, a police record is damaging to your job opportunities and to your personal relationships. If you feel yourself lonely, misunderstood, swayed or manipulated, seek help first. There should be local groups or organizations who will understand. Try your C A B.

that the legal system and the police can only function with the public's cooperation, and that, lacking the framework of the law, the weakest would go crashing to the wall with considerably more inevitability than at present. But it is always important for individual citizens to know their rights, provided that they don't at the same time forget their duties. To give scope for police infringement of the law is to damage the basis of the law itself.

Questioning and searching

If you're stopped in potentially damaging circumstances, here's what can happen.

If the police want information, or have reason to suspect you of committing an offence, they may *question* you. If you're driving a motor vehicle, you're legally obliged to give your name, address and age. Otherwise, there's no legal compulsion to answer, but you risk arrest if you don't. If you

feel you're being questioned as a suspect, you may want to say something to indicate your innocence. You may refuse to answer any further questions until you get legal advice. If you're under seventeen, the police may not interview you without the presence of a parent or legal adviser* or responsible adult of the same sex.

If you are asked to *go to a police station*, you may in theory refuse to go unless you are arrested. (But to refuse to go may be obstruction. The right of a private citizen here is unclear.)

The police have the right to *stop and search* you if they suspect you are carrying drugs, firearms, or –

* As long as you're aged under 17, *you are not automatically brought before the courts. Notice of the alleged offence will be passed to the Juvenile Bureau, who will interview you in the presence of your parent or guardian. If you wish to plead not guilty, the offence will be taken to court. If you admit guilt, the officer interviewing you will take into consideration (often after discussions with the social services or educational authorities) your background, studies, job, ambitions. If the Juvenile Bureau consider you are likely to commit a further offence (possibly because you have a string of offences in the past) you will be sent to court: but if you can give good reason to show that you are unlikely to commit a similar offence again, you will be officially cautioned by the police. If you commit no further offence before you are seventeen, all record of this offence will be destroyed. If you do commit a further offence, you will be sent straight to court.*

in some cities – stolen property. The police should have *reasonable grounds* for such a search. If you are stopped, ask what these are, ask what the police are looking for, and ask whether you are being arrested. If you feel there are no reasonable grounds you may refuse to be searched. Reasonable grounds do not include, for example, your hair or clothes. (This ruling does at present give very considerable licence, and is coming under criticism.) You need not be searched in the street. If the officer concerned is in plain clothes, it's sensible to insist on going to a police station.

Arrest

If you are *arrested*, ask what for. Once you are arrested, you can be compelled to go to the *police station*. Here you may be *searched* for offensive objects or for evidence connected with the crime for which you have been arrested. Women may only be searched by policewomen. Young people under seventeen may only be interviewed and searched in the presence of a parent or guardian or of someone who is not a police officer and is of the same sex.

If the police take property away from you, make sure it's listed and correctly described. Sign the list immediately under the last item. Ask for a receipt.

You are not obliged to have any *medical examination*, *except*, if you have been driving a motor vehicle, to give blood or urine samples. If otherwise you consent to be medically examined, you have the right to have a doctor, lawyer or friend present.

You have the right to make at least one *phone call*. If you know a solicitor, get in touch with him/her. However, few of us have a friendly solicitor's phone number at the tip of our tongue: in which case, ring a friend, explain what's happened, and ask for contact with a solicitor to be made. If you live in the catchment area of a Neighbourhood Law Centre, there is an emergency telephone service available day and night.

You should also be given *pencil and paper* if you ask. Do so. Write a detailed account of exactly what has happened. Date it, and include the time it was written. Sign it. If possible, have your signature and your statement witnessed, on every page. *This is very important.* If your case does come up before the courts, it may not happen for several months – ample time for you to forget important details.

If the police take a statement and ask you to sign it, don't unless you agree with everything in it. (In particular, watch out for the way police statements handle language. Often – probably through habit rather than with sinister purpose – defendants are described as having, e.g., 'admitted' instead of 'stated': a small difference, but one that could matter.) If English is not your mother-tongue, see the statement is made in your own language. (You can insist on writing the statement yourself – this could be especially important if you're non-English.)

The police should not offer inducements (e.g. hint of bail) in order to influence you into signing a statement.

Your *fingerprints* may not be taken against your will without a magistrate's order. (But in practice bail is not normally granted unless you consent to have your fingerprints taken.)

In some police stations you may be photographed. The rules governing this are not yet clear.

Release on bail

At the police station you will normally get *bail* – that is, allowed to go free on certain conditions. If you're not offered bail, ask for it. This will usually be granted unless it's serious, or you're under seventeen and there are strong reasons against, or because you'll be brought before the magistrates next day. If you're not granted bail at this stage, you *must* be brought before the magistrates within the next twenty-four hours (excluding Sundays, some holidays). Make sure you contact a friend or solicitor (see phone call,

p. 344). *Ask him/her to take to court anyone prepared to stand surety for you.* If you fail to get a solicitor, ask if there is a duty solicitor at the court who will act for you.

At court

When you are brought before the magistrates – in an adult, not juvenile court – what happens depends mainly on the offence with which you're charged. If it's a *summary offence* (e.g. drunk-and-disorderliness) it will be dealt with on the spot. (By far the greater number of summary offenders plead guilty. Lawyers advise you, even if you intend to plead guilty, to get legal advice. You may not be guilty of the legal charge, or guilty of a different charge.) If it's for an *indictable offence* (e.g. dangerous driving, some kinds of fraud) you may choose whether to stand trial in the magistrates' court or to be tried later by a judge and jury. (Here again you need legal advice to help decide which course would be best for you.) For the *gravest offences* (robbery with violence, arson, blackmail) you will automatically be sent – if the magistrates decide there is enough evidence to constitute a case – up to a higher court.

If you're pleading not-guilty, then either you or the police may choose to ask for an adjournment. If you have not already got bail, apply for it. *You must ask for it yourself*. The court will not necessarily offer it. Once asked for, bail must be granted for summary offences, unless there are certain special circumstances (e.g. you've no fixed address, you've broken bail before). For other offences, magistrates may or may not grant bail.

If bail is opposed

The police may *object*: because

Complaints against the police

All police stations should have copies of 'Police and Public: procedure for making a complaint against the police'. In practice they may not. Before making a complaint it's advisable to get (a) legal advice and (b) names and addresses of any witnesses who can support your statement. You may make a complaint in person or send a statement to the Chief Officer of Police (Chief Constable outside London, Commander A.10 branch, New Scotland Yard, inside): ask for the address at your Citizens' AdviceBureau. An investigation officer will then contact you. You may have this interview at your home or in your solicitor's office if you prefer this to a police station. After you have made a statement, you will be asked to sign this. Make sure it's accurate, and ask for a copy to be given to you. (This may not be offered to you unless you ask.) You may then be asked to attend a later inquiry.

There is considerable pressure at the moment – from members of the police force among others – to amend the methods of inquiry into complaints against the police. By the time of publication there may be changes in the methods available. Check with your CAB or the National Council for Civil Liberties.

(You may also wish to contact your MP or the press – but beware of giving opportunities for prosecutions for libel.)

they say you won't appear for trial, because you'll interfere with witnesses, because further charges might follow, because you may commit further offences. If you disagree with what the police say, tell the magistrate. Explain especially if *refusal of bail* might risk your job, cause hardship to any dependants, or lead to eviction. Relatives or friends may be asked to act as sureties. It is best if potential sureties are present in court. (Sureties must be over eighteen, have a fixed address, and enough money to cover the amount set for bail. They don't have to produce the amount in cash, simply prove that they could raise it if necessary.)

If it is refused, you may apply to a *judge in chambers* (a single High Court Judge). You can ask for an application form and leave it to the Official Solicitor: in practice, applications for bail to a judge in chambers rarely succeed presented in this way – it is better to apply through your own (or your friends' and relatives') solicitor. (This can be expensive. Legal Aid for this is not available whilst the case is in the Magistrates' Court.)

Legal representation

Whether you wish to plead guilty or not guilty you should, except for the most trivial of cases, be legally represented. Innocence alone is not necessarily enough

(see p. 345). If you're not guilty, or undecided whether or not you're guilty, don't be tempted to plead guilty 'to speed things up'. If your means are 'insufficient to pay for your own defence' you should apply for *Legal Aid*. If you are on bail, apply to the court office for the necessary forms. If you're held in custody, tell the magistrate you're applying for Legal Aid. Don't leave it to the last moment. Apply as soon as possible. (The court won't necessarily tell you you're entitled to Legal Aid. It's up to you to apply for it.) See also p. 341.

3 CIVIL QUARRELS

If you have a dispute or disagreement with another person or a company, then any legal action you take will almost certainly be under civil law. If so, it's up to you to sue: no one else can do it for you. (The police prosecute only in cases of *criminal law* – where, roughly speaking, offenders damage the community as a whole.) When you have complaints over faulty goods, altercations over motor accidents, quarrels with a landlord, what remedies you have depend on the letter of the law concerned and on what precise action you take. The CAB will advise you over this, and steer you through the initial stages. Again, in any but the most trivial cases you need legal advice (see also p. 340).

How to bring a complaint in the courts

For most young adults, probably the most frequent reason for going to law is to bring a complaint against a shopkeeper for failure to replace faulty goods. If you have already been through the stages suggested on p. 248, then ask your CAB or a solicitor for their advice on whether or not you should take your case to court.

If you decide to do so, and you live in England or Wales, get in touch with your County Court Office (find the address in your telephone directory under 'Courts'); if you live in Scotland, you should visit the Sheriff Court in your area. (The procedure in Scotland is in the process of being changed, and the Sheriff's Clerk will be able to give you the latest information.) You will have to fill in a form and pay a small fee (from 75p, depending on the size of your claim). If you're under 18, you can't sue on your own, but need a 'next friend' – generally a parent.

Because the legal procedures are now much simpler, your claim may be settled by arbitration in private. Even if it goes to court, you may still not need a solicitor. A free booklet, *Small Claims in*

the County Court, from any County Court office or CAB, will give you much useful information. How to Sue in the County Court, published by the Consumers' Association, 14 Buckingham Street, London WC1, at £1, goes into considerable detail, and has a practical introduction which looks at both risks and opportunities.

Provided you have a fair case, you now have a good chance of having it settled to your satisfaction *and* recovering your costs.

It's important in any kind of dispute to keep a record of what happens at the time it's happening. Make a note of dates and times of phone calls and what's said, keep all letters sent to you, take copies of letters you send. Keep any relevant documents – rent-book or receipt or whatever. Don't let time elapse between what happens and your record of it, or between letters and answers.

Racial discrimination

At the time of printing, the laws governing the treatment of racial discrimination are still those of the Race Relations Acts of 1965 and 1968. However, the current government White Paper (Cmnd 6234) proposes considerable changes both in the law and the way it's enforced. In particular, it's designed to widen the scope of racial discrimination to cover clubs and other voluntary bodies, to strengthen the powers of the individual to bring actions, and to give stronger powers of enforcement to a newly formed Race Relations Committee.

If these proposals become law, the section which follows will be out of date. If you're uncertain whether or not the law has changed, or what your position is, start by contacting your local CAB, Community Relations Office, Neighbourhood Law Centre, or the NCCL, 186 King's Cross Road, London WC1.

The Race Relations Acts of 1965 and 1968 make it illegal, in certain circumstances, to treat someone worse than someone else merely because he/she is of a different race.

If, therefore, you are refused goods, facilities or services; or if these are inferior; or if you are charged more for them; or if you are refused admittance to any public place; or denied the opportunity of employment; or the use of public transport; or the chance to rent or buy property; *because of your race*, then you should complain to the Race Relations Board. (There are exemptions: for example, private clubs and private houses may choose who they want on whatever grounds they please.) If you would like preliminary advice over this, or you're undecided what action to take, you may prefer to start by talking to your local Community Relations officer. Most large towns and London boroughs have a Community Relations Office staffed by a full-time helper or helpers. Ask at your Town Hall.

If you believe you have grounds, then you must bring a complaint *within two months of the incident* before the Race Relations Board (5 Lower Belgrave Street, London SW1) or a local conciliation committee. Neither can take up a case until asked to do so. You can either write or call directly, or you can fill in details on a special application form which you can get from the Board's offices, town halls, government Employment Exchanges, or Citizens' Advice Bureaux. If you want to make a complaint over employment, you may also write directly to the Secretary of State for Employment.

The Board or Conciliation Committee will do its best to seek conciliation between the two parties. (At the time of writing, its methods are handicapped by lack of certain enforcement rights.) If this conciliation process fails, the Race Relations Board may start civil proceedings in the County Court to seek damages (for the complainant) and an injunction (against continued discrimination).

You can read the NCCL's comments on the White Paper in

Report no. 10, price 20p, from the above address.

Sex discrimination

The Sex Discrimination Act first came into force on 29 December 1975. It will take time (and probably a number of test-cases) before it becomes clear how effective it is in practice.

In theory, however, these are its aims.

In *employment*: jobs must be advertised and open equally to either sex (except where sex is a genuine occupational qualification (e.g. acting)). This applies also to training schemes and apprenticeships. There are various exceptions (e.g. the Church, employers employing only five people or less), and protective clauses still operate in certain jobs.

In *housing*: each sex must be treated equally by building societies, councils and private landlords. (But a landlord/lady renting rooms in his/her house can specify what tenants are wanted.)

In *education*: both sexes should have the use of the same facilities and the chance to study the same subjects. The quota system should no longer operate in higher or specialized education.

In *buildings open to the public* (pubs, hotels, restaurants): admission can't be refused on grounds of sex.

You can get free leaflets dealing in more detail with all the above points from the Equal Opportunities Commission, Overseas House, Quay Street, Manchester M3 3HN. These will also tell you what to do in cases of complaint, and whom to approach.

How to get registered

As soon as you are over eighteen you are entitled to vote at any national or local election, but only if you are on the electoral register.

New electoral registers are compiled every autumn. Forms are distributed in September to every household. These should be completed and returned to include details of every person resident in the household on 10 October who is over eighteen (or will become eighteen during the period of the electoral register) and is entitled to vote. This includes all British subjects and citizens of the Irish Republic.

If you live in rented premises, often the landlord/lady will include your details on the general form – indeed, the form asks that this should be done. However, it is your responsibility to make sure that you are included. If you think you may not be/have not been, ring your local Town Hall, ask for the phone number of your electoral register office, and ask there for a form to be sent.

The provisional register is published during November. You

can find copies at the appropriate office, usually at your local Town Hall, at some main libraries and at some main Post Offices. If you are not included on this there is still time to apply, provided that you complete and send in the form before 16 December.

If you are already on an electoral register and move around the time the new register is being compiled, and fail to apply in time to be re-registered, you should write to the electoral registrations office dealing with your old address, and ask for a postal vote.

Juries

Anyone aged between eighteen and sixty-five, resident in the UK for at least five years, and appearing on an electoral register, is eligible without further qualifications to serve on a jury.

Most books dealing with the law are too involved and detailed to be easily understood. Two recent ones, dealing specifically with individuals' rights, are the *NCCL Guide* by Anna Coote and Lawrence Grant (Penguin, 1972) and *Women's Rights: a practical guide* by Anna Coote and Tess Gill (Penguin, 1974). Another, broader and more abstract, is *Freedom, the Individual and the Law* by Harry Street (Penguin, 1963). The NCCL produces a series of fact sheets on arrest, search, bail etc. Each set costs 14p plus postage.

ENVOI

You might think that once you had HELP! *under your belt, life would be a straight run-through from there to the grave.*

You would be wrong. HELP! *does no more than hint at what really matters. Many of the most important questions are those which have no answers. If* HELP! *gives you enough time to start asking them, it will have served its purpose.*

ADDRESSES AND TELEPHONE NUMBERS

I A ROOF OVER YOUR HEAD

YWCA Accommodation and Advisory Service, 16 Great Russell Street,
London WC1.
YMCA, 83 Endell Street, London WC2.
Beds-in-Homes, 44 Langham Street, London W1 (01–637 3251).
Self-Help, 17 Prince of Wales Crescent, London NW1.
Advisory Service for Squatters, 2 St Paul's Road, London N1
(01–359 8814).
London Tourist Board, 4 Grosvenor Gardens, London SW1 (01–730 0791).
GALS (Girls Alone in London Service), 69 Roseman Street, London EC1;
West Lodge, 190 Euston Road, London NW1 (01–387 3010).
Centrepoint Hostel, St Anne's House, 57 Dean Street, London W1.

II HOME SWEET HOME

Electrical Association for Women, 25 Foubert's Place, London W1
(01–437 5212).

III NOURISHING NOSH

Weight Watchers Ltd, 1–2 Thames Street, Windsor, Berks.

IV MEDICAL MATTERS

Ministry of Health, Alexander Fleming House, Elephant and Castle,
London SE1.
Health Education Council, Middlesex House, Ealing Road, Wembley,
Middlesex.
Family Planning Association, Margaret Pyke House, 27 Mortimer Street,
London W1.
Youth Advisory Centre, 31 Nottingham Place, London W1 (01–935 8870).
The Board for Information on Youth and Community Service, 67 York
Place, Edinburgh 1 (031–556 8671).

V OUTWARD APPEARANCES

High and Mighty, 164 Edgware Road, London W2.
Tall Girls, 32a Grosvenor Street, London W1.
D. H. Evans, 318 Oxford Street, London W1.
Narrow Foot League, 57 Abbey Lodge, Park Road, London NW8.
Lilley & Skinner, 358 Oxford Street, London W1.
Selfridges Ltd, Oxford Street, London W1.

VI FRIENDS AND LOVERS

London Village, 01–731 4366.
The Centre, Adelaide Street, London WC2.
National Federation of 18 Plus Clubs, 16–18 High Street, Dartford, Kent.
Youth Advisory Centre (see Section IV).
Campaign for Homosexual Equality, 28 Kennedy Street, Manchester M2S4BG.
The Albany Trust, 31 Clapham Road, London SW9 (Mrs Robertson, Parents' Enquiry).
Family Planning Association (see Section IV).
Brook Advisory Centre for Young People, 233 Tottenham Court Road, London W1.
Family Doctor, 47–51 Chalton Street, London NW1.
Pregnancy Advisory Service, 01–409 0281; (Manchester and Liverpool) 061–228 1887.
National Council for One Parent Families, 255 Kentish Town Road, London NW5 (01–267 1361).
Gingerbread, 9 Poland Street, London W1.
Child Poverty Action Group, 1 Macklin Street, London WC2.
Lifeline, 01–222 6392.
Let Live, 01–231 0271.

VII LIKING YOUR LEISURE

Ramblers Association, 1–4 Crawford Mews, London W1.
Youth Hostel Association, Trevelyan House, 8 St Stephen's Hill, St Albans, Herts.
Sports Council, 70 Brompton Road, London SW3.
The National Trust, 42 Queen Anne's Gate, London SW1.
Council for British Archaeology, 7 Marylebone Road, London NW1.
British Film Institute, 81 Dean Street, London W1.
Task Force, Clifford House, Edith Villas, London W14;
    Abbey House, Victoria Street, London SW1 (01–222 2955).
National Blood Transfusion Service (City Centre), Moor House, London Wall, London EC2.

VIII ABOUT AND AWAY

Cyclists' Touring Club, 69 Meadrow, Godalming, Surrey.

Automobile Association, Fanum House, Basingstoke, Hants.

Royal Automobile Club, 83–5 Pall Mall, London SW1.

RAC/ACU Training Scheme (as above for RAC).

National Travel (NBC) Ltd, Victoria Coach Station, 164 Buckingham Palace Road, London SW1 (01–730 0202).

NUS Travel, 117 Euston Road, London NW1.

Trust Houses Forte Reservations Centre, Paramount House, 71–5 Uxbridge Road, Ealing, London W5.

Interchange Hotels of Great Britain Ltd, 1 Victoria Road, London W8.

P & O Passenger Division, BI Educational Cruises, Beaufort House, St Botolph Street, London EC3.

The Camping Club of Great Britain and Ireland, 11 Lower Grosvenor Place, London SW1.

English Tourist Board, 4 Grosvenor Gardens, London SW1.

British Tourist Authority, 64 St James's Street, London SW1.

National Union of Students, 3 Endsleigh Street, London WC1.

Central Bureau for Educational Visits and Exchanges, 43 Dorset Street, London W1.

Acorn Camps (see National Trust, Section VII).

British Trust for Conservation Volunteers' Work, Zoological Society of London, Regent's Park, London NW1.

United Nations Association, 93 Albert Embankment, London SE1.

Quaker Youth Service, Friends Service Council, Friends House, Euston Road, London NW1.

International Voluntary Service, 91 High Street, Harlesden, London NW10.

Common Cold Research Unit, Harvard Hospital, Coombe Road, Salisbury, Wilts.

Passport Office, Clive House, 70 Petty France, London SW1.

5th Floor, India Buildings, Water Street, Liverpool.

Olympia House, Upper Dock Street, Newport, Mon.

Westwood, Peterborough.

1st Floor, Empire House, 131 West Nile Street, Glasgow.

Foreign and Commonwealth Office Passport Agency, 1st Floor, Marlborough House, 30 Victoria Street, Belfast.

Hospital of Tropical Diseases, 2–4 St Pancras Way, London NW1.

IX QUESTIONS OF COMMUNICATION

British Standards Institution, 2 Park Street, London W1.

X RISKS – ELEMENTARY AND ADVANCED

Youth Advisory Centre (see Section IV).
AA (see Section VIII).
Gamblers Anonymous, National Service Office, 17–23 Blantyre Street, Cheyne Walk, London SW10.
National Council on Alcoholism, 45 Great Peter Street, London SW1.
Alcoholics Anonymous, 11 Redcliffe Gardens, London SW10.
Health Education Council (see Section IV).
British Judo Association, 70 Brompton Road, London SW3.
Family Doctor (see Section VI).
Association for the Prevention of Addiction, Long Acre, London WC2.
National Council for Civil Liberties, 186 King's Cross, London WC1.
Release, 1 Elgin Avenue, London W9 (01–289 1123).

XI JUST THE JOB

CRAC (Careers Research and Advisory Centre), Bateman Street, Cambridge CB2 1LZ.
Educational and Career Analysts, Career House, 90 Gloucester Place, London W1.
National Advisory Centre on Careers for Women, 251 Brompton Road, London SW3 (01–589 9237).
Uncareers, 298 Pershore Road, Birmingham 5.
Community Service Volunteers, 237 Pentonville Road, London N1.
Open University, Walton Hall, Milton Keynes, MK7 6AA.
NCCL (see above).
TUC, Congress House, Russell Street, London WC1.

XII PENCE SENSE

National Union of Students, Cromwell House, Fulwood Place, London WC1.
Office of Fair Trading, Chancery House, 53 Chancery Lane, London WC2.

XIII IT'S THE LAW

Release (see above).
NCCL (see above).
The Law Society, 27–39 Red Lion Street, London WC1.
Consumers' Association, 14 Buckingham Street, London WC2.
Office of Fair Trading (see above).
Race Relations Board, 5 Lower Belgrave Street, London SW1.
Equal Opportunities Commission, Overseas House, Quay Street, Manchester M3 3HN.

METRIC AND US CONVERSION TABLES

Length

1 kilometre (km) = 1,000 metres (m)
1 metre = 100 centimetres (cm) = 1,000 millimetres (mm)
25·4 mm = 2·5 cm = 1 inch
30·5 cm = 0·3048 m = 1 foot
91·4 cm = 0·9144 m = 1 yard
1·6 km = 1 mile

Weight

1 kilogramme (kg) = 1,000 grammes (gm)
25 gm = 1 ounce (oz)
450 gm = 16 oz = 1 lb
1 kg = 2 lb 3 oz
6·3 kg = 14 lb = 1 stone

Liquid Measure

1 litre = 10 decilitres (dl)
3 dl = $\frac{1}{2}$ pint
6 dl = 0·56 litre = 1 pint
1 litre = 1·76 pint
4·5 litres = 1 gallon

Velocity

1 k.p.h. = 0·621 m.p.h.
1·609 k.p.h. = 1 m.p.h.

Temperature

To convert °C to °F multiply by $\frac{9}{5}$ and add 32
To convert °F to °C deduct 32 and multiply by $\frac{5}{9}$
Freezing point = 0°C = 32°F
Boiling point = 100°C = 212°F
Body temperature = 37°C = 98·4°F

USA Measures and Equivalents

The definitions for the international pound and yard adopted in 1959 bring USA weights and measures into correspondence with those of the UK, with the exception of the USA measurements of capacity, which include both dry and liquid pints and quarts, the dry derived from the bushel (64 dry pints = 1 bushel) and the liquid from the gallon (8 liquid pints = 1 US gallon).

The short ton of 2,000 lb and the short hundredweight of 100 lb are used more commonly in the USA than in the UK.

USA Dry Measure Equivalents

1 pint	= 0·9689 UK pt	= 0·5506 litres
1 bushel	= 0·9689 UK bu	= 35·238 litres

USA Liquid Measure Equivalents

1 fluid ounce	= 1·0408 UK fl oz	= 0·0296 litres
1 pint (16 fl oz)	= 0·8327 UK pt	= 0·4732 litres
1 gallon	= 0·8327 UK gal	= 3·7853 litres

CLOTHING CARE LABELS CODE

 Washable. The top number refers to a laundering washing code; for practical purposes you can often ignore this.

The bottom number tells you the maximum water temperature in °C. This is important. 40° is warm (i.e. warm-wash only at your launderette, or by hand); 50° is hand-hot; 60° hot.

 Hand-wash only.

 Not washable.

 Don't use bleach.

 The number of dots in the iron shows the *correct ironing setting.* One dot means cool; two dots warm; three dots hot.

 Don't iron.

 Dry-cleanable.

 Don't dry-clean.

INDEX

If you want help with managing your money, look up 'money'. You will see many headings to help you, and you may decide to look up 'planning spending'. At the bottom of the list, you will see '*See also banks*', where you will find more information about money.

A book or publication is shown in *italics*, organizations in **bold** type. Organizations known by their initials are listed at the exact alphabetical position of the initials.

About The Author

Barbara Paterson became a copywriter after leaving
university. She worked her way through several agencies and
thinks advertising is useful, interesting and good training.
She then turned to freelance writing – mainly short stories and
articles and writing extensively for *Petticoat* (as Barbara Olive).
She has taught, translated and worked as a foreign
language guide. Much of the information included in *Help*
has been gained through personal, and painful, experience
and she hopes that the book will make starting off on your
own a little less traumatic.

Some Other Peacocks

And Some Penguins you Might Enjoy